Produced by Scottsdale Multimedia, Inc.

YOU CAN IF YOU WILL

HOW TO SUCCEED

THROUGH COMMITMENT & ACCOUNTABILITY

KIP KINT

DEDICATION

This book is dedicated to my son, Kasen Avery Kint, who was living proof that you can make a significant impact in the lives of others in a very short period of time. I miss you, son.

CONTENTS

FOREWORD

There have been moments in my life when I knew that the task I was engaged in was exactly what I was meant to be doing at that time. I believe these moments are divinely guided when I attempt to live my life in a pattern of doing good things. One such moment occurred a few years ago in my first meeting with Kip Kint. An associate of mine knew that I had a deep desire to advance my organization, the School of Life Foundation, to the next level. At the time we were experiencing success with our mission and were ready and seeking direction on how to grow to a scalable and sustainable entity that could impact many more individuals. This same associate also knew from previous interactions with Kip that he possessed the skills necessary to assist in my endeavor. During my initial time spent with Kip, I quickly realized that he had a vast knowledge, wealth of experience and true desire to share proven tactics of how to improve people's lives in any circumstance. I knew immediately that I was experiencing one of those moments of being precisely where I needed to be.

Over the next several months, Kip and I met and went through a methodical and enjoyable process that led to engaging his services for assisting the progress of the Foundation. Since joining together I have never looked back nor given a second thought to that decision. The School of Life Foundation continues evolving toward the vision I have, with a large portion of the success due to the efforts and guidance from Kip. Something else has happened while on this journey. Kip has become one of my dearest friends. This cherished friendship has developed through Kip's sincerity of wanting to make the world be a better place, and how he lives what he teaches. It feels like we have known each other forever.

As I write this, I now encounter another one of those moments when I have no doubt that I am literally doing what I am supposed to be doing as I present this Foreword to you. I am enjoying firsthand the victories that have come by my aligning my actions with the principles outlined in this book, You Can If You Will. I am confident your life will change forever as you follow the path described in these pages. You have an opportunity to reach for and achieve what matters most to you. Through this book, Kip becomes your coach, guiding you along that path.

As you move forward, with the help of these timeless principles, you may find yourself experiencing one of those "moments" in your own life, just as I have. In fact . . . You Can If You Will.

Jack Rolfe

Author, *Learn to School Your Toughest Opponent*

CEO & Founder, School of Life Foundation

ACKNOWLEDGMENTS

Gratitude is one of the most important elements of a happy and successful life. Grateful people are happy people. I have found this to be true in my own life, even during the most difficult times. When I focus on what I am grateful for, rather than what I am lacking, my happiness goes up. With that said, I want to express my gratitude to several people. First, I am grateful for my wife, Becky. It may seem cliché to you, but she truly is my best friend, my partner in life, my advocate, my confidant, my cheerleader, and my inspiration. Even when I may doubt myself, if she believes in me, then my own belief is strengthened. I'm not sure how she does that, but I am glad she does. Thank you, Honey.

I am grateful for my children. Ashley, my oldest, is my thoughtful one; so considerate. She pays attention to the details, and does the little things that are so sweet. Whitney, my confident one. She could hold an audience's attention in the most engaging and articulate way from a very young age. She is talented in so many ways, and is driven to succeed. Kannon, my third child and oldest son, is a talented athlete, and so intelligent. He has a way of figuring things out and solving problems that I did not possess at his age. He has his grandfather's hands, able to take things apart and put them back together (and they work). Brynley, my youngest daughter, is my artist. Her paintings are special treasures to me. She is so loving and sensitive to those around her, and such a bright light, from her smile to her attitude. Finally, my youngest son, Kasen. Though we only had him for four years, he has forever changed me. This book is dedicated to him. During his short time on this Earth he made a big impact. I love him, and miss him, and can't wait to see him again.

I would like to give a special thanks to my Mom and Dad. In my many travels I have been privileged to meet and associate with a great number of people. I can honestly say I have never met two more giving, loving people. Of all the gifts I've been given, am truly grateful for my capacity to love, which I attribute to my Mom and Dad.

Introduction

I was eleven years old in the spring of 1977, and in my second year of little league baseball. The year before we had finished just ahead of the middle of the pack; we weren't bad, but we weren't great either. This particular year, however, we did really well, and took first place in our division.

At the team awards dinner, with all the parents present, is where it happened: I received my calling in life. During the awards ceremony, each of us on the team received a little trophy for our participation. As luck, or destiny, would have it, I was called up last, and my coach introduced me with the words:

"Last but not least, Kip Kint... 'The Mouth.'"

My mother still loves to share that story. By the ripe, old age of eleven, I was already known as a talker. I earned this distinction partly because I was pretty quick to offer my advice, including to the coach, but also because I was always shouting encouragement to the other players on my team. It didn't matter if the other boy was the worst player on the team, I was there to give him my vocal support. I would call "heads up" when it looked like a teammate might be daydreaming. I would rally the dugout to cheer the team on. Understandably, my coach may have been occasionally annoyed by my tendency to provide unsolicited coaching—after all, I was just a kid, right?

From a young age, it was clear that communicating with others was as natural to me as breathing. I had no fear about cheering people on, or helping them work through difficulties. In fact, as much as I enjoyed playing, I enjoyed coaching even more.

Looking back now, it's not surprising to me that I have since evolved as a trainer, public speaker, effectiveness coach, and now author. But to be honest, the sailing wasn't always so smooth. While I have never been shy about being vocal to those with whom

I am close—like teammates—speaking to larger audiences in more formal settings wasn't quite as natural for me.

Evolution of a Public Speaker

The first time I had a true public speaking opportunity, I was literally sick to my stomach. I was more nervous than I had ever been to that point in my life. It was January of 1984, and I was 18 when the bishop of our congregation asked me to speak in church on the topic of "Service to Others." There were at least two or three hundred people in the congregation. I was very nervous, and very intimidated.

I don't remember all the particulars any longer, but I do remember my bishop waved away my hesitation by telling me "Kip, you were born to do it." Up to that point in my life, I had never hesitated to be encouraging to others—individually or in small-group settings. This quiet leader felt that I had something of value to share, and encouraged me to give it my best. My fear was holding me back—inwardly focused, self-absorbed fear of rejection—but my bishop knew, if I could just get outside of myself and focus on others, I would have valuable insights to share. He knew that if I could forget myself, I would forget my fear.

"Courage is not the absence of fear, but rather taking action in the face of fear."

(Author Unknown).

I remember stepping up to the microphone—still very nervous—swallowing hard, then sharing the message I had prepared. After only a minute or two I forgot myself and my fear, just as he predicted. While it would still be years before speaking, training, and coaching would become my passion and career, and there would still be bouts of fear, my courage was found that day.

For the next two years, I served on active duty in the Army in West Germany during the Cold War. While I had ample opportunity to coach and mentor other soldiers, my teaching experiences were all informal, unofficial, and individual. That said, I had one experience in particular that shaped my perception of the impact I could have as a mentor.

Being "The Man"

For our unit, the worst assignment you could get was guard duty. It involved staying up all night guarding the tanks in what was called the "Track Park," a sort of gigantic parking lot for tanks. It was long, boring, weary work, and we would do anything we could to avoid being assigned guard duty, especially in the winter when it was snowy and freezing cold.

As it turned out, one of the best ways to avoid guard duty was to be "The Man." To become The Man, we had go through both a physical and mental "inspection" by our unit leaders. Your uniform had to be perfect—every crease pressed, meticulously cleaned and starched, without wrinkles, shoes shined so bright you could see your face in them, etc. Perfection was the standard.

When the leaders narrowed the group down to the top two or three whose uniforms were perfect, they would start asking questions about anything and everything related to your military assignment, such as the chain of command from the individual soldier all the way up to the President of the United States, or perhaps a quiz on the Preventive Maintenance, Checks, and Services of an M-1 Tank. If there was still a tie, we might be timed on how quickly we could field strip an M-16 rifle, or Colt 45 pistol.

Happily, my best friend and I basically took turns being The Man. We pulled very little guard duty because we prepared and earned the right to "immunity." Once in a while, another of the soldiers would win, but it was mostly my friend and I.

There was one guy, however, who was never The Man. He was perhaps a little more right brained, so he was never concerned enough with his appearance. The sergeants were always getting on his case about his uniform. To make matters worse for him, he was very shy and quiet, so even if he knew the right answers, he would fold under pressure. In the first year and a half that I knew him, he'd never been The Man. I decided to change that.

I helped him with everything. I taught him how to press his clothes, how to shine his boots, and how to get everything looking perfect. I drilled him on questions, we studied together, and I coached him on how to answer without freezing up. It took about a month and a half of working together, but he finally got The Man.

The interesting thing for me was that I felt better about his win than I had ever felt about any of the times I got The Man. I had learned to experience sweet victory through helping others achieve victory for themselves.

Getting Technical

Following my time in the military, I went to college and then on to the real world. My first job was at WordPerfect. I started on the registration team but worked my way up to the technical support team, and eventually, a technical advisor position. At this point I became a coach, teaching WordPerfect employees about our software or about customer service. This was new and different to me in that it was the first time my training responsibilities were officially part of my job description—and I loved it.

Helping my coworkers perform better in taking customer service phone calls was enjoyable, but what motivated me wasn't the fact that my coworkers were better service agents because of *my* efforts. What drove me to love what I did was that I got to help people be better at what *they* did. I got to help them overcome their personal performance roadblocks and find more satisfaction in their jobs. In other words, I was deriving great personal satisfaction helping others become The Man.

I eventually moved from that job to a contract position with the United States Department of Justice (DOJ). This move took my training ability to a completely new level.

At WordPerfect I had trained small groups in fairly informal settings—usually half a dozen people sitting around a couple of computers. With my work at the DOJ, I was teaching in a more front-of-the-room, formal, classroom-style, instructor-led setting. I would have 20 to 30 "students" at a given time, and I was responsible for running the program and getting everyone up to speed on the technical side of the software they were using. Every time I moved to a new geographical center, I would have the US Attorney for that region in my classroom.

I remember the first training I gave for the US Attorney in Washington, DC. Beforehand, I was in the bathroom doing all I could to not lose my breakfast. In some respects, it was like that first public speaking experience all over again. It took nearly everything I had just to get myself into that classroom to start that first training. My fears were for naught, of course, because it went great. The moment I got started my mind shifted from my self-centered fear to a selfless concern about how I could help the DOJ employees be more productive. I started to think about them and their needs and what I could offer them. And, just like with that first presentation years before, the fear and nervousness melted away as I focused on others.

I started to train them on more than just the nuts and bolts of the software package they were using; I started to give them insights on how to leverage the program features to improve communication and efficiency in the office. I saw that there was more value to be had than simply a how-to lecture, so I customized the curriculum and matched the coaching to meet their particular needs.

Franklin Covey

Ultimately, I took a job with Franklin Covey, coaching employees on the technical side of their software and productivity tools. Shortly after I started there, Franklin Covey partnered with Novell and the DOJ contractor I had previously worked with to put together a training program for the platinum resellers of Novell's products.

That program took the shape of a typical coaching protocol: once a week for 30 minutes for 12 weeks. The wrinkle came from the unique need to do all the coaching over the phone instead of in person. Because of this, Franklin Covey wanted a specialized trainer; someone with solid interpersonal communication skills, adaptive training skills, and aptitude for the coaching skills that Franklin Covey cultivated in-house.

That became my job. I was responsible for not only teaching the technical side of the software over the phone to resellers, but also teaching the sales techniques to help those resellers move more product. This included skills like building rapport, communication, problem solving, consulting on the product, etc. As a result of this new coaching program there was a significant increase in revenue from those resellers that year.

Surprisingly, after only a year, some management changes resulted in the program being cut—despite its success. I suddenly thought I was out of a job.

The people at Franklin Covey, however, came to me and told me that my performance hadn't gone unnoticed. The program I'd been running had been cut, but that didn't mean I was going down with the ship. As it turned out, Franklin Covey provided the coaching personnel to teach a wide variety of programs—both in-house programs and contracted programs from other management thought leaders.

Over the next five years I did a lot of coaching. I was teaching programs from *Time Management* and *The 7 Habits for Highly Effective People* to Zig Ziglar, Tom Hopkins, Brian Tracy, Denis Waitley and more. I wasn't training on my own curriculum anymore, but I was coaching nearly 100 clients each week across a diverse array of programs.

It wasn't too long before Franklin Covey decided to codify their coaching methods, and I became their first Master Coach, responsible for training and coaching the other coaches. In conjunction with this opportunity, I got to help design and write some of the training materials, including materials for the Coaching Certification Program. As a side note, Franklin Covey no longer offers their Coaching Certification Program, so there are only 200 Certified Franklin Covey Coaches (CFCCs) in the world.

All of this experience built on a preexistent, natural ability to help people clarify what matters most, establish commitments to reach those goals, and hold themselves accountable. My experiences had cultivated what I now consider one of my greatest strengths: the ability to hold people accountable by balancing strictness and leniency. I am able to call people to task without being confrontational—but also without backing down and letting them off the hook. While this skill may not be unique to me, it is a rare skill to exercise effectively.

Back to the Basics

I was going strong. I had coached well over 2000 clients, created a training program to teach coaches how to coach, and become a Certified Franklin Covey Coach. I had worked with government officials, private organizations and management thought leaders. Everything seemed to be going well, but I'd hit a wall of sorts. I was coming to realize that it was less about the number of people I could coach at the same time and more about the level of quality I could provide in my coaching.

This was the point in my life where I realized that what I had to offer—this rare blend of clarity, commitment, and accountability—was best offered on an individual, highly customized basis, so I broke off and decided to sail under my own power. I wanted to focus on relationships and true personalization of the material. In fact, my most common coaching program is a one-year, one-on-one program.

Since 2002, I have been doing what I do best: helping others find personal balance in order to achieve business success. I have been refining the tools and methods I have in order to help my clients better reach the potential they've always possessed.

The fact of the matter is that my clients are able to do what they want to do without me, but they haven't. They were able to do it before they ever met me, but they didn't. Now that we've met, they'll still be able to do it without me, but if it wasn't something we moved forward on, they will most likely continue to procrastinate.

That's what I bring to the table; the ability to help others clarify, commit to, and be accountable for their goals.

Why Write This Book?

Which brings me to why I want to write this book. The truth is, I've again hit a wall in how far I can stretch myself; to take on hundreds of simultaneous clients again would adversely impact the quality of the relationship I could build with each one, so that's not really an option. In order for me to truly help my clients find business success, I have to get to know them and customize the program to match their needs. I can't offer a "one size fits all" approach because one size only fits the handful of people who are that one size—by definition.

This book is the solution to my dilemma. Many books are written in that "one size fits all" format. This one is not. As we go through, I will provide you examples and exercises to help reinforce the concepts and principles. If we are talking about something that isn't appealing to you right now, skim it. Don't skip it entirely, but feel free to move quickly through that section and get to the parts that are more relevant to your specific needs and aspirations.

This book is designed to be the closest approximation of a one-on-one mentoring experience that a book can be. I have tried to fill these pages with the principles, concepts, and applications you need to balance your life in the pursuit of business success. The logical extension of that intent means that readers will each need a slightly different mix of the principles to get from where they are to where they want to be. I will provide the guidance. It will be up to you to employ the appropriate level of focus for each concept.

Which brings us to a discussion of how to use this book to get the most value out of it.

Making the Most of this Book

The value of this particular book is not in the introduction of some crazy, new, hot-off-the-press psychological research. We don't need to deal with fringe science to find success. Instead, I will be drawing on decades of tried, proven research and principles that *will* change your life, if you let them. The true value of this book is in the application of these concepts—in how, together, we can change your *life*, not just your mind.

Because of my background in coaching, I can't just share valuable insights and then walk away. I live and breathe accountability, and this book is designed with that in mind. When your mother used to ask you to clean your room, did you do it? Sure. What if she asked you on her way out the door to go out of town for a week? Would that change your response?

The fact of the matter is, we can't create value for you unless we stimulate action, and the best way to drive action and change is through accountability. With that in mind, I have created a series of Coaching Assignments related to the principles of the book. At the conclusion of each chapter, I will share a number of 'homework' assignments with you; I will also list 'bonus' assignments and additional, external reading opportunities from other experts.

The idea behind these assignments and readings is to help you activate yourself. Together, we want to push you to finally do those things that you've always known you could. If I could jump out of the book and into your living room to help you stay on target, I would. These Coaching Assignments will help you commit to an action which will either help you be more effective, help you progress toward a goal, or give you some other valuable benefit for the time you invest.

Two Approaches for this Book

Now that you know who I am and where I'm coming from, let me suggest that there are two possible ways to approach this book: you can read it straight through or you can take it slow and treat it like a coach. Obviously, I would recommend the latter approach, but the choice is yours. There are certainly pros and cons to each method.

If you decide to read straight through the book, you will have a number of 'a-ha' moments as you go. You may not attain the same depth of understanding overall, but those principles will help you to become a better person. What's more, in taking in the whole book in a fairly short period of time, you will get a great view of the 'lay of the land.' You'll have a high-level view of all the principles and how they integrate with one another. And the book will always be here—patiently waiting—for when you want to come and refer back to a portion. This is definitely a valid, valuable way to use this book.

As a coach, myself, however, I have to champion the use of this book as a coaching tool. Whether you choose to take this approach right out of the gate or whether you prefer to read through once and then come back for a second pass is not the important thing.

Either way, the book is designed to be an interactive coaching companion to you; to use it as anything else (over the long term) is to have the book fail to live up to its potential. So, for whenever the right time comes along, allow me to describe the second method of "reading" this book.

The Coach Approach

Instead of hurrying from one cover to the other, consider taking your time to appreciate the journey. Rather than a chapter a day (or hour), try reading just one chapter a week—and not just reading the chapter but really *studying* it. Focus on it. Absorb it. Read and reread. Highlight key phrases. Reflect and introspect. Do the homework at the end of the chapter. Set goals, make commitments, and track your progress.

The homework and activities in this book will help you to uncover your potential to set and meet commitments and goals. The accountability framework revolves around you keeping track of your progress—and, at the appropriate times, the book will provide you places and instructions on tried-and-true ways of documenting everything. Feel free to create a companion notebook or computer file if you prefer to not write in the book; however, to maximize the benefit of the exercises, you *must* record your answers and progress somewhere. The mind is too fickle to keep track of everything at once (when was the last time you forgot something on your shopping list because it wasn't written down?).

The choice of which approach you use is yours and yours alone. There is value in a direct, straight-trough read. I would recommend, however, that you take this coaching approach at some point. I want these principles to provide as much value as possible, or I wouldn't have written this book. You want these principles to provide as much value as possible, or you wouldn't be reading this book. The best way to harness the full potential of this opportunity is to treat it like a true coach.

Three-Person Teaching

Regardless of whether you decide to read this book straight

through like a normal book or decide to use the book as a coaching tool, I would like you to consider making use of a technique called "three-person teaching." I am borrowing this idea from Stephen Covey[1] but the concept is that the best way to learn a principle is to teach it.

In three-person teaching, the first "person" is the source—whether that source is an actual person, a book, a video, an Internet site, or some other medium. The second person is you, the person learning directly from that original source. The third person in this process is the one that you turn around and teach the concept to after you learn it.

Again, the idea is that, in a "classroom," no one learns more or better than the teacher. That classroom can be your living room, the hall at work, or a real classroom; the principle applies just the same. In order for you to effectively teach something, you have to learn it at a much deeper level. You have to be ready to answer questions, expound on ideas, and integrate concepts. You have to know the concept well enough to communicate it to someone else.

Three-person teaching will help you think deeply enough about the principles in this book to receive more than just an 'a-ha,' which you might forget in a month; it will help you come up with your own life experiences, analogies, and applications of the principles. The objective is to give you a better understanding on a more personal level, leading to more significant insights, which will help you better apply these principles in your life. I want this book to be more than an interesting read. I want it to help you achieve the success and results that deep down you've always known you were capable of.

The best way to make that happen is for you to teach these principles. You don't have to teach the same person every time (though a spouse/significant other, adult child, or close coworker would be a great candidate), but every time you have one of those 'a-ha'' moments, teach it. Every time you come across a principle you don't quite understand, teach it. You may find your 'a-ha' in

---

[1] Covey, Stephen R. *The 7 Habits of Highly Effective People.* New York: Free Press, 2004.

the course of preparing to teach a concept.

Admittedly, it takes a little more time to read with a three-person teaching frame of mind, but if you really want this book to help you improve your life, it will be time well spent. If your goal is simply to read and understand the principles, then don't worry about this extra step for now. Save it for your next trip through these pages.

Credit Where Credit's Due

Before we move on, I wanted to briefly touch on two more points. The first is about the number of diverse perspectives represented in these pages. The second relates to a little axiom called "the 10 shortest words that lead to success."

As I mentioned earlier, this book is about the application of time-honored, battle-tested principles. It is a refinement of a story that predates the modern, nonfiction, self-help era, but it is not a new story. Various portions have been told and retold in the past by wise and insightful authors, experts, and philosophers. I'm not trying to claim that I invented *the* path—or even a *new* path—to personal efficiency and business success. I'm just saying I have a sustainable, replicable method for helping you reach it.

Still, because of those who have gone before, we now have the privilege of citing numerous perspectives and paradigms, creating a better, clearer vision by harnessing their insights. I consider many of these thought leaders as mentors because, either in person or through their written words, they have influenced my life for the better—much as I hope to help you influence your own life.

In order to provide a more comprehensive view, I will be referring to these ideas as we go along. To be clear, I have no wish to claim their insights as my own.

The idea of learning from others leads us right to the 10 shortest words that bring success: "If it is to be, it is up to me." While drawing on the experience and insight of others can help us clarify, strengthen, and guide our commitment, in the end, that commitment must come from within. The only person who can change you is you.

I sincerely hope that as you read through this book you will be bombarded with insights on how to improve your effectiveness, make and keep commitments, and balance and center your life; but that all depends on you. I can't force you to do anything you are unwilling to do—in fact, I wouldn't try. In some respects, the experience of reading this book will be like an empty box: it's only as good as what you put into it.

I can promise you that the principles will help you change your life—they've worked for thousands of people like you—but only if you take charge and use them. I will lay out the path and teach you the technique, but if you want to experience the success you have to do the work.

Homework

Decide whether you will (1) use the full, step-by-step coaching program in this book, or (2) read straight through first to get a feel for the overall structure.

If you plan on using the coaching program, answer the following questions:

1. Will you commit to reading one chapter per week?
    ___ Yes ___ No

    If yes, how much time will you commit to your coaching program on a daily basis (30 minutes or more per day recommended)? _____

2. Will you commit to completing the homework assignments at the end of each chapter?
    ___ Yes ___ No

3. Will you commit to three-person teaching (*i.e.,* will you share at least one principle you learn with at least one other person at least once per week)?

    ___ Yes   ___ No

Principles of Personal Balance

If you have decided to use this book as a coaching tool, pay special attention in this section. If you have decided to read straight through, remember this section for when you come back for coaching. The principles we're about to cover are tightly connected to all of the personal change contained in this book.

Balance, in life, is reflected by eight major pillars, or facets, of every person's individual existence. Those categories are Business/Career, Personal Finance, Health/Fitness, Family/Friends, Romance, Personal Growth, Physical Environment, and Fun/Recreation. Everything in life can be sorted and categorized into one (or more) of these eight areas.

For the next little bit, we're going to walk through these topics one at a time. In doing so, I'm going to ask you to self-assess, on a 10-point scale (1 being low and 10 being ideal), how you are doing with regard to certain aspects of these categories. Before we do that, however, I need to explain a few details about how this process works.

First, try not to over-think the questions. They will be fairly simple and very straightforward, so they shouldn't take long to answer. I'm not trying to be your psychiatrist here; you don't need to second-guess yourself. I just want you to take a moment and give an honest answer to each question.

That said, we will be using this information to help you catalyze change in your life later, so don't skip a question even if you think it's irrelevant. I've left you space to record your answers, or, if you prefer, you can tuck a slip of paper into the book here (or use that paper as your bookmark going forward) to record these numbers on—just be sure to record them with enough detail that you can remember what they refer to later on.

Second, the questions will be essentially the same for each category. You will be self-rating your level of performance for a given segment of your life and then rating your level of satisfaction with that level of performance. Allow me to go into a little more detail about that process.

Performance

In terms of your performance for a given category, a score of "10" does *not* mean things are perfect; it doesn't mean you've "reached your destination." A 10 means that things are on track, heading right where you want them to go—you're following your 10-year plan. In other words, you are saying how tightly you are staying on course and how quickly you are moving in achieving your current vision, not how close to the "destination" you are.

Many goals in life take years of effort to reach, but if you're doing everything you can do right now to reach that goal in the future, then you're on track and deserve a 10. If you're putting things off because the goal will take so long anyway, or because you've let other concerns distract you, then you probably don't deserve a 10.

Be honest with yourself. The coaching program in this book *will* help you drive balance to achieve effectiveness—but you'll get the best results if you are honest.

Satisfaction

The second element you'll be scoring yourself on is your level of satisfaction. In effect, what was your level of discomfort in giving yourself the performance score. If rating your performance was quick and easy, you are probably fairly satisfied with it and, therefore, will probably have a fairly high score for satisfaction (regardless of whether your performance score was high or low). If, however, you agonized over how to rate your performance (or were embarrassed by what you were putting), then you likely have a low level of satisfaction with your performance in that facet.

Keep in mind that your level of performance is only loosely tied to your level of satisfaction with that performance. I can be a homeless transient and recognize that I've given up every opportunity to change my situation, but still be completely satisfied with my level of achievement in life (low performance, high satisfaction). Or I can be the CEO of a Fortune 500 company, recognize that I'm nearly meeting all my goals, and yet be dissatisfied with my level of performance because I expect more from myself (high performance, low satisfaction). In fact, it's often the case that those in humble circumstances are content to remain there, whereas high-powered people are rarely content to accept the *status quo*.

This can also work in other ways, however. I could be the manager—and maybe not even the owner—of a small retail store, and if that's my goal in life, rate myself high in both performance and satisfaction (high performance, high satisfaction). Alternatively, I could be that same retail manager, recognize that I have sold myself short compared to what I could be doing, and be totally disappointed in myself for it (low performance, low satisfaction).

Remember that these ratings are personal to you—no one else gets to rate you on your behalf. Also keep in mind that different types of people will rate themselves differently across different categories. For instance, artists or other creatives might be tempted to give themselves low ratings in Business/Career because of the conditioning that society places on them. However, if an artist is on track, meeting predetermined goals, and making progress to reach his vision, that artist should be self-rating closer to an 8, 9, or 10 for performance.

Lastly, don't be surprised if, for at least some of the categories, your rating for performance and your rating for satisfaction vary from one another by a wide margin. Just remember that you are rating two very different aspects of a segment of your life. That's the reason these two scores are taken and recorded independently.

Are you ready?

Let's get started.

Business/Career

For many people, this category is the one they spend the most time on. It may not occupy their attention and concern in the same way that, say, Family/Friends or Romance might, but most people in Corporate America spend at least 40 of their 168 weekly hours at work—and that doesn't include commuting or overtime. And then there are the entrepreneurs, many of whom would call 40 hours a week a "vacation." Anything that takes up 25 percent or more of your life deserves some attention. Because we spend so much time with this aspect of our lives, we all tend to inherently understand what success means from a societal perspective.

However, the key to this facet is knowing what *you* are trying to accomplish in life; *i.e.,* What do you want to be when you grow up? What is your vision for the future? This goes beyond simply wanting to be a firefighter or doctor or movie star or football player, or 'being rich'; this is about what you *can* do and what you *are* doing now to achieve the level of success of which you know you are capable. Your vision is that level of success, and it will be different for every single person on the planet. The hardest part of accurately rating yourself in this category is correctly defining what success means to you—instead of taking the definition of success that society would otherwise give you.

How are you doing in achieving your vision? Are you still stuck in that desk job when you've been dreaming about starting your own business for years? Or did you start a business a couple years ago and now you've decided that self-employment isn't all it's cracked up to be and you want to find a steady job? Or did you just earn the top box for performance reviews and your career is progressing right on, or even ahead of schedule? Did you just change your marketing emphasis and now your business has really taken off?

With respect to your career, where did you think you would be at this stage in your life? Where are you actually? How do those two ideas align? Now rate yourself on a scale of 1-10, with 1 being low and 10 being high.

How close are you to being on track in achieving your business and/or career goals?

(1-10) _____

How satisfied are you with the number you just answered for the last question?

(1-10) _____

Last, average the two scores to create a composite score for Business/Career.

_____

Personal Finance

After Business/Career comes Finance. Many people get a little confused at this point and ask what the difference is between Finance and Business; after all, doesn't the money for your personal finances come from your career?

The answer to that question is "yes." The money you make comes from your career; however, the category of Personal Finance *isn't* about where you get your money or how much you get. Personal Finance is a question of what you *do* with your money once it's yours. This is a question of how well you budget, save, and plan with your finances. How good are you at managing the money that comes in, whatever that amount might be?

Allow me to explain by giving you some real-to-life examples. These examples are based loosely on real clients I've had in the past, so obviously, I've changed any names and some of the other vital statistics in order to protect confidentiality.

First, let's consider a neurosurgeon I worked with. We'll call him Henry. He had his practice in the southwest of the United States but owned multiple homes in resort locations around the nation. He had a number of cars—all new, of course—and made just over $1.2 million per year. He had a nice little family and, by all appearances, everything was going smoothly.

Contrast Henry with a young man I coached in North Carolina at about the same time. We'll call him John. John was in his early twenties, hadn't been to college, and only made about $40,000 per year. He made his money primarily from a lawn-servicing business he ran, cutting the grass for local strip-malls and business parks. He was single and lived alone.

Which would you say was better off? Well, if you answered that you don't have enough information, you answered correctly.

As it turns out, Henry the neurosurgeon was up to his eyeballs in debt. He was stressed about how he was going to make his next mortgage payment. Believe it or not, he also had more than $150,000 in unsecured credit card debt. To further complicate matters, his only source of income was his work, so he had no recourse if something prevented him from going in; he was a slave to his job and his paycheck. Even making $1.2 million, he was barely making ends meet each month. While he may have looked like a 9 or a 10 from the outside, in reality, Henry was more like a 2—at best.

John, on the other hand, had three employees in his lawn-care business. He wasn't even the one going and doing the lawn care; he only spent about 15-20 hours a week on the management aspects of the business (networking, marketing, accounting, empowering his team etc.), but he got his paycheck anyway for being the business owner.

He was also invested in two other ventures in the area and had some money in paper assets like stocks and bonds, diversifying his income sources. The net result was that his income was nearly completely passive—he made it whether he worked or not. What's more, his cost of living was only around $24,000, meaning he made significantly more than he needed each year on 15-20 hours of work per week. John still had plenty of room to grow, but he was already at a 9 or 10.

Now who would you rather be?

So let's come back to you. Do you live paycheck to paycheck? Do you have money set aside in an emergency fund? Are you putting away for retirement? Do you carry balances on multiple credit cards? Do you feel stress and anxiety over where the money for your next meal will come from? When you see something you have to have, do you save up and buy it down the road, or do you buy it right away and worry about the payments later?

What this all boils down to is, "Do you have a budget? Do you live by that budget?" Again, this isn't about your total amount of income; it's about how you manage what money you do make.

How effective are you at managing your personal finances?
(1-10) _____

How satisfied are you with the number you just answered for the last question?
(1-10) _____

Last, average the two scores to create a composite score for Personal Finance.

_____

Health/Fitness

In the movie *The Princess Bride*, Count Rugen says, "If you haven't got your health, you haven't got anything." While the situation in the movie is somewhat ironic (the count is about to go and torture a prisoner to "mostly death"), the quote stands true all the same. Health is one of those aspects of life which we so often take for granted until it fails. The danger we run into is that health and physical wellbeing are much easier to maintain than to regain.

This section is about your level of fitness, your muscle tone, your level of energy, and your overall sense of wellbeing.

For the purposes of this section, we're looking at Health in the sense that everything is 'under control.' If you have a medical condition, that doesn't mean you have to have a low performance score in the same way that having a low-paying job doesn't mean you have to have a low Personal Finance score. The real question is, How you are doing with your Health? Are you taking any required medications? Do you see your doctor every year for your physical—no matter how uncomfortable or inconvenient that might be? How is your diet? A diet, by the way, is defined as the food you eat, not the food you *don't* eat. Do you dream of well-balanced, homemade meals while you wolf down a burger and fries every day? Do you eat your fruits and veggies? Do you meet your recommended daily fiber intake? Do you wear sunblock when you go outside?

The same idea holds true with Fitness—and be honest with yourself about it. Packing gym clothes and thinking about the corporate fitness center is not the same as actually going and lifting some weights. Being at the start of a New Year's resolution *might* count, if you stick with it. Some questions to ask yourself might sound like the following:

Do you work out hard enough and long enough to break a sweat at least three times a week? Can you climb several flights of stairs without stopping? Do you get frustrated when you can't find a parking spot right next to the doors or do you intentionally park fifteen rows back to give you that opportunity to walk? Can you touch your toes? That might sound funny to some of you, but for others, it's serious business. An easy way to consider your fitness is to answer one simple question: Can you go out, right now, and run a mile without stopping? Not a marathon, just a single mile— but you have to run the whole thing. If the thought of going and running one, single mile right now sounds like failure in your mind, you probably need to make some changes.

You don't need to be a professional athlete or have a personal trainer to score well here though. The real question is how are you doing on all the health and fitness things that we all know we *should* be doing? Basically, how are you doing on taking care of the one asset that you can't ever replace?

What is your level of performance with regard to your Health/Fitness?

(1-10) _____

How satisfied are you with the number you just answered for the last question?

(1-10) _____

Last, average the two scores to create a composite score for Health/Fitness.

––––––––––

Family/Friends

There is a somewhat famous, often unheard poem by John Donne called "No Man Is an Island." The central message of the poem is that, as a human family, we are all interconnected by the way we live our lives and by our natures as human beings. Mr. Donne ends with the famous part of the poem: "Therefore, send not to know / For whom the bell tolls, / It tolls for thee." The point he is trying to make is that none of us is alone or disconnected from others. We all need companionship in life, and to lose a chance for friendship is to lose a chance to be more than you already are.

Our next category refers to the people with whom you choose to surround yourself, but let me make three important distinctions. First, your significant other/spouse is *not* included in this category; he or she will be covered in the next section. Second, we're going to break up this category into three subcategories and have you rate yourself in each independently.

Friends

Last, I want to emphasize the choice aspect of this category. Your coworkers or employees are only included in this section if you choose to include them. Many of us have amiable, positive relationships with the people we work with, yet we wouldn't consider those people *friends*. This is totally acceptable. For the purpose of this first subsection, consider your friends to be the people with whom you choose to have friendships.

To be clear, we're not talking about "friends" in the sense of social media. This facet of your life is not dependent on whether you have 1 follower or 100,00 followers; rather, this segment of life is defined by the closer, higher-quality relationships we share with others. We'll look at friends as those people for whom you would be willing to expend time, effort, and energy to remain in contact. This doesn't mean you have to see them on a daily or weekly basis, but it means you should have some level of regular interaction—and it should be more regular than a Christmas card. That time requirement often becomes the limiting factor in this particular category.

Do you have people you can turn to, outside your family/ significant other, for conversation, advice, or entertainment? Do people interact with you of their own initiative? Depending on who you are and your personality, you may have many friends or few. Again, you are looking at *your* perception of your performance. Also, for this first set of ratings, don't consider your family (they will come in a moment); just consider your friends who are not also family.

Do you feel like you have enough friends, or do you find yourself wishing you had more? Do you feel like your friendships have a deep enough level of quality, or do you feel that your friendships are on the shallow side?

How is your performance with respect to making and maintaining friendships?
(1-10) _____

How satisfied are you with the number you just answered for the last question?
(1-10) _____

Extended Family

Friends are, obviously, different from family. This doesn't mean you can't have enriching, valuable relationships with your family—quite the opposite, in fact—but it does mean that you can have friends without regard to your family, and *vice versa*. For that reason, we are going to look at family relationships apart from your friendships (though I hope none of you will think this means you can't be friends with your family).

Family relationships are, genetically, closer than friendships and typically fill a different niche in our lives. For one thing, because we don't exactly pick our families—yet we're "stuck" with them— we tend to approach those relationships with a different frame of mind. Also, because family relationships tend to be instinctively closer, we tend to guard our family more closely. In some cases, though, the opposite is true. Some families become dysfunctional, upsetting that natural order.

This subsection includes your parents, siblings, extended family, and any of your older children who have moved out of the house. This subsection does *not* include any children you may still have at home (we'll cover them in a moment).

Do you avoid these people? Do you treasure the time that you're together? Can you speak freely around one another, or are there topics that can't ever come up for friendly discussion? Do the holidays end in tearful goodbyes, or begin with tearful arguments?

How are you doing on keeping in touch with family and managing those relationships?

(1-10) _____

How satisfied are you with the number you just answered for the last question?

(1-10) _____

Children

The third subcategory has to do with live-at-home children. If you have no children at home—either because you don't have any children or because they've all grown up and moved out—then skip down to get your final average score below.

How do you do as a parent? Do you spend time with your children? Do they talk to you about their problems and concerns? Are they glad to see you when you get home, or do they leave the room when you enter? Do you have a warm, loving relationship, or do you have trouble talking with one another? This relationship can be a very hard one to rate, but make sure you're honest.

What is your performance as a parent?

(1-10) _____

How satisfied are you with the number you just answered for the last question?

(1-10) _____

Scoring

At this point, you should have either two or three performance scores for the different facets of Friends/Family. If you have no children at home, go ahead and average the performance and satisfaction scores for Friends and Extended Family and input those averages below, then move on to the next Principle (Romance). If you have children at home, we're going to do things a little differently.

To get your overall average, add your Friends and Extended Family performance scores, then add your Children score twice.

That's right, add it in twice.

Now divide the total by four. What we've just done is create an average performance score for you, but we've weighted your Children score more heavily than the other two. Write the new composite on the line below. Now do the same for your satisfaction scores.

The idea here is that your ability and drive to be a parent is the most important of these three facets—and the most time consuming—so it should be accounted for proportionately. If you are doing a great job with your children, that can "make up" for lackluster scores in the other two subcategories. If, however, you are neglecting your children, no amount of friendship or extended family relationship can entirely make up for that.

Your average level of performance in the Family/Friends Category.

_____

Your average level of satisfaction with your performance in this category.

_____

Last, average these two composite scores to create an overall score for Family/Friends.

_____

Romance

Somewhat aligned with the Family/Friends category is that of Romance. Romance is about the most important relationship in your life. Romance is about the communication and connection in that critical relationship; it's the level of understanding you share and the fulfillment you give and receive. Romance is about trust and compassion and forgiveness and deep love. However, this is *not* about romance as Hollywood portrays it. This section isn't just about passion or sex or physical gratification. We're talking about commitment and depth.

Specifically, this section refers to your significant other. If you're married, I hope this person is your spouse. Otherwise, your significant other could be a boyfriend/girlfriend or, if you don't have one of those, whatever efforts you are making to acquire a significant other and fill that inherent need for an "other half." The idea is that we all, on some level, have an instinctual craving to share our success with someone we view as equal to ourselves.

Now, before you go rating this category low because you don't think you're getting what you want, remember, you are rating *your* performance in all these categories. When you rated your Personal Finance performance, you rated your ability to manage your finances, not your finances' ability to manage you. The same holds true in this life facet. How are you doing in living up to the ideal of what *you* should be?

Are you being the kind of spouse/boyfriend/girlfriend that you know you should be? Are you doing all the things you know you should be doing to support, deepen, strengthen, and increase your relationship? Are you staying true to the trust that serves as a foundation for this kind of relationship? Do you take your significant other on dates? Do you make time for your significant other? Remember, we're talking about *you*.

How well are you performing in your role as a significant other? (1-10) _____

How satisfied are you with the number you just answered for the last question? (1-10) _____

Average the two scores to create a composite score for Romance.

_____

Personal Growth

This section is actually comprised of two sub-categories and is somewhat related to the Health/Fitness section we covered earlier. The idea is that the human organism is a changing, growing, advancing creature. Just like the need to exercise our physical bodies to keep them in shape and healthy, we also need to exercise our minds and spirits to keep them alive, vibrant, and healthy. Because this kind of activity takes time, effort, and energy, people often forget or put off focusing on their mental and spiritual health. However, doing this weakens a person just as surely as putting off or forgetting about an exercise routine.

A lot of adults, even successful ones, score low in this area. Typically, a low score is the result of always needing to 'get a round to it.' Inherently, we all recognize the importance of personal growth and finding meaning in life, but life is often so frantic that we put off everything that seems "nonessential." In fact, very successful people are often more guilty of this than less successful people because the busier people get, the less time they take for themselves. They get so caught up in everything else that rather than seeking balance, they decide that "something has to give," and they give up Personal Growth.

So let me ask you this: What would happen if you never

changed the oil in your car? It would run just fine for a long time, right? Eventually, though, the oil would break down and the engine would start to have problems. Is it convenient to get an oil change? Not usually. It takes time and money. Yet how many of us change the oil in our cars (or take it somewhere to have the oil changed)? The point is, eventually, the mind and spirit will wear out and break down in the same way a car would. It may not always be convenient to take time to reinforce our minds and spirits, but the danger is an eventual, almost inevitable, breakdown.

Mental

This subcategory is all about the mental side of your personal growth. This is about taking your intelligence and working it out like a muscle. All of us develop a set of specialties as we go through life, but not everyone tries reaching beyond those foci to further enlarge and strengthen the intellect. Some people exercise their minds by learning new languages or facts, reading histories, doing puzzles, taking online or correspondence courses, writing in blogs, traveling to new places, studying new cultures, etc. The options are limitless—so long as you are focusing on expanding the horizons of your mind.

Do you do the same things day in and day out with little to no variation? Do you stimulate your mind by learning new things? Do you explore new ways of thinking and new methods of problem solving? Do you take time to learn things unrelated to your job or just focus all your bandwidth on work? Do you read books (fiction or nonfiction), newspapers, and magazines (or their online equivalents) for pleasure? What do you do to expand and strengthen your mind?

How is your performance in Mental Growth?
(1-10) _____

How satisfied are you with the number you just answered for the last question?
(1-10) _____

Spiritual

Let me take a moment to qualify this section. Most people in the world have some belief in deity, but not all people believe in a religion or church. That's fine. This segment of your personal life revolves around your personal view of life's purpose, not your view about a higher power. To be sure, for those of you who are religious, this will likely be tied into those beliefs. For those who are not religious, spirituality doesn't necessarily need to be connected to a God figure. I have known many people in life who were deeply spiritual yet had little or no belief in divinity. In many respects, this subcategory is the concept of "stopping to smell the roses." Do you take time to pause and contemplate the deeper, less-defined aspects of your existence?

Again, this is not about your adherence to any specific religious observance(s); it's all about your understanding of the meaning and purpose in life. Do you take time to think about life's purpose? Or do you get so caught up in the rush of daily life that you ignore anything beyond the immediate? Do you meditate on your existence and what it means? Can you seek inner peace even in the face of turmoil around you? Or do you feel empty inside, lost or confused?

How is your Spiritual Growth performance?
(1-10) _____

How satisfied are you with the number you just answered for the last question?
(1-10) _____

Last, average the four scores from this section to create a composite score for Personal Growth.

_____

Physical Environment

Physical Environment is just what it says: your physical surroundings. This can be your office, your home, your bedroom, etc. We want to restrict the scope of the category to just those locations where you have some control, however. Physical Environment does not include the grocery store or mall or local park unless you work in one of those places and have some control over its physical organization. The reason this is important is because your Physical Environment can impact both your creativity and your productivity.

Interestingly, the human mind craves physical order—organization. Now, some of you are probably putting on the brakes right now and saying, "Hold on. Have you seen my desk? I'm the most productive person in my office, yet my desk is an utter mess. I don't need order to be productive." Others might be saying, "You can't organize and sort creativity. Creativity is an inherently messy process. It's a right-brained, crush-random-ideas-together-to-get-something-new-out process. How can that possibly have structure or order?"

To be fair, both those trains of thought are correct. You can be productive in spite of a mess, and creativity can be a messy process. That said, I repeat, "The human mind craves physical order." Allow me to prove it to you through a little thought experiment.

Let's say you show up in Los Angeles for a convention at the Ritz Carlton. Earlier in the day, there was a minor earthquake. Though no real damage was done, it messed up all the rooms in the hotel: books fell off their shelves, couch cushions flew around, desk chairs tipped over, towels fell off the shelves and got unfolded, and the bedding—sheets and blankets—got messed up. Now, the dutiful workers at the hotel have been hurrying to get everything cleaned up and ready to go all day.

You are one of the last guests to check in that night, and they give you a choice. They have two rooms left. Both are on the top floor with beautiful views of the surrounding area. Each costs the exact same amount of money per night. Both have all the amenities that you'd expect from a top-of-the-line hotel like Ritz Carlton. However, they've only had time to clean, straighten, and organize one of the rooms. The other room is still a disaster—clean on a health-hazard level, but messy and disorganized. You can have whichever you want. The choice is yours.

In my experience with thousands of clients, I have *never* met a person who would pick the messy room over the clean one. Why? Because the human mind craves physical order. We can function without it, but that doesn't change the craving. Otherwise, there would be segments of the population lobbying to have garbage collection discontinued.

Let me put it another way. Let's say that I have a magic wand which is only good for one thing: organizing. With one tap of this wand, your entire office would be magically organized; everything would go to its proper place, and you would know where every proper place was. Swish it through your home and everything would be where it belongs—right where you'd expect it to be. Now, tell me, if I offered to let you use this wand *for free*, who would accept my offer? I guess the better question might be, How much would you be willing to pay to use this wand?

When I hear people say that they don't mind having things a little cluttered or messy or disorganized, what I really hear in translation is that they don't have the desire or inclination or willpower to clean it up themselves. Now, we may all have different ideas of organization and cleanliness, but deep down, we're all human and we all crave order. It's instinctual. And this leads us to an important key of productivity and creativity.

Subconscious Interference

Have you ever had a dream in which you were trying to run away from something—but couldn't? Or maybe you were trying to open your eyes or move your arms or talk or scream—but couldn't? I have a theory about why this occurs, and the reasoning is fairly simple.

When you are asleep, your brain naturally releases a neurotransmitter that paralyzes your body. Actual, physical paralysis. It does this, of course, to protect you from the damage you could do to yourself—or others—if you started acting out your dreams. Have you had the dream where you could fly? That might not end so well if your sleeping body tried it out in real life while you sleep. But while your conscious mind and physical body are sleeping, your subconscious comes awake, taking over and creating dreams for you.

At some level, there is communication between your subconscious, dreaming mind and your almost-but-not-quite-all-the-way-asleep conscious mind. Your conscious mind, asleep though it is, recognizes that your body is paralyzed and transmits that information to your subconscious, which adds that detail to your dream. Suddenly, you can't run because your subconscious mind is getting that feedback from your body through your sleeping, conscious mind.

But what does this have to do with organization, Physical Environment, and productivity/creativity? Well, my theory is that the same unable-to-move-while-dreaming concept happens in reverse. Subconsciously—instinctively—we all want to be in an organized, ordered place. We want to be able to feel harmony with our surroundings (this is the root of the Chinese philosophy of Feng shui). So, when the subconscious recognizes that our surroundings aren't so ordered, it wants to motivate us to organize things—just like the conscious mind tells the subconscious that the body is immobile.

The conscious mind is strong enough to continue on task regardless of the input from the subconscious—just like the subconscious can keep dreaming even though the conscious mind says nothing is happening—but a little disconnect occurs. This disunity between the levels of the mind detracts from creativity and productivity. In fact, current research into unconscious thought suggests that the subconscious is better at the abstract, random-connection thought required for creativity.[2] But if your subconscious is focused on how messy things are—and on trying to clean up—then it's not focusing its creative superpower on the same work as your conscious mind. This also means that your subconscious is not working together with your conscious mind to be as productive as possible.

Alternatively, if you stop and take a moment to clean things up, then you can sit down and your whole mind can work together.

---

[2] Zhong, Chen-Bo, Ap Dijksterhuis, and Adam D. Galinsky. "The Merits of Unconscious Thought in Creativity." *Psychological Science* 19, no. 9 (September 2008): 912-918.

Your subconscious no longer fights your conscious mind in an effort to get you to straighten up your desk. Instead, your subconscious will lend its creative efforts to the task at hand—to whatever project you are completing or problem you are solving.

The point here is that you can't stop the instinctual craving of your mind for an organized environment. You can try to ignore it—and suffer the ill effects—or you can organize your Physical Environment and get both levels of your mind working together again. Recent research from Princeton University supports this theory and shows that having an organized workspace will boost creativity and productivity by removing distractions.[3]

How are you doing on your organizational ability? How are you doing on *using* your organizational ability? Do you feel like you are always working in a barely-controlled-chaos environment, or can you put things in order and feel at peace in your surroundings? When you go to get something, do you find it right where you expect it, or do you have to search high and low—losing time and energy in the search?

What is your level of performance in maintaining order in your Physical Environment?

(1-10) _____

How satisfied are you with the number you just answered for the last question?

(1-10) _____

Last, average the two scores to create a composite score for Physical Environment.

_____

---

[3] McMains, Stephanie and Sabine Kastner. "Interactions of Top-Down and Bottom-Up Mechanisms in Human Visual Cortex." *The Journal of Neuroscience* 31, no. 2 (January 2011): 587-597.

Fun/Recreation

Last but—contrary to popular belief—not least is Fun/Recreation. This is the "less than" category, as in less than Business/Career or less than Romance, right? Similar to the idea of putting off Personal Growth, many people feel that fun and recreation are filler activities—only to be included if there is nothing more important to do. However, let's look for a moment at the word recreation—or re-creation. If you discharge a set of batteries, are they worth anything until you charge them again? Not unless you need a paperweight.

Everyone's batteries are different size—some are like car batteries and others are like a 9V—but all of us run out of steam eventually and need a recharge. The reason your car starts each time you get in is because the vehicle automatically converts some of the energy the engine makes back into electricity to recharge the battery. Anyone who's ever had alternator problems can tell you how frustrating it is when you introduce dysfunction into the process. Denying yourself the opportunity to re-create yourself—to renew or recharge—is like willfully damaging the system that keeps you going.

So Fun/Recreation is actually an *equal* eighth with all the other categories. It does not (nor should it) take a backseat to the other facets of your life—if you want balance. Neglecting this aspect of your life can be just as damaging as neglecting any other facet—like Romance or Business/Career. Thankfully, being equal in importance does *not* mean it needs to be an equal draw on your time. Where Business/Career might take 40, 50, 60, or more hours a week and Family/Friends and Romance should also be given significant chunks of time, Fun/Recreation might only require a couple of hours a week.

Even better, those hours can often overlap with time invested in other categories. For instance, if I go on a date with my wife, that can strengthen my Romance facet and also count as Fun/Recreation. For some, Fun/Recreation will take the form of intense activities like hiking or skiing or swimming—which also contributes to Health/Fitness. For others, that re-creation might come through quieter, more contemplative activities like reading a book, having a philosophical discussion, or prayer/meditation—

again doubling up with the categories of Personal Growth or Family/Friends.

What's more, Fun/Recreation doesn't necessarily equate to "wasted time" the way some people think. If you take great pleasure in yard work, maybe mowing the lawn each week can be a part of your re-creation. The same goes for home repair or other housework. However, your source(s) of Fun/Recreation should *not* be the same as your work. If you work as an accountant, providing free accounting services for a local nonprofit is not really recreation. I love coaching, but coaching is still my work, not my recreation. Of course, if you really enjoy the work you do, you may need less time to re-create yourself than someone who slogs away at a job she dislikes day after day.

The idea here is to figure out what recharges you, and then make sure you are incorporating those sorts of activities into your life—and not just on an "as needed" basis. You should be proactive and preemptive in re-creating yourself in order to avoid putting yourself in a breakdown situation. Don't wait until you "just can't take it anymore and have to get away"; take time regularly and "life" won't build up in quite the same way. You'll find that you have the energy and willpower to keep going when you take time to balance this aspect of your life.

So what are you doing to renew yourself? Do you just work, work, work all the time? Do you take time to relax and recharge? Do you take time to have fun? On the other hand, do you spend too much time in this category? Would it benefit you to be more focused on other aspects of your life? Remember, you should be seeking a balance, and while that balance will be different for every person, balance inherently means that no category can operate to the exclusion of any other category.

What is your level of performance in participating in effective Fun/Recreation?

(1-10) _____

How satisfied are you with the number you just answered for the last question?

(1-10) _____

Average the two scores to create a composite score for Fun/Recreation.

_____

The Wheel of Life

We've all heard the idea that "life's unfair," or that the road of life is long, twisty, and often bumpy and rough, right? If you hadn't heard that before, you have now. The road of life can be a bit bumpy at times, but I contend that the issues don't lie solely with the road. Let me put it to you this way: Have you ever been driving on the freeway and gotten a flat tire?

Freeways are usually—though not always—paved fairly smoothly, yet, if you get a flat tire while you're driving, it can make the car jostle and shake and vibrate in nearly every direction. Well, life may be a road that we're driving on, but that means we have wheels to drive with. This is where the concept of the Wheel of Life comes in.

Take a moment and gather your composite scores from the previous sections. I've created a place to reenter those numbers below.

Business/Career   _____

Finance   _____

Health/Fitness   _____

Family/Friends   _____

Romance   _____

Personal Growth   _____

Environment   _____

Fun/Recreation   _____

Now, using those numbers, plot them on the blank Wheel of Life diagram on the next page; then fill in the segments in sequence around the Wheel.

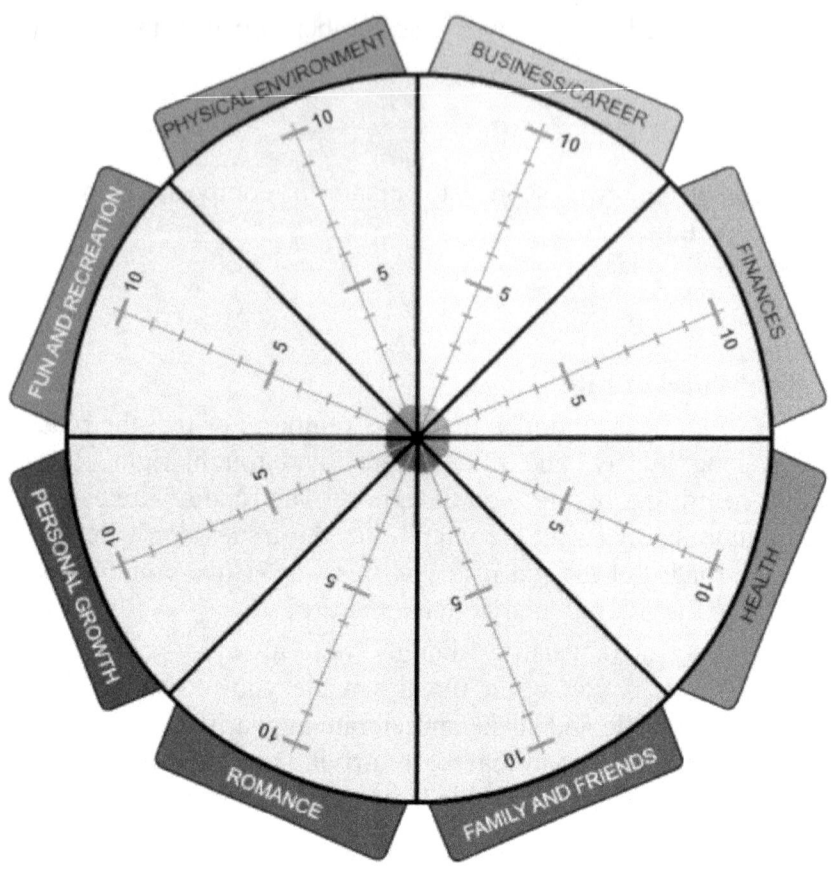

How does your Wheel look? Is it nice and full and round and smooth, or do you have some "flat" areas? Most people, until they learn and apply the concepts in this book, tend to have some unbalanced Wheels. Most will naturally have an area or two where they do well and an area or two where they don't do as well, with the rest of the categories spread somewhere in between—like the example Wheel on the next page.

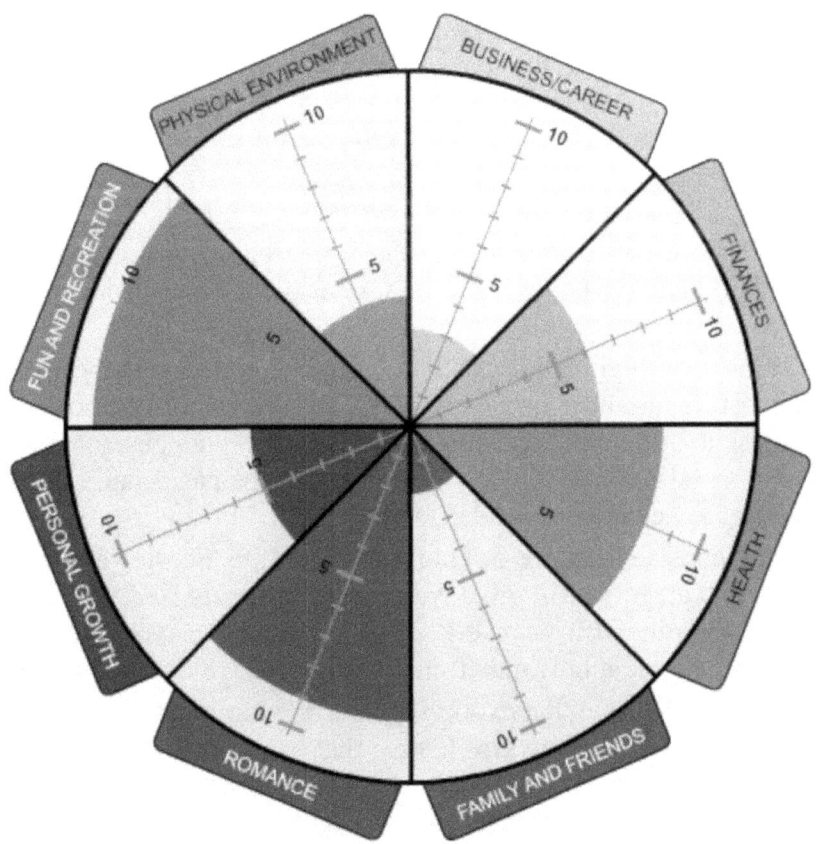

Look at your own Wheel for a moment and let me ask you a question: would you be comfortable driving your car down the freeway with four wheels shaped like that? Would you be comfortable driving at speed, or would you need to drive more slowly in order to compensate for the wheels?

Life is unfair and a little bumpy all around, but do you think the people who are really flying up the Road of Life are doing so with unbalanced Wheels? If you want that same kind of success, what's the obvious solution? The remainder of this book will be structured around helping you to balance your Wheel.

The Myth of Small Wheels

Before we get into that, however, I need to take a moment to dispel a myth that some of you may be considering: if you just score a four in every category, your Wheel will be balanced, right? Quit trying in everything and be content with that abysmal performance. Your performance drops to a 1, your satisfaction goes to a 10, and you get a 5.5 average in every category, right? Two problems.

First, you wouldn't be reading this book and trying to improve yourself if you were content with that kind of apathy. You're better than that, and you know it. Second, consider a brief analogy with me.

Think of a high-end sports car. Something sleek and beautiful and most importantly, fast. This would be a Ferrari or Lamborghini or Porsche—something exotic and expensive and guaranteed to exceed the speed limit at the slightest tap of the gas pedal. Do you have that image in your head? Good.

Now consider the size of your Wheel of Life. Scoring a 9 or 10 in every category will give you good, normal-sized, balanced wheels. Scoring a 3 in every category will give you balanced wheels, but look at how much smaller they are.

Do you still have that exotic supercar in your mind? Okay, now take away the sleek, low profile tires that would normally come on it and attach some skateboard wheels. How does that car look now? More importantly, how fast do you think it can go? How do you think we've just altered the performance and handling?

You are a high-performance 'vehicle.' Just like that exotic sports car, you are built and wired to fly down the Road of Life. To move comfortably—and safely—at speed, do you want your wheels to be full-sized, balanced ones, or would you prefer the skateboard wheels? Do you see how shrinking your wheels to find balance short-changes your ability to perform and achieve success?

Additionally, I'll freely admit that life is unfair, that the Road of Life does have some bumps and rough patches. There's a reason that cars have tires as big as they do. There's a reason that monster trucks have tires as big as they do. Wouldn't it be nice to be able to absorb the bumps—and even boulders—of life because your Wheel was big enough to roll right over the obstacle without slowing down? The best wheels for tackling uneven terrain are big, full ones: 9 or 10 on the scale.

So let's talk about how to take your Wheel—your scores in

these Principles of Personal Balance—and push them to full scores. Remember, a full score (a 10) does not mean you're perfect—that would be virtually unattainable. Instead, a full score represents being on track and going in the right direction—which means that it will change over time. Once you find yourself at a 10 in performance, you won't be there long before your vision of a 10 evolves into something even greater—giving you a new vision to achieve.

As you continue, remember that a full score represents something a little different for each person, but it also represents something achievable for each person. My goal, for the remainder of this book, is to help you understand your true vision, chart your course toward that vision, and then get on track to achieve your success through personal balance. So hang on to this Wheel; we'll be referring back to it again and again as we go on.

Homework

Complete your Wheel of Life Diagram. Be sure to plot your scores and shade the various segments, so you can see how your Wheel looks overall.

Spend a little time thinking about your Wheel and what you can do to fill and balance it. We'll be coming back to those thoughts later, so be sure to record them somewhere safe (a notebook, computer file, or in the blank note pages provided at the back of this book), and don't just try to keep that information in your head.

You Can If You Will

The dictionary defines Will as a noun: "the power of choosing one's own actions."[4] I agree with that definition in some respects. I believe Will has two major usages in today's society. The first is the common usage where we indicate something we "will" do in the future. In this respect, the word becomes a replacement for "am going to," as in, "I am going to go to the mall on Saturday." The sentence could also be said, "I will go to the mall on Saturday."

Other common occurrences are statements like "I will take out the trash," "I will get that report to you on Thursday," or "I will start exercising next month." This particular usage of Will is a weak form. In fact, it's so weak that many of those sentences probably felt a little awkward to read. This is because in hiding the Will of the underlying situations, we often contract the subject (I) with the helping verb (will) to form "I'll." Why do we do this? Because we don't want to feel obligation to actually exert our Will, and it's easier to ignore the opportunity if we don't say the full word.

But this brings us to the *real* meaning of "Will"—the *dictionary* meaning. Go back two paragraphs and reread that definition. Thank you. Now, let's dissect it for a moment. This doesn't mean power in the sense of ability. The *ability* of "choosing one's own actions" is a divine right. No one can take away your ability to make your own decisions (though we do apply penalties to certain actions to make them less appealing—but that's another subject for later).

Instead of ability, we want to talk about power in the sense of

---

[4] Will. *Random House Webster's College Dictionary.* Random House, 2010.

energy and strength. In our case, the definition could be tweaked to read more like "the power gained from and expended in choosing one's own actions." We're talking about old-fashioned Will; the kind of 'grit' or 'gumption' or 'courage' that so many of our role models seem to possess in spades. When we admire people who pushed hard for a seemingly insurmountable goal, we are typically admiring their Will. This kind of Will manifests in the form of determination and perseverance. This is the idea of pulling yourself up by your bootstraps—of taking on a task and seeing it through to the end in spite of the difficulties. We often refer to this as "strength of Will" or "force of Will"—or even "the Will to survive." In its purest form, Will stops you from giving up on something because you Willingly, Will*fully* forget how.

So, when I say in the chapter title, "You can if you will," I don't mean "you can if you are going to." The concept of "if you are going to" doesn't even make sense in this sentence. No. What I mean is that "You can if you exert your effort and energy to make it happen": "You can if you *Will*." We're not talking about intention for future action; we're talking about power and determination that you bring to bear on a current action.

As it turns out, humans are remarkably versatile, adaptable, capable creatures. You, as a human, are probably capable of just about anything you set your mind—or Will—to. Does that mean that anyone on the planet is capable of being an Olympic athlete? Or designing a fully functional rocket ship? Or winning a bid to be President of the United States? Or break the world record for the 100-meter dash? Maybe, maybe not. But it *does* mean something more profound:

"Of course you *can*, but Will you? It is not your ability but your *account*ability that ultimately determines your success."

Now, to answer the question about everyone being able to break the world record for the 100-meter dash or not, let's consider the idea of natural talent and what it means in life.

Leveraging Talents

In life, we each have a set of talents—predispositions, if you will—which make us different than anyone else. This is why some people make good politicians while others are just good at the 'game' of politics, and still others want nothing to do with the political arena at all. Talent and predisposition indicate why some people study business and others study art or science or music. Why do some people love to exercise while others seem adamantly opposed to the idea? You guessed it, at some level, there is a disposition toward one or the other.

Thankfully, there is no cosmic law that says you can't change your disposition(s). If you would rather get a root canal than go jogging, there are steps you can take to overcome your aversion to exercise—one aspect of which might be to pick an activity other than jogging. If there is something out there that you've always dreamed of doing—but which you haven't ever really worked at— you don't need to give up that dream. Chances are, you can do it; you have the ability. Just make sure you're realistic in what it will take to reach the level you dream of reaching. Da Vinci spent his whole life painting and sculpting and inventing. If you haven't been doing those things up until now, it's going to be very difficult to reach his level.

So, can I go out and paint the next Mona Lisa? I'm not da Vinci, so I probably can't. Could I go out and learn to paint? Certainly. And, with enough time and effort, I could become quite good at painting; I'm just not sure that I could reach da Vinci's level. The idea is to find your talents and interests and then leverage them, rather than trying to become a "Great" at something you have no predisposition toward.

Keep in mind that, most often, the reason people fall short of their dreams is that they don't have the strength of Will to stay the course. No path in life is easy, so any direction takes effort and energy and determination. If you want to learn to sing, you can probably do that. Just don't let your Will falter when you don't land that platinum recording contract. Most people don't get that contract—go watch American Idol or The Voice, if you don't believe me. Not landing the contract doesn't mean you can't still develop a wonderful ability to sing—don't believe me? Go listen to the people who *do* land those platinum contracts.

Consider the case of Michael Phelps, the most decorated Olympic athlete of all time. Was Michael Phelps born as a 22-

medal-winning Olympic athlete? No. Was he even born knowing how to swim? No. In fact, he didn't really start swimming until he was seven.[5] However, was he born with some talent for swimming? I would say yes. Did that talent mean he was automatically world-record fast once he learned to swim? No. That's why Phelps didn't compete in the Olympics until nearly a decade later at the Summer 2000 games when he was 15. By the way, he didn't win any medals that year. His success started two years later at some non-Olympic world competitions.

What Phelps *did* have, aside from his innate talent, was Will. He had the Will to work at swimming. He didn't just go down to the pool and float around; he pushed himself. He got a personal coach, Bob Bowman, to help him focus on proper technique. Phelps practiced and went to the weight room. He put in countless hours of time and effort and energy to hone and perfect his innate talent. He didn't just settle for what he was born with; he leveraged that gift and made it something more.

So, do you need to be born with some level of innate ability in order to do something? Sure. But we were all born with an innate level of predisposed ability to do nearly anything we want. What is it that you want to do? What do you want to be good at? What do you Will to happen?

As Henry Ford said, "Whether you think you can or you can't, either way, you are right."

As I mentioned in the Introduction to this book, I didn't have any desire to be a public speaker when I was growing up. The idea terrified me. But I had that ability deep within, and, through time and effort and energy and coaching, I've been able to cultivate that talent and turn it in to something worthwhile. Once I realized that the direction I wanted to go in life was going to require me to speak publicly, I started joining different coaching organizations, taking classes, talking to other successful speakers, and entering speaking competitions. I actually won third place in a contest in my home state for humorous storytelling.

---

[5] Michael Phelps. *Wikipedia: The Free Encyclopedia.* Wikimedia Foundation. Last Updated 20 April 2013. Accessed 23 April 2013. https://en.wikipedia.org/wiki/Michael_Phelps

What really matters in all this, however, is that I exerted my Will. I had the ability to be a good public speaker, but I never would have become one if I hadn't made a conscious effort. I had to make the decision and then stick with that decision—even when things were difficult or scary.

So the question is "Will you?" Will you "will" yourself to do the things that you already have the ability to do, but for which you may still need to train up skill to execute? Because if you have the "will" to do it, you can do it—and the converse is also true: if you don't have the "will" to do something, you are highly unlikely to get it done. More than simply wanting something to happen, you need to harness your inner desire and drive and then work to make that thing happen.

In the early 1900s, Thomas Edison said, "Genius is one percent inspiration, ninety-nine percent perspiration." His proverb is still true today. Edison was a true optimist with an amazing attitude. In fact, his attitude, which was a reflection of his will, kept him going when most other people would have quit.

Edison didn't have his success with the light bulb until he was 32, and it was not an easy journey to get that far. At another point very late in life, his lab caught fire and burned to the ground.[6] As the fire spread through the lab Edison told his son to go get Edison's wife and daughter and bring them. The son replied that it was too late and that the shop was already gone. Edison excitedly told his son again to go and get the rest of the family because "they'll never see a blaze like this again for as long as they live."

In the New York Times the next day, Edison was reported to have said, "Although I am over 67 years old, I'll start all over again tomorrow. I am pretty well burned out tonight, but tomorrow there will be a mobilization here and the debris will be cleared away, if it is cooled sufficiently, and I will go right to work to reconstruct the plant."

Edison is a great example of a person whose will was strong enough to keep him pushing forward even when "forward" pushed

---

[6] "Edison Sees His Vast Plant Burn." The New York Times, December 10, 1914.

back on him. That drive to succeed is a critical precursor to achieving success. In so many ways, your attitude really does determine your altitude.

Doing Hard Things

So now I want to change gears a little. Back in the early 1900s, Watty Piper published a story called *The Little Engine That Didn't Think It Could.* Have you heard of it? I thought not. You see, it never sold very many copies. Nobody bought it because you would open the book and the story was only a page long. It read:

> "The Little Engine didn't think it could. So it didn't."
> The End

Obviously, this book was a complete flop, so the publishers decided to go back to the drawing board and rewrite the story from a completely different perspective.[7]

This time, the story was about the very same Little Engine that was assigned the very same, very difficult task: take the toys up over the mountain to the kids in the village on the far side. This particular Little Engine wasn't rated for such a large load. Normally, a Bigger Engine would have been assigned to the job, but all the Big Engines were busy with other work, so the job fell to this Little Engine.

Well, the Little Engine wasn't about to let all those kids down, so it got hooked up to the load and started toward the mountains. At first, the job wasn't too hard and the Little Engine was able to gain a little speed. Then it reached the mountain, and it got a lot harder to keep going.

To keep itself going, the Little Engine started repeated the mantra "I think I can; I think I can" as it struggled up the mountain. It was hard, but the Little Engine was having some success; it was climbing the tracks, so it kept talking to itself: "I

---

[7] Piper, Watty. *The Little Engine That Could.* New York: Platt & Munk, 1961.

think I can; I think I can." Then, before long, the Little Engine was having enough success—even as the mountain got steeper—that its language changed: "I *know* I can; I *know* I can."

And you know what? That Little Engine successfully delivered the presents. As it crested the mountain and started down the backside, it said to itself: "I knew I could; I knew I could."

Now *that* particular story sold, and sold well. Since it's first printing a hundred years ago, that book has sold more than ten million copies in English alone. But why has it sold so well? Because people love a good story that resonates with truth: you can if you truly believe that you can.

It is also an example of the next concept I want to go through with you.

In life, every possible action can be grouped among four categories. Depending on which category a given opportunity falls into will determine whether or not you should even do it in the first place and, if you should, what kind of mental and emotional attention your should give to the task. Those categories are easy and worth it, difficult and worth it, easy and not worth it, and difficult and not worth it.

Worth *vs.* Difficulty

The idea here is that we want to make sure that we're channeling our Will—our energy, attention, time, and effort—into the right things, so we need to be able to eliminate some of the options right from the start. It doesn't do much good to set your mind to accomplishing something if that something is worse nothing, right?

So, let me introduce a little matrix diagram to help you visualize what we're talking about, and then we'll get into the details of how to approach these concepts.

Worth/Difficulty Matrix

	Easy	Difficult
Worth It	I Don't worry about it; just do it	II Do it; your focus will determine your success
Not Worth It	III Don't do it	IV Definitely don't do it

We'll start in Quadrant I and work our way around counter-clockwise to Quadrant II.

Quadrant I: Easy and Worth It

This quadrant includes things like calling your mother on her birthday, eating a healthy breakfast in the morning, telling your kids that you love them, etc. These are things that are not difficult but still provide value to us. How hard is it to pick up the phone and call your mother—especially since it's her birthday? How hard is it to pour yourself a bowl of high-fiber cereal in the morning— even if you have to force-feed yourself to get it down? How hard is it to give your daughter a quick hug and tell her you're proud of her? These are things that we sometimes forget to do because they are so simple and easy.

When presented with a task that falls in this quadrant, you should just do it and be done with it. There is no reason to stress over the opportunity because it's not hard to do it and then move on. Don't let yourself stress or agonize over these things; just get them out of the way.

So, for this quadrant, remember the Nike slogan: "Just Do It."

Quadrant III: Easy and Not Worth It

What do you do when, in the middle of dinner, the phone rings and the caller ID comes up "Unavailable"? With about 90 percent confidence, who is on the other end of that line? Do you answer it? Most people would say no. And why not? It would be easy. Just pick up the phone, nothing hard about that. But is it worth it to you? Most people would again say no—at least in most cases.

The difference between this quadrant and the last is that the actions in this quadrant are *not* worth it. This quadrant would include picking up a new vice, like gambling, drinking, or smoking, but also includes more innocuous things like spending the whole day in front of the TV, ignoring your spouse, or calling in sick to work when you aren't actually sick.

Just because something is easy to do doesn't mean you should do it. It would be easy to ignore all traffic signs for the rest of my life—but my life would likely be much shorter as a result. It would be easy to walk out of the grocery store with a cart full of food—but the jail time and criminal record wouldn't be worth it.

In other words, if it's not worth it, *don't do it*. Ease, in this case, is irrelevant. End of story.

Quadrant IV: Difficult and Not Worth It

How you treat something in this quadrant is kind of a no-brainer. If you're not going to do something that's *easy* and not worth it, how do you think you should react to something that's *hard* and not worth it? That's right. *Don't do it.*

This would be any number of activities that teenage boys participate in, organized crimes, cheating on a spouse, or most of what you see in reality TV these days. Less severe examples would be building a house without any tools (try driving nails with your hands), running for public office against a wildly popular incumbent, learning to throw a full deck of playing cards—all 52—into a hat from 10 feet away, or building a rocket ship in your backyard. To most of us, a lot of these ideas sound so ridiculous as to be outright stupid. Typically, people only end up caught on something like this if someone else has made a challenge of pride. Don't let yourself get suckered in—by yourself or anyone else.

If it's hard to do and there's no payoff or purpose? Don't waste your time on it. That's just common sense.

Quadrant II: Difficult and Worth It

Last, we have those things that are difficult but still worth it. To be clear, this doesn't mean heaps of effort for small rewards. This is the category for hard things that have a real payoff at the end. Maybe you're working on a multi-million dollar deal with a sensitive client. Maybe you're trying to fall in love with the right person and then buck the trend and make the relationship last. Maybe you're trying to raise kids. Maybe you're contemplating doing night school to expand your training and marketability while still maintaining your current job. Whatever the case, what you're doing isn't easy—but it's worth it in the end.

At the risk of sounding Machiavellian, these are the instances where the ends really do justify the means—or at least the time and effort. Often, these things require overwhelming amounts of time, energy, and attention, but they also pay off big. Usually, the only way to accomplish these things is to walk straight into them and work your way through. Typically, shortcutting the process would short-circuit the end result.

Imagine being old and gray—sitting across from your sweetheart after decades of love and support. Then imagine your kids coming to visit not because they feel obligated but because they love you and want to come see you. Now think of that comfortable retirement you secured by putting in the time to land big deals while also advancing your career through that night schooling. Sure, there's a lot to enjoy along the way, but don't we all have a dream kind of like this?

Focus Locus

If you find that mental image motivating, or can imagine it being motivating, then you have struck the nail on the head for where your focus needs to be. Remember that story about the Little Engine? Why do you think the Little Engine could make it up that mountain with that heavy, heavy load? Do you think the Engine was focused on how heavy the toys were? Or how steep or tall the mountain was? Think again.

What we focus on largely determines our success or failure when the task is both difficult and worth it. If we focus on our ability to pull the load and the inevitable smiles on the faces of all those kids, then we can struggle up the mountain and get over without losing hope—without breaking our Will. If, however, we focus on how heavy the train cars are behind us and how precipitous the mountain is rising up in front of us, our fear will choke our hope.

For a moment, let's imagine the narrative of *The Little Engine That Didn't Think It Could*. If the book had been longer than that single, hypothetical page, the story would have gone along these lines:

The Little Engine set out from the station thinking how heavy the cars were. It tried to pull, but gaining speed was so hard. And then the Little Engine reached the mountain. It started up at first, saying to itself, "This is hard; I don't think I can." Pretty soon, as the grade climbed and the going got tougher, the Little Engine began saying, "This is *too* hard; I know I can't." And then the Little Engine stopped, blaming its failure on the difficulty of the journey.

Kind of a morbid tale, isn't it? It's so depressing to read because we've all seen people who think like that Little Engine—or maybe we've *been* those people at times. As the Little Engine sets out, you just know that it has already decided to fail. That's what focus on the difficulty is: a decision to fail. You can look at that attitude as focusing on something—anything—to be an excuse. Since we don't really want the reward—even though the reward is worth it—we look for a way out of the difficulty.

Focusing on the end reward, however, is like telling yourself that you've already accomplished the task. Sure, in some small way it's like brainwashing yourself—but isn't focusing on the difficulty a form of self-brainwashing too? When you focus on the reward, it's much easier to stay positive. As it turns out, studies show that happy, positive people are more productive and effective in their work.[8] Optimism doesn't mean the work is easier, but it does mean that you're better at doing the work.

In some respects, Will—true Will—is all about keeping the right perspective. Remember, no matter how difficult this task is, you already know how worth it the result will be. Few of the truly valuable things in life come easily; most require blood, sweat, and tears. If you are unwilling to bleed, sweat, and cry along the way, you'll end up taking the easy path and missing out on all the "worth it" things you might have otherwise had.

Instead, keep your goals in mind and push forward. Focus on the good in life. Focus on what "it" is. Which, of course, raises the question of what "it" *is*.

What Is "It"?

"It" is, as it turns out, the difficulty. In other words, if something is difficult but worth "it," we're simply saying that the end value is worth all the difficulty through which you must pass to reach that end value. What level of difficulty any given end result is worth to you is entirely up to you. You might be willing to walk through a burning building to rescue your child; most of us wouldn't be willing to walk through that same building to rescue a TV.

Essentially, we're describing a cost-benefit analysis. So, at some point before you begin an endeavor, stop and decide whether it is worth it. What is the reward you hope to achieve? What will success bring you? Fame? Money? Happiness? Family? Security? A clean, clear conscience? What is that reward worth to you, and are you willing to bleed, sweat, and cry to earn that reward. If so, then the task is worth "it" for you—though it may not be worth it to someone else. That's fine.

As Ralph Waldo Emerson said, "Whatever course you decide upon, there is always someone to tell you that you are wrong. There are always difficulties arising, which will tempt you to

---

[8] Myers, David G. *The Pursuit of Happiness: Who is Happy--and Why.* New York: Avon, 1993.

believe that your critics are right. To map out a course of action and follow it to an end requires courage."

Remember, courage is Will. You can if you Will, and the way to maintain your Will is to focus on the worth, instead of the difficulty. If you start to listen to your detractors or question yourself or focus on the doubts, difficulties, and insecurities along the way, you are setting yourself up to fail. Focus on the worth and "it"—the difficulty—will melt away, just like the Little Engine that could.

If you want to fill your life with all of that worth and value, Quadrant II is where you need to focus your effort. If something is easy and worth it, just do it and be done; that doesn't take much effort but usually doesn't bring much reward either. If it's easy but not worth it, don't do it; inaction takes no effort. If it's difficult and not worth it, *really* don't do it. If we do the math here, all of your effort is still left over after those three quadrants—left over to focus in Quadrant II.

This is one of the critical keys to success: you need to balance your life so you can focus your efforts on reaping the worth from the difficult endeavors, rather than wasting effort in the other quadrants. The rewards from activities in Quadrant II tend to be proportionately higher than the rewards from Quadrant I; *i.e.,* you'll get more out of Quadrant II for the same effort than you would get out of Quadrant I; it just takes a lot more effort to reach the much larger reward in Quadrant II.

What I'm really trying to help you understand is that successful people do hard things. If you want to be successful, you can't just do the easy things; you will have to roll up your sleeves, put on your gloves, and go to work. I'll say it again; successful people do hard things. It's really that simple. These people are successful because they're willing to put in the effort to achieve results that everyone else thinks are too hard to get.

Watch Your Mouth

Successful people don't indulge in deflationary talk about whether they can or can't. Successful people just focus on the reward, grit their teeth and, like the Little Engine that could, pull.

Your language about a task will often indicate your likelihood for success; your language is very revealing about your Will. If your language is focused on the difficulty, where do you think your mind is focused? Don't indulge in talking about how hard things are or you will simply end up talking yourself out of success.

This is something you can monitor in yourself, conveniently. Listen to your language when you talk about things. Do you use weak, distancing words and phrases—things like "I can't...," "I wish...," "I need...," "I want...," or "if only..."? Phrases like this indicate a lack of Will on our part and are unbecoming of successful people. If you "wish" for something, what you're really saying is that you want the reward, but you want someone or something else to deliver that reward to you. To "need" or "want" something doesn't even imply any intent; these verbs just state the "fact" of your desire without indicating any action or effort on your part.

Don't reinforce weakness in your Will or cultivate a reactive, victimized mindset. If you want something, take responsibility for it. Use words and phrases that empower you and help motivate you. Talk like you're going to make something happen. Instead of "I don't think I can," say "I think I can"—and then go prove yourself right. This is the concept of the self-fulfilling prophecy and psychologists have found powerful connections between positive language and overall ability. If you call someone a victim, they'll become a victim. If you call someone strong, they'll become strong. If that someone is you, then the strength of your language is doubled because it reinforces itself every time you speak.

If you say, "I need a glass of water," then I'll say, "That's nice. What are you going to do to get that glass of water?" You'll reply, "I'm going to get a cup out of the cabinet and go to the sink." Now we're talking. Instead of just giving up and hoping someone else will do the work, plan out the actions and then do them—and let your language reflect that intent.

Unless the action requires a skill set that you don't currently have—I can't pilot an airplane (because I've never tried to learn)—using the contraction "can't" is really just saying "won't." Do you know what "won't" is a contraction of? Will not. So when you say you can't do something, you're completely right—because what you're really saying is that you Will it to not happen. Wishing for something, wanting something, is not the same as going out and getting that something. To put this in perspective, let me tell you a story from my childhood.

Back in my little league days, I went on a long car trip with my family. Being only about 10 at the time, it wasn't too many hours before I was tired of the drive. So, of course, I did what every kid does. "Dad, are we there yet? I wish we were there."

"Dad, are we there yet? I *really* wish we were there."

"Dad? I wish we were there already."

After I'd been whining this over and over for a while, my dad stopped me and said, "Son, open both your hands. I want you to wish in one and spit in the other and then tell me which one fills up first."

The lesson was clear: I wasn't going to get any results by wishing into my hand, but I was certainly going to get some kind of result by taking action—by spitting in my other hand. Now, between you and me, just like for little Ralphie, my dad didn't say "spit." But, either way, that lesson stuck with me all these years since: wishing doesn't get you much.

Have you ever heard the phrase "all bark and no bite"? Well, the same concept holds true here. Wishing and wanting and using weak, defeatist language is just bark. It's all just "talk." It doesn't do anything, so it's not worth it. In fact, as easy as it is to speak this way, it's a Quadrant III activity: easy but not worth it. You're just wasting energy. Have you ever seen a little kid throw a fit about wanting something simple—something the parent would be happy to provide it asked nicely? Or the kid will throw a fit about not wanting to clean the bedroom? How much energy do they waste throwing that fit—and the bedroom still needs to be cleaned in the end?

When we give in to language like this, we do the same thing. We waste our energy and, in the end, the task still needs to be accomplished. Instead of making up excuses and wasting time, if we just buckled down and got started, we'd find ourselves climbing the mountain and then over the other side—and have energy to spare because we didn't waste it all throwing the fit first.

Parable of the Farmer's Bull

Now, I've been hinting about how where you focus will largely influence your tendency to make excuses for yourself—excuses which inevitably lead to failure. To help you better understand that concept, I want to tell you a little story—a parable.

This is a little tale of woe. Once upon a time, not so long ago, there was a gentle and kind-hearted farmer. Though he lived in meager times, he had an industrious mind and an entrepreneurial spirit. He was quite successful in his farming business, having specialized in such crops as corn, wheat, barley, and hay. He also enjoyed a small but thriving dairy farm.

One day this farming entrepreneur was struck with an idea: "Cattle ranching could be quite profitable," he thought to himself, "This could be just the thing to add to my small but growing enterprise."

He already had a fair number of cows from his dairy business that he could begin with, but what he was lacking was a quality bull to act as sire for a growing herd. So, the farmer conducted some research and diligently shopped around. Finally, he found a rancher in a nearby village that had a quality bull for sale. One thousand dollars was the asking price. Not cheap for the time period, but then again quality never is.

The farmer and the rancher conducted their business and closed the transaction. The farmer paid the rancher one thousand dollars cash and promptly began his journey home with his new bull in tow, mulling over his plans with excitement along the way.

About a week later the rancher from whom the farmer had purchased the bull came to call. He said to the farmer, "I know this is going to sound strange, and I am sure you will not be pleased, but I need you to pay me another thousand dollars for that bull."

The farmer was indeed not pleased. In addition, he was also confused. Had he not already paid one thousand dollars for the bull? Hadn't the price already been agreed upon? Was the bull not already his? All these thoughts and more went through to the farmer's mind. Finally, all he could bring himself to ask the rancher was, "Are you sure I need to pay you another thousand dollars?"

The rancher replied, "I am sure."

And with that the farmer reached into his satchel, retrieved another thousand dollars, and handed it to the rancher.

Trying to ease his troubled mind regarding the circumstances surrounding the purchase of his bull, the farmer quickly immersed himself back into his new cattle business and soon forgot all about the rancher and the extra thousand dollars.

However, after another week had passed, the rancher came to visit the farmer once again. He began much the same way as he had during the previous visit. "I know this is going to sound strange …" said the rancher as he went on to explain that yet again he required *another* thousand dollars for the bull.

All the same thoughts again went through the farmer's mind about having already paid, the bull already being his, and also about how expensive this was getting. But, once again all the humble, honest farmer could bring himself to ask was, "Are you sure?"

"I am sure," said the rancher. And with that the farmer paid the rancher yet another thousand dollars for the bull.

This continued for several weeks until eventually the farmer had no more money left to pay. In fact, the farmer found he was bankrupt. He lost his new cattle business, his previously successful farm, his beautiful home, and all that he possessed. The farmer was left with nothing. He was destitute.

The End

Now, in the beginning I told you this was a tale of woe, and I was true to my word, but this sad little story is not without a moral for the rest of us.

The moral of the story is …

… Never, *never*, buy your own BULL!!!

My dear friends, I am fully aware that my little parable is blatantly corny, maybe even a little too obvious in its play on words. And even though you may have rolled your eyes, I am pretty sure you won't forget this story any time soon. The truth that it speaks is quite plain.

There is an old saying, "Fool me once, shame on you. Fool me twice, shame on *me*."

It is one thing for us to buy our "own bull" once, maybe even twice, but to buy our "own bull" again, and again, isn't that just too expensive? To fool ourselves over and over, isn't the price just too high?

The choice is ours, but we have to be awake and aware as to what our "own bull" really is. We must be willing to acknowledge within ourselves that we are responsible, that we are accountable for the choices we make. Ultimately it was the *farmer* who was responsible for the demise of his business and financial well-being, not the rancher. Sure, we could rightly say, "Shame on the rancher" for fooling the farmer once, but shame on the farmer for being fooled time and again until everything was lost.

> *So as my little parable draws to an end,*
> *keep this poem in mind my friend.*
> *Over your own eyes never pull the wool,*
> *and don't continue to buy your "own bull."*

Cowboy Up

So it's time to, in rancher terms, "Cowboy Up," and stop buying your own bull. What exactly does this mean? Allow me to tell you a true story to demonstrate it.

I had a client, we'll call him Jed—though that's obviously not his real name—who was about 50 pounds overweight. A common enough plight, but he'd been 50 pounds overweight for the better part of 20 years, he *knew* he was overweight, he *knew* he was completely able to lose the weight, and he really wanted to lose those 50 pounds—but he always had a reason not to. He hurt his knee or was too busy with work or needed to spend time with his family or whatever. He had all these reasons—*aka* excuses or "BULL"—so he just kept putting off what he knew he needed to do.

The reality of the situation was that his Will was too weak for him to tackle the mountain of losing the weight, so in order to console himself instead of recognizing the weakness, he made up these excuses and bought his own bull, over and over. And that happens to be the answer for eliminating the bull from your life: strengthen your Will. By strengthening your Will and eliminating your excuses, you can start to replace all that negativity with positivity; you can start to replace the bad with good—because it's the good in life that makes the difficulty worth it.

So how do you decide on what's worth it? How do you know if something belongs in Quadrant II or Quadrant IV? Well, a wise place to start is by learning to see worth in the things and events and people around you. In other words, you need to learn how to recognize good in your life and then seek more of it.

Recognizing Good

Whenever I take on a new client, I have a simple question for them: "Why would you engage in a coaching program?" The answers are numerous and varied.

Many people want to reach their business goals. Some want more balance in their lives or want to make more money. Some people are more concerned about lifestyle changes so they can lose 30 pounds and keep it off. Some want to strengthen their relationships. The list goes on and on.

When you take a step back and look at all these reasons from a higher level, they all share something in common: they are all good. In essence, all of my clients answer my question by telling me they want more "Good" in their lives. They see things that are "worth it," but they aren't sure how to achieve the results. What many of them don't realize is that there is a step even before going out and actively working for more Good.

First, if I want more Good in my life, doesn't it follow that I also want to be good at recognizing Good so I can account for the Good I already have? Otherwise, how can I be sure I won't miss any new Good I might create going forward? It takes time and effort to create Good in my life, so why would I want to recognize any less than 100 percent of what I create?

It doesn't make a lot of sense to put forward all the effort to create 10 "units" of Good if I am only going to recognize 2 units worth. That would be like building 10 houses and pretending that 8 of them didn't exist. Or closing 10 important sales and only recording and getting paid on 2 of them. Yet, for whatever reason, we do this to ourselves all the time.

It turns out, this is a talent or skill—being good at recognizing Good—which means that we can increase our capacity to recognize the good all around us by developing this talent. One of the easiest ways to increase our capacity to see and appreciate more Good is to be grateful for the Good we already see and appreciate. Gratitude is an extension of humility and a vital precursor to really refining your ability to see the Good around you.

Life's a Beach

How important is gratitude? Important enough to make it a conscious process every day of your life. This isn't a once-a-week or once-in-a-blue-moon type activity. Gratitude is something you need to do all day, every day. Allow me to illustrate through a little analogy.

Imagine that you are standing on a broad, beautiful beach.

In your right hand, you have 100 pounds of seaweed. It is wet, heavy, messy, smelly, tangled, slimy, and has bugs crawling in it. It is generally unpleasant in virtually every way. It is heavy enough that you are straining your whole body to keep from dropping it. But you don't want to drop it because you perceive that, mixed in with the unpleasant seaweed, are many important things you would not want to drop. So, despite the effort, you hang on.

In your left hand, you have one tiny, shiny grain of sand. Though it is small, it is very pleasant to look at as it catches the sunlight—haven't you ever noticed how a beach sparkles in the sunlight? If you were to look at this shiny grain of sand under a magnifying glass, you would see that it looks almost like a jewel or gem because it has been polished by the pounding waves for thousands of years.

So what weighs more? The seaweed or the grain of sand?

Of course the seaweed far outweighs the grain of sand. You could put the seaweed on your bathroom scale to weigh it. The grain of sand, on the other hand, requires specialized scientific instruments. How many grains of sand did you carry home from your last beach trip—without even realizing they were stuck to you?

But now take a step back. What does each represent?

The seaweed represents all the problems, trials, challenges, annoyances, frustrations, inundations, obligations, and stresses that often accompany some of the weighty, urgent, and/or important matters in our lives: the next staff meeting, the oil change for the car, the commute to work, the plans for your kid's next birthday party, the deadline for that upcoming project, how to surprise your significant other for your next anniversary, etc.

The tiny, shiny grain of sand represents the little things in life that we feel good about, all the little "wins." It could be anything, big or small—as small as cleaning your sock drawer and feeling good about it, to landing that big account without compromising your integrity, to helping put a new roof on the garage of that widow up the street. Whether you're doing a good deed for someone, celebrating a workplace success, getting a hug from a friend, taking time to play with your children, or appreciating the beauty of a rare double rainbow, you are making another "win." You may not have created the rainbow, but you can still win by pausing to appreciate the beauty of it. You may not put any of these things on the evening news, but they still help you feel good.

Now, as nice as these victories are, and as good as they make us feel in their moments, that 100 pounds of seaweed still far outweighs any individual grains of sand, right?

Actually, where did I say you were standing? That's right, on a beach. And what weighs more? The 100 pounds of seaweed? Or the entire beach? Obviously, it's not even close.

The beach may weigh millions of *tons*. The seaweed pales in comparison. There is an old saying: "I can't see the forest for the trees." Well, sometimes we can't see the beach for the seaweed. Sometimes we get so caught up in staring at the bugs and slime that we forget to be grateful for the beautiful, shimmering beach all around us. We need to count the tiny, shiny grains of sand in our lives so that they can accumulate in our hearts and minds, thereby forming a beach of happiness, peace, and success.

Let me also take a moment to point out that not all of these victories are so small. Some are quite large, in fact—large enough even to make you forget the seaweed for a time. Think of the rocks and boulders you sometimes see on the beach. These would be things like a big raise or promotion, the success of that new product line you introduced, a college graduation or wedding, a top box score on your performance review, the birth of a child, or finally taking that trip to Europe. Now, these things may or may not balance the weight of the seaweed on their own for a time, but even these big victories can't compare to the vastness of the beach. Think how many huge boulders you could make if you glued together all those tiny grains of sand. It is by truly appreciating the number of those little grains of sand that we truly appreciate the beach of life whereon we live.

The seaweed will still be there—there is still value wrapped up in those smelly strands, remember—but I can promise you that it will shrink in comparison to an entire beach full of the wonderful things in your life. And that's something to be grateful for.

Victory Journal

Allow me to extend to you a call to action—a little accountability, if you will. By the end of the day, create a Victory/Gratitude Journal. This can be electronic or paper, whichever you prefer, but it cannot be just a "mental list." Short-term memory of the average human brain can only store between five and nine different items. That's not a long enough list to record all the victories you experience in a single day, much less a week or more.

This journal is a place to record the small things that are victories in your life—the shiny, priceless grains of sand. You will be amazed at how much more you have to be grateful for when the small things don't go unnoticed and uncounted.

Also, your gratitude journal should include more than simple tally marks, which are easily forgotten when the great "eraser of life"—also known as the seaweed—comes along. Don't leave yourself in a position where, when asked about the little victories in your life, you simply hold up that fistful of seaweed and say, "Victories? No. Nothing but seaweed here."

It's too easy to get caught up in the day-to-day challenges and forget all the little victories if we only try to remember with our minds. That said, you don't need to write a paragraph about each one either. These are little victories so little entries are just fine—as few as two or three words, even. You need only enough description so that you can look back on these things and remember them: "Cleaned sock drawer." "Nailed presentation." "Called Mom." "Helped Jimmy." "Finished project." "Double rainbow."

Interestingly, as you begin to track your victories in your journal, you will also begin to accumulate that beautiful beach in your mind. Slowly, subtly, but steadily, your paradigm will shift to be more grateful—and that will help you have perspective to be more effective.

Remember, Life's a Beach—and it's wonderful.

A "Good" Bucket

Now that you can see around you all the things you can be grateful for, allow me to share another analogy to relate this back to treasuring up the Good in life.

Imagine that Good is actually some kind of physical liquid, like water. It's beautiful, pure, clean, clear, and delicious. To drink a little can set you at ease in the most uncertain times, strengthen you when life's challenges seem impossible, and help you focus when the world is in chaos around you. Clearly, Good is a precious commodity.

Well, as it turns out, each of us has a bucket to carry around our Good in, and we go around trying to collect Good to fill our buckets with. Ideally, we want to keep that bucket as full as possible, right?

So, when given the choice between two buckets, do you pick the bucket with lots of tiny holes in the bottom (like the holes in a colander or sieve), or the bucket with no holes at all? It's not a trick question, just an easy answer: we want the bucket with no holes in the bottom.

This isn't to say that you couldn't make the bucket with holes work, but for me to keep that kind of a bucket full, what would I have to do? That's right; I'd have to put Good in faster than Good was dripping out the bottom. Again, not impossible, but possibly more effort than necessary, and we have other places we need to direct that effort. To make matters worse, I'm losing a whole lot of Good every day.

Clearly, you want the bucket with no holes. That way you can fill it, and keep filling it, without it draining all on its own. With this kind of bucket, you can fill it until your bucket "runneth over." I don't mind so much if it's running out the top—that just means I'm carrying all the Good I can possibly contain. What I don't want is to have it draining out the bottom to where, one day, I might find myself in need of a drink only to have my bucket empty.

If I can keep my bucket mostly full, then I don't mind when I need to take a little drink. I don't mind if a little evaporates away naturally. I don't mind if I need to share a little with a friend. That's all fine because I can keep filling. I just don't want it draining out the bottom because it ends up being too much effort to keep my bucket filled.

This all seems like common sense, right? Well, as it turns out, most people's Good buckets have holes in the bottom. Kind of like being unable to see the vast, beautiful beach for that hundred pounds of messy seaweed, many people aren't getting the benefit of the good they experience because it is running out of the holes in the bottom of their buckets. The real problem is that all too often, they don't even see the holes in their buckets.

What about you? Do you have holes in the bottom of your bucket? If so, how do you fix that? The only solution can't be to run around collecting Good faster than it runs out the bottom, can it? Thankfully, no. It is possible to plug the holes in the bottom of the bucket.

In effect, the bucket is your memory. It can only pick up so much Good unless you specially tune your mind to see the Good. The rest of the Good—the part you don't see—is like the Good that runs right out through the holes in the bottom. By making a focused effort to see, understand, appreciate, and remember the Good you experience, you begin to plug those holes. You start to retain more of that Good so you can make use of it later.

As we start to focus on the Beach and plug the holes in our

buckets, we put ourselves in a position to appreciate all that life has already offered—and all that it will still offer, if we'll just allow ourselves to see it.

In doing this, we become better at discerning what's "worth it" and what's not. We also treasure up that precious Good, strengthening our Wills for when things get difficult. Looking for the Good in life will also help you be more optimistic and shift your language to be more positive. Making changes and putting your life back into your own hands isn't necessarily an easy thing, but it's entirely possible for you. *You can by using your Will.*

Homework

Will you commit to focusing your effort in Quadrant II— Difficult and Worth It?

___ Yes ___ No

Write a list of all the Quadrant I obligations you've been putting off. As you fulfill these obligations, cross them off the list. Carry this list with you until you have completed each task. And remember, don't stress about these things; they're easy.

Now think of one of the Quadrant II activities that you've been putting off because it seems too difficult. Record it on the line below.

_____

_____

Will you commit to accomplishing that thing this week?

___ Yes ___ No

Language Journal

From the time you wake up in the morning, listen to the way you talk. Every time you say something negative, reactionary, or weak-willed, write down the negative portion; *i.e.*, "I can't do that report this week" becomes "I can't" in your journal. Then, each time you reuse that defeatist language, add a tally mark.

The idea here is to track your language use so you can work on controlling and changing it. This journal will help you be more aware of what you say and, in turn, how that affects your outlook and actions. As you record your speech patterns, you will be able to reduce your reliance on weakness and strengthen your Will instead. Essentially, you will learn to express what you can and will do, instead of offering excuses.

Will you start a Language Journal (either in a physical notebook or an electronic file)?

___ Yes ___ No

Will you keep it with you at all times to record what you say?

___ Yes ___ No

Gratitude/Victory Journal

Start a victory journal and carry it around with you. In the journal, record the date and a three-word description of each victory you experience. Don't leave out the tiny victories (like the sock drawer) and feel free to spend a little more time and a few more words on the large victories (that huge deal you just landed). Just remember that you only need to record enough to remind you of what the victory was.

Will you start a victory journal (either in a physical notebook or in an electronic file)?

___ Yes ___ No

Will you keep it with you at all times?

___ Yes   ___ No

The Common Denominator of Success

I'd like to share with you a simple yet profound experience I had. It was as simple in the sense that I was just reading an article, but it was profound and life changing as I went through because it opened my eyes to a way of thinking I'd never considered before. I've included the entire article as *Appendix A* in the back of the book, but I'll just cut and paste some excerpts here as we go along.

This text comes from Mr. Albert E. N. Gray in an address he gave back in 1940.[9] Mr. Gray was an insurance salesman for the first part of his life, transitioning into public speaking about life insurance subjects as his life progressed. This particular address, *The Common Denominator of Success*, details some simple principles that set apart the successful from the unsuccessful.

I'm going to share this experience by highlighting some key quotes and how those quotes impacted me. In doing so, I hope to capture the emotions I felt as my paradigm was shifting—in hopes that you can experience a similar shift.

"The common denominator of success – the secret of success of every [person] who has ever been successful – lies in the fact that he [or she] formed the habit of doing things that failures don't like to do."

When I first read that, my thought was "Well, that makes sense. Obviously successful people are doing things that unsuccessful people aren't doing." In fact, I started to wonder, at this point, whether I should even continue reading. I wanted to be enriched, not to waste my time reading true-but-painfully-obvious stuff.

*"If the secret of success lies in forming the habit of doing things that failures don't like to do, let's start the boiling-down process by determining what **are** the things that failures don't like to do."*

After I read this, I started to think "Oh. Maybe there's some

---

[9] Gray, Albert E. N. *The Common Denominator of Success.* National Association of Life Underwriters, 1940.

value here after all. He's about to give me a list of all the things that failures don't like to do. Once I have the list, I can start checking the boxes as I form the habits. This'll be great." Now I was interested, so I kept reading.

Second Nature

"The things that failures don't like to do are the very things that you and I and other human beings, including successful [people], **naturally** *don't like to do. In other words, we've got to realize right from the start that success is something which is achieved by the* **minority** *of [people], and is therefore* **unnatural** *and not to be achieved by following our* **natural** *likes and dislikes nor by being guided by our* **natural** *preferences and prejudices."*

To which my response was "Hmm. This could change things for me." Now, in the real world, when someone says the word "natural," do we think it's something good or bad? All-natural foods, herbal remedies, naturopathic medicine, wildlife refuges, etc.

Typically, when we think of things being natural, we think that it's a good thing; it's good to embrace what's natural. This quote starts to tell a different story. Let me demonstrate with a question: Is it natural to brush your teeth?

No. It's not natural to brush your teeth. Animals—in all their natural goodness—don't brush their teeth. So why do you brush your teeth? So that your spouse/significant other will come within five feet of you? So that you don't get tooth decay leading to heart disease? So that you look better for pictures? These are all valid reasons, but they're also all wrong.

Think about it. Were you married, or even dating, when you started brushing your teeth? Did you even know what heart disease or tooth decay were when you started brushing your teeth? Were you worried about your appearance in pictures when you started brushing your teeth? Think back. How old were you when you started brushing your teeth?

Whatever your reasons for continuing to brush your teeth now, the reason you started brushing your teeth is because someone taught you to. At first, your mother brushed your teeth for you.

Then, as you grew up, she stood nearby and let you brush them yourself—though she retained the right to check that you had brushed well. As time continued on, she would just check on you while you were brushing. Then, eventually, she stopped checking altogether. You had formed the habit, and she didn't feel the need to enforce something unnatural on you anymore.

Someone helped you develop a habit that ran contrary to the natural order of the world. As a side note, most acts of hygiene are "unnatural" in their nature. I call this situation your Second Nature. Your first nature includes all the things that would have happened spontaneously—things like eating, sleeping, and using the restroom (whether a restroom was involved or not).

Your Second Nature is comprised of all the things you do which aren't natural but which have become so ingrained into your identity and consciousness that you no longer question why you do them. These are the habits that you don't even think about anymore. At this point, these habits feel just as natural as any natural instinct you were born with.

Now, to be clear about Second Nature, it's not a bad thing. Second Nature is actually really great—if it produces a result that you want. Many of your behaviors today would not be part of you if you'd been raised by wolves in a completely "natural" manner. The key to remember is that Second Nature habits are learned behaviors, meaning that you can always learn more.

Going back to the quote now, successful people form habits to do the things that failures don't like to do. In other words, failures want to do the natural things when successful people are doing the unnatural things that lead to success. Successful people overwrite their first nature with a more effective second nature.

For instance, is it natural to plan? Is it natural to keep a calendar and write down goals and events and track them? Before you say yes, think about how many people you know who can't ever seem to remember what they have going on that day, much less in the future. It is very much *not* natural to plan ahead or keep an appointment book. But how many successful people do you think keep track of their schedules? If it's not all of them, it's pretty close.

Is it natural to subordinate your feelings to your values? In other words, is it natural to do what you know is right even when it makes you uncomfortable or anxious? Yet this very quality is basically a requirement if you want to be able to make the hard decisions that lead to success.

The point in all this is that your natural tendencies are more than likely working against you. Only by overcoming those natural inclinations and rewriting your programming with an effective second nature can you come to have the success you want. Why? Because, naturally, I don't like to do hard things—like getting up early to go to work or working out hard enough to break a good sweat. Naturally, I don't like to delay my gratification—like waiting to buy that new car/boat/motorcycle until I can afford it cash instead of credit. Naturally, I don't want to exercise self-control—like saying no to that cookie/brownie/ice cream sundae.

Commitment

Now, back to Mr. Gray.

You're not going to plan your day's work when you know in your heart that you're not going to carry out your plans. And you're certainly not going to keep an honest record of things you haven't done or of results you haven't achieved.

My emotional response to this one was, "That makes sense. I agree with that." After all, do people like to fail? No. People don't like to fail. But do you know what people like even less than failing? Written proof that they have failed. Right? It's like a bad letter grade on your report card. It's not enough that you didn't learn the subject matter, now someone has labeled you with that failure.

Who in their right mind is going to set up a plan unless they intend to see it successfully through? Why would you plan out your day if you weren't going to carry out the plan? All that does is set you up for failure *with a written record of that failure.* This is the primary reason that people don't write out their goals. It's easier to let yourself off the hook if there's no real evidence of your goal in the first place. Once it's written, there is an added level of accountability.

It's not that we don't want the goal or that we don't want the success; it's because we don't want a record of our failure in the off chance that we're unsuccessful at achieving the goal. The problem is, it's natural to not want to work for a goal, so we need commitments to help us stay on track.

For example, imagine you just took out a mortgage and bought a house. Is the bank going to let you take their money and move into the property without signing anything? Not likely. The bank wants to see you make a commitment to repay. And even if you pay cash, you still have to sign the title documents to demonstrate your commitment to the purchase.

The extension of this is that you are not going to write out your goals—a series of commitments and outcomes—unless you are truly committed to completing them. And that works in reverse too. If you're truly committed to a goal, there's no reason why you shouldn't be willing to write it down. In fact, if you *don't* write it down, you've just betrayed and minimized any commitment you may have been feeling.

Purpose

Any resolution or decision you make is simply a promise to yourself, which isn't worth a tinker's dam unless you have formed the habit of making it and keeping it. And you won't form the habit of making it and keeping it unless right at the start you link it with a definite purpose that can be accomplished by keeping it.

When I read this, my thought was, "I think I feel an epiphany coming on. I've got to like the purpose with the plan. I've got to link the resolution and the method in my mind, not separate them. And then, when they're linked, I finally have a shot at making promises to myself *and keeping them.*"

So, are you ready to receive the secret to success in life? You'd better sit down for this one. I know we haven't been together long, but the time has come to give you this very important bit of knowledge. The secret to success in life and everything else boils down to one simple principle:

Your ability to make *and keep* commitments *to yourself.*

It's that simple. I know, good thing you were sitting down, huh?

Now, it's very easy to make a commitment and, when that commitment is to someone else, keep it. When our promises become public domain because we involve another person, we don't often have problems doing whatever it takes to maintain our integrity, right? You may know (or know of) a few people who have issues with keeping their word, but most of us understand this concept and follow it.

But why then is it so easy to break a commitment made to one's self? Is it because we value ourselves less than we value others? Perhaps. I think it has more to do with the accountability side of things than whether or not we respect ourselves. Think about it, if life gets busy and "something's gotta give," what commitment are you going to give on first? The one to your boss or the one to yourself?

You're only accountable to yourself if the only person involved in the goal is yourself. You don't lose any public face for giving up on that goal, and, since the goal was probably never written down, no one else ever has to know anything happened. You can always just recommit so you can put it on the back burner again some other time right?

It's sad, but setting commitments for ourselves and then not following through has become almost a cultural phenomenon. If you don't have some "goal" you're working toward, then you must be a lazy vagrant, right? Everyone's got *something* to work on, right?

The catch is, without accountability, it's far too easy to make ourselves promises when, in reality, we have little-to-no intention of keeping those promises. We sometimes call these things "New Years Resolutions." Sometimes we "turn over a new leaf"—for a week or two. Why aren't we better about keeping these commitments to ourselves? I believe it has to do with maintaining vision—remembering why we embarked on that particular journey in the first place.

This is the reason why, as you've grown up, you've looked for reasons to keep brushing your teeth. As we said, it's unnatural to brush your teeth, so the natural thing is to quit brushing your teeth once there's no longer a reason. This concept works the same way for many people with diet or exercise programs: once they start to see the results, they quit the program because they've "achieved" the reason.

As you cultivate the skill to connect your purpose with your goal, you will be more inclined to keep your commitments to yourself. If you can keep commitments to yourself—the hardest client—then you will have no problem keeping commitments to others. So, as you develop your ability to make and keep goals for yourself, you'll be in a better position to work with others and achieve success.

Okay? Well, then keep your seat because we're about to cite our last quote from Mr. Gray's address.

Results Versus Methods

*Successful [people] are influenced by the desire for **pleasing results**. Those who experience failure are influenced by the desire for **pleasing methods and are inclined to be satisfied with such results as can be obtained by doing things they like to do**.*

When I first read this, I was mad. I was *so* mad about this because it cut me to the core—but it was true. I didn't want to hear it because of what it meant I would need to change, but, once I read it, I couldn't deny it. My life was forever changed, and my blissful ignorance had been peeled away permanently.

I believed that I hadn't found the level of success I wanted because I hadn't found the right method for me yet. I had met successful people and tried out their suggestions and decided that there must be a better way for me. Their methods worked for them, but I needed something specially designed for me.

The truth is, up to this point, like most people, I wanted an "easy road" to success. I wanted someone to come along and say, "Kip, you're a perfect match for this job. It's a perfect blend of all the things you like to do—and only the things you like to do—and it'll bring you all the success you ever wanted." It's not that I didn't want to work; I just didn't want to do some of the hard work that was required to have the kind of success I wanted.

The other truth is, there is no "easy road" to success. Life isn't fair, and it isn't easy. That's all there is to it. Life is a struggle, but it is totally worth it. The good things in life are absolutely worth the struggles—but that doesn't mean the struggles will be any easier. This is what makes keeping commitments to yourself so valuable—and so difficult.

Looking for a more appealing method is fine if there are a hundred ways to achieve success in that venture. Just sort through them all and pick your favorite. The issue comes up when there are only a handful of ways to achieve success on a certain front *and you don't like any of those methods*. What are you going to do now?

Let me put this into perspective: how do you lose weight? A million different diets and/or workout plans out there but there's really only way to lose weight: burn more calories than you take in. That's it. People might claim there are surgical alternatives, but that's not *losing* weight, that's cutting it off—and without a change in habits, the weight will just come back.

Every diet and exercise program in the world is aimed at either taking in fewer calories or burning off more—all in an effort to get you burning more than you take in. It's that simple. Don't like any those methods? You're in big trouble if you're methods motivated. Don't plan on losing any weight. Ever. You can eat 10,000 calories in a day and still lose weight; you just have to burn 11,000 off. That's a *lot* of cardio, by the way.

Want to get your finances under control? You need to spend less than you make. It's that simple. You can increase your income or curb your spending or some combination thereof, but the root of financial stability is to spend less than you make. You will have to keep a budget and make sure to stay within that budget—or exactly match it—across every category. Overspend in any category and you start to go out of control again.

The point is, success is like the summit of a long mountain climb. You can take an existing path or try to blaze your own, but you have to keep struggling upward with your eye on the top. If you are more focused on pleasing methods—a pleasant alpine stroll—you will never reach the top. Ever. If you want to be successful, you have to be willing to do the things that failures won't do: you have to be willing to focus on the results and put up with the methods to achieve those results.

Don't like that method? Too bad. There's not another way to make your own success.

The good news is that once you start to achieve those results you want so badly, your feelings about the methods required will improve. You'll be grateful for the method—even if it isn't any more fun—because it will get you to where you really want to be. And there's more good news: as Emerson said, "That which we persist in doing becomes easier for us to do; not that the nature of the thing itself is changed, but that our power to do is increased."

As you focus on the results and exercise your Will to push through the methods, your ability to repeat the task in the future will increase. So, for you, the methods will seem easier the next time around, and the next after that.

So you may not *like* going jogging every morning (or night), but, as you do it and your health improves, you'll start to appreciate it more. You may not *like* keeping track of where you spend every penny each month, but, as you do it, your finances will start to come together, and you won't mind the methods so much.

Risks of Methods Motivation

But wait! There's more! Did you know that there's an entire industry built around making money off people who are heavily methods motivated? Now, it's not that these people don't want pleasing results—they do—but, even more than results, they want the method of getting there to be pleasing. The industry is that of the health and fitness infomercial.

It's a little later in the evening or early in the morning on Saturday. Your favorite fitness icon walks on screen and makes you an offer you can't refuse: Buy this new, scientifically advanced doohickey and squeeze it under your arm for 15 minutes a day, 3 days a week and you'll look just like the fitness icon.

Never mind the fact that the fitness guru is basically paid to go and spend hours every day in a gym, working on a variety of machines/weights. Never mind the fact that it's illogical to think that one $60 device could possibly make you look like a model. Deep down, we all know that person is lying through their teeth. It should be illegal, right?

Well, it's not illegal because of something called a money-back guarantee. If you don't have the promised results within six weeks, just return the product and they'll send your money back. No questions asked, right? Well, maybe they'll ask some questions.

In any case, we hear that we can be fit and trim and look amazing in just 15 minutes, 3 times a week and the natural instinct within us rises up and says, "Sign me up!" We all know it's not going to work—but what if it does? The chance is too good to pass up, right? Besides, there's a money-back guarantee. It's not like we're really risking anything.

So a methods-motivated person will order this new abs-inator extreme 3000, and, for a limited time, get the arms-inator extreme 3000 to go with it. Then what happens? Do they use the product? Maybe a couple times. What is cardinal reality of exercise, however? It's *work*. A subset of the population is addicted to the endorphin high they get from working out. For the rest of us, exercise is *work*. If you're more concerned with pleasing methods, how long are you going to keep up with the work?

But whether or not the product gets used is irrelevant. You're not going to end up looking like a gym bunny/bodybuilder by using some mail-order product. So, if everyone is calling in for a refund after 60 days, how do these infomercial companies make any money?

Let me answer that question with another question: if you're truly methods motivated, is it a pleasing method to call the telemarketers from a company and request a refund? The result (getting the $60 back) might be pleasing, but the method isn't. So how many of these people do you think actually call in to get their money back?

And that's why these infomercial companies make money hand over fist. The very people enticed by the get-fit-quick scheme are the same people who don't want to go through the hassle of getting their refund when they didn't get fit.

Retailers are doing the same thing now. You buy a product and spend a couple hundred dollars but get some sort of manufacturer's mail-in rebate. But how many people bother with mailing in the rebate? And, of the ones who do, how many actually follow all the necessary steps to qualify themselves to receive the rebate? That's right. Not many. People will let themselves be sold on the expensive product because they know they can get a rebate (that means the product is actually much less expensive, right?), but then they don't bother with completing the process to redeem the rebate because it's too much effort.

Have you ever sat down to do something important only to get partway through, throw up your hands, and say, "this isn't worth the hassle"? That's an indicator of being pleased by the methods. If it isn't worth doing, don't ever sit down to do it in the first place. If it *is* worth doing, then you need to see it through to completion. To give up partway is to give in to the nature of people who fail.

And that's why reading this address cut me so deeply. It cut me because I realized that, if I wanted to be successful, I had to learn how to make good goals and then keep those commitments to myself. I had to set goals to do hard things—hard things that would achieve good results—and not get dissuaded along the way by the methods. I not only had to be like the Little Engine in keeping my eye on the prize, but I also had to be willing to write down my plans and stick to them along the way.

Up until that point in life, I'd been a pleasing-methods person, which worked okay for many things. However, if I wanted to launch myself into real success, there were only so many ways to reach what I wanted, and I couldn't let myself stall out over the method; I needed to pick a lane on the highway and go for it.

Levels of Competence

We'll come back to the highway in a moment, but first, we need to talk about what happens when we try something and find the methods to be difficult. Specifically, we need to take a moment to talk about how we adapt to new situations and new challenges so that you understand how to take control of your motivation.

What happens when, going through life, we run into a situation in which we are unable to perform at the level we want? On rare occasions, the inability to perform is because we're attempting a task that, on an individual level, we'll just never be able to do. However, I am a firm believer that all of us can do nearly anything we put our minds and Wills to—just perhaps not to quite the level we might dream.

More often, I believe when we hit one of these difficult times, it is because we haven't yet developed the necessary skills and abilities to perform at the level we expect from ourselves. In some cases, we may even believe we *do* already have the necessary skills. We're just wrong. To illustrate how this happens, I turn to another matrix. The components are often attributed to Abraham Maslow, and are presented in diagram form here just you help you see the relationship.

Competence Quadrants

	Incompetent	Competent
Conscious	**II** You are still unable to perform the task but you are now aware of the deficiency	**III** You are able to perform the task but only through concerted, conscious effort
Unconscious	**I** You are not only unable to perform the task but also unaware of the deficiency This is First Nature	**IV** You can not only perform the task but also do it without needing to think about it This is Second Nature

This matrix explains how we can sometimes be unable to do a thing without even realizing that we are unable. The thing to keep is mind is that this matrix applies every time we want to improve ourselves. This diagram is, in no way, a judgment against you or your abilities. Obviously, you've gotten as far as you have just the way you are. The idea here is to help you see how you can go further.

Quadrant I: Unconscious Incompetence

Translation: You stink, and you don't even know that you stink (for an extreme example, think reality TV).

Quadrant I is us anytime we need to learn a new skill (or advance an old skill). The idea here is that, regardless of any preexistent ability, our efforts are insufficient to meet the requirements placed upon us. But, worse than simply being insufficient to the task, we don't even realize that we're insufficient. Our incompetence (lack of developed skill) is unconscious to us. This would be the business executive who thinks he's an amazing communicator and that he understands his colleagues so well, but his 360-degree feedback reports that he is impossible to work with because he never listens. In some respects, this quadrant can be compared to First Nature or hubris, depending on how you look at it.

Maybe you need to learn a new program to stay current in your industry, or as so often happens, maybe you *think* you already know the new program, yet everyone else in your department seems to be able to work at a much higher rate of output. Maybe you think you're a wonderful parent, yet your kids try to avoid you. Maybe you just think you're in great shape—but only because you haven't tried to do anything strenuous for a while.

The point is, until you know what to work on, you aren't going to improve. You can't very well set a goal to get better about something if you don't know what goal to set. You can't choose to move forward if you don't know where to go. At some point, however, your awareness will enable you to move from this quadrant into Quadrant II.

Quadrant II: Conscious Incompetence

Translation: You stink, but at least now you know you stink.

This tends to be the painful stage on this journey. After all, it's not exactly pleasant to see our own faults, but it's a necessary step on the path to improvement, balance, and success. Similar to any number of "Anonymous" 12-step programs, the first step forward is admitting that you have steps in front of you to take. If you believe you are already the pinnacle of perfection, you are unlikely to see room for improvement—and you're most likely stuck back in *un*conscious incompetence.

This is that moment when you get in the driver's seat of the car for the first time ever. You go to push the gas (or manipulate the clutch for the brave ones out there), and the car bunny-hops, so you freak out and slam the brakes and give everyone whiplash—and maybe even stall out. Most people come away from that experience thinking something along the lines of "I suck." The truth is, you only suck[ed] at driving (hopefully that's no longer the case, right?).

Now, be careful here to give yourself credit where credit's due. You've accomplished any number of things in life. You've grown and developed and cultivated skills. Take comfort and credit in those things. Don't let your recognition of opportunity cloud your vision of all the victories you've already had. Also recognize that seeing your inability will humble you so that you are open to learning, growth, and change.

That said, once you see room for improvement, you have moved into this second quadrant. No sustained, positive change ever happened in ignorance. Now that you realize your "incompetence," you can work on it. This is the stage of action. This is where you begin to develop the habits that will set you apart from unsuccessful people. This is where you set your goals and hold yourself accountable in order to move toward competence. Then, slowly, over time with lots of practice, you'll develop new aptitude and ability.

Quadrant III: Conscious Competence

Translation: You don't stink anymore, but it's not automatic yet.

At this point, you're reaching the level for which you aspired. You've gained the level of ability you needed to perform the task. In some respects, you've arrived. However, this isn't the final destination for your skill level. After all, at this point, you still have to focus closely on what you're doing. You have to remain consciously engaged in order to perform the work. The good news is, you've started to reach the goals you set.

This is like those paint-by-the-numbers books. You can get a nice-looking picture if you just pay attention and stick to the directions. Or think of the last time you cooked something from a new recipe. You could make something reasonable, but only if you focus and follow the recipe closely. This is the stage once you've "learned" to drive where you can make the car go, but it's not the smoothest drive your passengers have ever experienced—and you can't even think about talking to anyone else in the car or you'll lose your concentration.

Maybe you recognize that you have anger issues, but you consciously, constantly work to keep your temper under control. Maybe you know that you don't like to make sales calls, but you make a conscious effort to make them anyway. Maybe you see that you've been a bit absent as a spouse or significant other, but you're working to spend more time—and quality time—with your partner.

Basically, you've fixed the problem, but only if you stay focused. For that reason, this isn't the end of the process; it's the beginning. You want to be able to take that focus and effort and direct it somewhere else, right? Besides, your competence is based on your focus. If you stop focusing on the change, you'll easily regress to where you were before you started.

The catch is, you can't consciously move to the next stage. Why?

Quadrant IV: Unconscious Competence

Because this stage is all about being an expert but being unconscious about it. You develop this kind of expertise by focusing your efforts in Quadrant III. You'll be doing whatever it is day after day, time after time, until one day, you'll wake up and say to yourself "Whoa! Whoa! I just did that without even thinking about it!" And that's how you'll know you've arrived in this fourth stage. The transition will be slow and unnoticed; you'll only see it as you look back over all the blood, sweat, and tears you put into learning and growing.

This is the stage you want to reach. This is the Second Nature we talked about back in Chapter 2. At this point, your change effort is essentially complete—for now. You've reached a level 10, and the change has become internalized to such an extent that you no longer have to think about it. At some point in the future, you'll realize that there is another, higher level to work toward, but, for now, you've earned a little victory celebration.

Want an example? Have you driven anywhere today? What was it like? Are you still in Driver's Ed mode? Or can you drive without even thinking about it? When you think of driving, do you think about all the attendant components of driving (signaling before turning, using the clutch, maintaining a safe following distance, changing lanes, etc.) or do you just conceptualize "driving" as an aggregate of all those components without needing to focus on any given part?

You don't have to think about returning phone calls from your friends; it comes natural now. You don't have to worry about gossiping about your coworkers because you've rooted that out of your personality. You don't have to think about using less negative vocabulary because you've reprogrammed yourself to be positive. You don't have to worry about giving up halfway through worthwhile endeavors; you've trained yourself to instinctively focus on the results, not the methods—the reward, not the difficulty.

So let's take a look at how this Competence Framework comes together and functions in our lives by going back to our highway analogy. You already know you're a high-performance sports car, like a Ferrari. Doesn't it make sense that you want a nice, smooth, wide highway to cruise down? Well, there's more truth to that than you might expect.

The Neural Highway

As it turns out, the concept of a highway in the mind closely fits the actual, physical architecture of the neurons in the brain. In some respects, the brain is like a massive interchange between roads and highways of all sizes. On a most basic, physiological level, we function because our brains transmit impulses around our bodies to tell them what to do.

How does the brain decide what to transmit and where to send it? The brain works by selecting neural pathways that trigger actions in response to a stimulus event. In other words, each time we're presented with a situation, or stimulus, our brain checks for the best neural pathway and triggers that pathway in response. How does your brain choose the best pathway? It basically just chooses the pathway it's chosen most frequently in the past.

Effectively, every time you respond to something, you create an actual, physiological neural pathway—like blazing a new pathway in a forest. The pathways for the actions you pick most often become wider, thicker, and stronger, allowing impulses to travel down them more quickly—like a Ferrari down a highway. When you're presented with a stimulus, the brain will look to the most established pathways to send out its response.

So I'd like to tell you a story about your journey through life.

Try not to close your eyes, but picture that you're cruising down a six-lane superhighway in a Ferrari. You've got the wind in your hair (it's a convertible), the sky is clear and blue overhead, and there's no traffic. You have a free pass to push the pedal as hard as you'd like and go as fast as you want. There are no restrictions on how fast you can go because this particular highway is like the Autobahn—and you're the only car on the road, which means no police officers either.

So you are just flying down this highway, enjoying the drive, when you finally look up ahead and realize something a little alarming: the highway is taking you to the wrong place. You're not on the right course to reach the destination you had in mind. You look around, trying to figure out why you got on the wrong highway and realize that you're not even driving—you're in the passenger seat. Your brain is driving.

So, feeling a little confused, you look over at your brain and say, "Brain, why are we on this highway? Pull over. I don't think this is the way I want to go."

And you brain looks around and replies, "HA HA HA!! You? Think? That's why *I'm* driving."

So you sit back in your seat, feeling a little hurt, and think about that. Well, a moment later, you're looking out your window and you see, off the side of the highway, a broad, thick jungle. It looks like no person has ever touched this jungle before. It's thick with undergrowth and vines and trees and all kinds of plant life. But you don't really look at the jungle for long because, beyond the jungle, you can see the place you really want to go peeking out from above the trees. And it looks amazing.

So you address your brain again, "Brain. You see that over there? That's where I want to go."

And your brain looks out your window and says, "You want to go to the jungle?"

"No. Beyond the jungle. Can't you see that place on the far side?"

And your Brain looks again for a moment and says, "Oh. Yeah. Hey, that does look nice, doesn't it? But that jungle is in the way. I think we're just going to stay on this highway. Can't you see how fast we're going? Why would you want to slow down? Don't you know how hard it's going to be to cut through there? It's much easier to just go this way."

And now you face a problem. You've seen where you really want to go, but your Brain isn't interested in changing course, and it's still driving.

So, after a bit you decide that you're going to take back control of the wheel. Like a scene from an action movie, you climb over into the driver's seat, take the wheel, and push your Brain into the passenger seat. Then you pull over on the shoulder and get out.

Your Brain asks, "What are you doing?" But, instead of answering, you just pull your machete out of the trunk, grab your brain by the collar, and start toward the jungle.

The undergrowth is thick and tough and it's hard to sweat your way through, chopping a path with your machete. As if that wasn't hard enough, your Brain is kicking and screaming the whole time, telling you how much easier it would be to just stick to the highway. In spite of all that, because of your perseverance and Will, you manage to hack your way through and reach the destination on the far side of the jungle. Pretty nice, right? Well, the story isn't done yet.

What happens if, the next day, you take the passenger seat in the Ferrari again? That's right, you're going to end up on the wrong course again. What's more, how quickly can a thriving jungle swallow up every trace of your passage through? Maybe a day? Two at most? So if you don't slog your way through to that special place again, the pathway will disappear. Which means you're going to have to take the wheel again. You're going to have to pull over at the side of the road again. You're going to have to get out your machete and drag your brain back through that jungle again, bleeding, sweating, and crying as you go.

And you're going to have to do it again and again, day after day.

The good news is that after a while, the jungle won't close in quite as quickly. The path you've chopped to the place you really want to go will stay open just a little. Then, after a little longer, the footpath will get wide enough for two to walk side by side—though you're still just dragging your brain behind you. Then, after a while, you have the way clear enough to put down a little gravel. Then more gravel. Eventually, you're able to pave that little path into a one-lane road. And before you know it, that little trail you hacked through the jungle will become a new, freshly paved, six-lane superhighway.

Now you can finally drive your Ferrari again, and even better, you can toss your brain the keys again. As it turns out, that old superhighway—the one that took you to the place you *didn't* want to go?—is breaking down. It's in disrepair. So when your brain goes driving down this highway, it'll take the new route to where you want to go—and you'll have to humor it while it tells you all about the great idea it had to pave that new road to the better destination.

Building Competence

Aside from being an entertaining story, this account is the best way I've ever found to conceptualize the shift through the competence stages. Allow me to elaborate.

In Quadrant I, unconscious incompetence, you're sitting in the car and just enjoying the drive. You're not really paying attention to the destination or anything else; you're just relaxing and having a good time.

When you look around and realize you're going to the wrong place, you start to shift into conscious incompetence, Quadrant II.

You realize you're not going where you want, but your brain is quite content to do what it's always done. We've talked briefly already about the different levels of the mind. Well, as it turns out, the subconscious has a lot of strength. It's not some scrawny little force to be laughed at. The subconscious (or "Brain" in our story) is a huge, muscle-bound bodybuilder. It's strong and powerful—and it doesn't particularly *like* to be pushed around.

But once you cultivate the Will to reassert the dominance of your conscious mind, you can take back the driver's seat and start moving into conscious competence, Quadrant III. Remember though, you're going to have to exert your Will to drag your brain, kicking and screaming, through that jungle while you cut the path. Also remember that your brain still wants to take the old superhighway. It wants to send impulses down the most developed neural pathways, not down fragile, tiny, new pathways. So you will have to remain the boss of your brain, your subconscious, and continue to drag it where you want it to go.

The brain is less concerned with what's effective and more concerned with what's efficient. It wants to use the path of least resistance because that pathway will move the impulse most quickly. Your subconscious doesn't want to think about what it's doing; it just wants to receive a stimulus, process a response, and send it out as quickly as possible. It's a reflex reaction to keep everything going and it's going to go down the path of least resistance.

Which sounds like less resistance to you: a Ferrari on an open superhighway or a machete in the jungle? Dumb question, right? But only failures take that path of least resistance. Successful people will use their Will to do the things they don't naturally want to do. If you want to make a change, you can't do what feels natural to you because what feels natural is only a function of your established neural pathways. If you do what feels natural, you're just cruising down that original six-lane superhighway, not blazing the new trail to the destination you really want to reach.

Instead, you need to keep blazing that trail, over and over, day after day. Eventually, it'll get easier. Eventually, it'll become the new superhighway; it'll become second nature. Until that time, you can't let up on your Will or your emotional, subconscious mind will want to slip back to what it's always done before. Thankfully, no matter how strong or stubborn your subconscious is, it's still subordinate to your conscious mind. You are the boss of you; your subconscious isn't. So be the boss. Strengthen your Will and start making your own decisions instead of riding in the passenger seat.

This section has covered the secret to building habits and the secret about what habits to build. Now it's time for you to take control of what habits you form and act instead of reacting. It may not be easy, but *you can now that you understand.*

Homework

Write a short list of some habits you would like to develop; habits you've always wanted to have but which you've never really tried (or always failed) to achieve.

Now pick one of those habits and write it on the line below.

_____

_____

Will you commit to staying in the driver's seat on that one habit for the next week? Don't let your subconscious steer you anymore; be in control.

____ Yes ____ No

You Can If You Are

Can you build a house without a foundation? Many of you probably said no, but some of you might have said yes. Well, the truth is you *can* build a house without a foundation. So the real question isn't whether you can or can't; it's whether you should.

Suppose you just earned/won/inherited/discovered enough money to finally build that dream house of yours. The one with the walk-in closets, the indoor hot tub, the wrap around porches, and maybe even that swimming pool in the basement—or whatever other wonderful features you want in your dream house. What's that going to cost you? A million dollars?

Well, it turns out that I'm a General Contractor, and I really know the laws and regulations in the area where you plan to build this dream house. I happen to know about some loopholes that will allow us to build your house without putting a foundation underneath. Now, before you tell me "no," listen to the deal I have to offer you: I can save you 30 percent off the construction costs—that's about $300,000—if we just skip the stage where we build the foundation. It'll save on excavation, concrete, materials, and labor—and we won't have to clear as much of the land before we start, so you can leave more of the natural plant life in place. Additionally, if we skip that step and go straight into building, I'm confident we can have your house built and ready to go a whole month earlier. Sounds good right? Do you want to take my offer?

No? Why not? I can still use all the same premium materials inside: the tile floors in the bathroom, the granite countertops in the kitchen, the plush carpets in the bedrooms. I can still make it look just exactly the same from the outside too. The view from the street or backyard will be identical. It's not like anyone's going to know that there's no foundation underneath. Besides, it's *your* dream house, not theirs. Who cares what they think anyway, right?

You still won't do it? Not even if it could save you $300,000? Good. Why? Because you already understand what might happen to the house if it were built without a foundation. It would be more likely to settle over time, jeopardizing whole sections of the house and potentially making it structurally unsound enough that the house would collapse. You also understand the potential for mold, insect, and water damage that a foundation normally keeps out. The fact of the matter is that you understand the value of having a solid, secure place upon which to build the things that are supposed to last.

And what about "saving" that $300,000? By not putting down a foundation, don't you risk the $700,000 that you're still spending on the rest of the house? When that house settles, you'll have to tear the whole thing apart and start over. It won't take long to spend far more in repairs and remodeling than you would have spent on the foundation in the first place.

We're working on building a different dream right now: you. We're working on building your effectiveness at creating personal balance, so you can achieve business success. Do you think you should be building without a foundation?

The Foundation for Personal Effectiveness

The foundation for personal success is comprised of three things: Mission, Vision, and Values. You may have already heard different organizations or people talking about these concepts.

My grandfather was a dairy farmer, so naturally, when we would go to visit him, I would go to help him milk the cows. My grandfather had a three-legged stool for when he was milking, and that stool was always stable and secure. He'd move it around across sometimes-uneven ground without any problems. No matter where we were, that stool would stand firm.

Now, I've heard of some dairy farmers who prefer one-legged stools. I just wanted to dispel that myth. A one-legged stool seems like a good idea in terms of flexibility and movement, but you give up all the stability. If you shift your position in such a way that you lose contact with the stool, it will slip out from under you and leave you in the dirt. This is because, when you really think about it, *your* legs become the second and third legs for the stool. If you get separated from the stool, it can't stand on its single leg anymore.

In all my years, I have yet to see a two-legged stool. Most likely because it would offer no advantage over a one-legged stool while also being heavier and less versatile.

I have seen four legged stools, and they are wonderful in certain circumstances. The problem with a four-legged stool is that all four legs have to be perfectly, exactly the same length or the stool will wobble and be unstable. What's more, if the ground is at all uneven, a four-legged stool won't stand properly, resulting in wiggling, wobbly, or other foundational issues. And what have we already said about the rough and uneven nature of life? Your wheel may be a critical factor, but the road plays a role in the bumps too.

A three-legged stool, however, is stable on uneven terrain _and_ stable, albeit sloped, even if the legs are slightly uneven. This is why you need Mission, Vision, and Values for your life. These three concepts form that solid foundation upon which you can build your dreams, and like the three-legged stool, they are adaptable to the environment and stable under any conditions.

Mission

A mission is a personally empowering statement about who you desire to be and how you desire to get there. It serves as a personal constitution by which you can evaluate decisions and choose behaviors. In effect, this becomes the cornerstone of your foundation and the centerpiece of how you frame your life. Your Mission is no more important than your Vision or Values, but the Mission tends be the trunk from which the other two pieces naturally grow.

Ideally, it's concise but powerful. It should be not only memorable but also memorize-able. It should be short and compact so you can remember it easily in a moment. Think a sentence or two, not a page or two—though there are people and organizations out there with lengthy Mission Statements. There's no right or wrong length, but you need to be able to say this Mission to yourself in a moment of choice so you can make the decision in alignment with your Mission. I find that a sentence, or maybe two, is best. Does that mean longer ones are wrong? No. We can memorize entire songs. Stage actors (like the kind you find on Broadway, not in Hollywood) memorize their entire part in a production that might last two, three, or even four hours. The human brain has a stunning capacity to memorize and reproduce material.

But there are two big reasons why conciseness is better. First, you can't afford to pull out a piece of paper in order to remember your Mission just because it's too long for you to memorize. If you can't remember it without help, how are you going to use it? If you do need to pull out a piece of paper and read an entire document, chances are that you'll make the decision without bothering to check your Mission because the process of checking your Mission is too cumbersome. Second, even if you *can* memorize a long mission statement, the point is to be able to use it in an instant. If you have to recite two pages of Mission in order to make sure you're making the right decision, you're probably not going to bother with reciting your Mission.

You need to be able to call up your Mission at will at a moment's notice. You need to be able to make decisions quickly while also keeping those decisions in line with your Mission. You can't make quick decisions if you have to belabor your Mission for five minutes every time a choice comes up.

Now, if you have a mission statement already, and it's a page or two in length, that's okay. The Mission writing process I'm going to take you through will output a long-ish document to begin with. The remainder of the process, however, is designed to help you refine your Mission to become something more concise and powerful. My Mission, for instance, started out as a solid page, maybe a bit more. Now, it's just nine words long. I'm not going to share it at this point because I don't want to inadvertently influence your own Mission-creation process, but I know a number of people whose Missions have fewer words than those people have fingers; *i.e.*, some can count off their Mission on a single hand.

But, again, your mission won't start there. It will start longer and we'll work it down from there. If your first run is a page, that's okay for starters.

The reason I make a big deal out of little length is because life has a way of holding a gun to your head when decision time comes around. According to Laurie Beth Jones,[10] author of *The Path*, World War II soldiers had to know their Missions well enough to be able to recite them without hesitation in the dark of night. They couldn't fumble for a piece of paper to remind themselves. If those soldiers didn't know their Missions, they would end up shot.

Today, we don't get shot for being a little unsure of our Missions. However, as I said, life has a way of putting a lot of pressure on us, and, if we don't know our missions well enough to recite them in the dark of night, that pressure is likely to break us. So, unless you want to find yourself falling victim to your natural instincts and the path of least resistance, you need to know your Mission well enough to engage it whenever you are faced with a decision. And we're not necessarily just talking about big decisions here either. If you add up lots of little decisions, they shape your course as much as the big ones.

So you can choose to make decisions in the heat of the moment out of urgency, expediency, or indifference, or you can choose to plan ahead, have your Mission written in your heart, and make decisions accordingly.

Creating Your Mission

Now, as we get into the exercise of actually building your Mission, I'd like to pause and do a little activity with you. Normally, I would have you close your eyes but, since you'll need to read this, closing your eyes wouldn't work very well. Those of you taking advantage of the three-person coaching technique we talked about at the beginning of the book might be able to use your coachee to help you now.

To start with, I want you to clear your mind. Take a deep breath and try to relax. We're going to do a little word association game,

---

[10] Jones, Laurie Beth. *The Path: Creating Your Mission Statement for Work and Life.* New York: Hyperion, 1996.

and I want your mind to be ready. I'm going to "say" a word, and I want you to tell me the first image that comes to mind. Okay, are you ready?

Blue.

Now, tell me what you saw. Describe for me, in some detail, just what came to mind when I said the word blue. Good. Now pick an element of what you just described and tell me more about it. Does it have length? Width? Height? Depth? Temperature? What kind of texture, if any? How many? One? Hundreds? Use your words to paint for me what you saw.

Good. Thank you. Now, were there any feelings associated with what you envisioned? When you hold that thought in your head, how do you feel inside? Happy? Sad? Content? Agitated? I'm not trying to psychoanalyze you here, but I want you to think about something more for just a moment: Wow. All that from the word blue? I say one word and you can go into all that depth and description?

Okay. Now I have some startling information for you. I've done this exercise more than 3,000 times. In all those instances, about two-thirds of my clients have said sky in response to the word blue—and that's true even if the client doesn't speak English as a primary language. Another fifth said water. The rest have described any number of different things from flowers to clothes to cars. But do you know what none of them ever described for me? The letters b-l-u-e. Not one. I'm guessing you didn't think the letters b-l-u-e either—even though you'd just read them off the page. Why?

Because the human brain thinks in reference and symbol. Even these letters and words you're reading right now only have meaning because we've made them symbols for sounds. The brain—even for you "left-brainers"—doesn't think in letters and words; it thinks in pictures and emotions and memories and experiences; we just use words as an economical way to, as best as we can, attempt to convey the meaning that the brain attaches to things. So how much truth is there to the idea that a picture is worth a thousand words? Could you write a thousand words about what you thought of when I said blue? If you're taking this book seriously, I bet you could.

That old saying doesn't capture the full power of itself though: how many pictures is a single word worth? I told you to think about blue and you came up with all that description and detail. If you thought about blue again now, do you think you'd see the same image as before? Even if you did, could you come up with another image pretty quickly? Another interesting thing about all the times I've done this with clients is that I've never heard the same sky described twice. I've heard more than 2,000 different skies described, yet no two were the same.

The right words can trigger associations with dozens, or even hundreds, of pictures. Think about words like "mother," "school," "America," or "happy." I'm willing to bet that at least one of those words triggered multiple images, each image being worth more than a thousand new words. This is the secret to creating a powerful Mission. If you can find the right words, you won't need to rely on lots of them to remind your brain of the message you're trying to send. A few, choice words can convey all that meaning in a much smaller package.

Allow me to elaborate with another example. What kind of car do you drive? Do you have any idea what it weighs? The average car nowadays is easily 3,000 pounds; trucks and SUVs are easily 5,000 or more; even motorcycles can weigh 500 pounds or more. Pretty weighty, right? But let's say we take it down to a local scrapyard and put your car in their crusher. In a few minutes, they can turn that vehicle into a three foot by three foot by three foot cube, and, if they did so, how much would that cube weigh?

If you said anything less than your original answer, think again. All we've done is take that car and squeeze it down into a much denser, more compact package. It would be a bit harder to drive home in that form, but it would be a lot easier to park. The point is, though, that everything in your original car is still there—just smaller.

A mission statement is the same. You can have a long, two-page statement, or you can use the right words to trigger that same series of powerful images and get all the same weightiness in a much smaller package. The right words will remind you, in an instant, who and how you desire to be. In fact, this concept of triggering the right images is so powerful that I have actually had 3 clients, out of that 3,000, whose mission statements contain zero words. None. How's that even possible?

Well, it turns out that those three are very talented artists, and they found that the most powerful way to convey their Missions to themselves was to draw or paint or sculpt their Missions into existence. Now that creation serves to trigger all the thoughts, emotions, and images they need to guide them in making decisions. Of course, I still had them come up a with a short list of powerful words to help them remember that piece of art when they couldn't be home looking right at it, but the proof of concept is there.

And, because of the economy of words, a short mission statement that conveys the same images to you as a longer version can actually be *more* powerful. It becomes more powerful because you can actually remember it, recite it, and use it in a moment's notice.

Personal and Business Missions

Now, I know you're chomping at the bit to get started on writing your personal mission statement, but I want to clarify one final point before we do that. In these next few pages, we are going to build for you a powerful, motivating mission statement. It will start out a little long and then work its way shorter. Keep in mind, though, that you are creating *your personal Mission.*

I sometimes have clients who want to skip the personal Mission part of my coaching because they are focused on their businesses and making those businesses more effective. I have two things to say about that. First, this personal Mission will help you dictate your actions in *all* aspects of your life—remember the Wheel of Life we made? Second, only effective people can run effective businesses.

So, first, I need to dispel the idea that you need multiple mission statements for your life. You don't. Let me put it into perspective this way: how many people are you? If you answered that you are more than one person, I might recommend you seek counseling. Of course, we all sometimes *wish* we were more than one person, or that there were more hours in a day, because we have so much to get done and only one self to do it with, but the fact of the matter is that each of us is still an individual. You aren't one person at home and a different person at work. You are still you, no matter where you happen to be. If there's only one you, why would you need more than one mission statement? Wouldn't that be like having more than one boss? What happens if those two bosses disagree?

Your mission statement should be impactful enough to you that it applies to every aspect of your life, not just family or friends or romance, but also fitness and business and mental/spiritual growth. Does this mean that you shouldn't create a mission statement for your business? No. Your business needs an overarching, guiding statement just as much as you do. What I *am* saying is that you don't need more than one for yourself; there is no "home self" and another "business self." The mission statement you design for your business may be similar to the one you design for yourself, but the way the two integrate is that you will work toward the Mission of your business within the bounds and guidance of your personal Mission. You can't put aside either for the other.

The idea here is that, in an ideal world, if you have a workplace with a thousand people in it, each one of those thousand people will come to work each day with a personal mission statement. Additionally, the business will have its own mission, and each of those people will seek to fulfill the business's Mission by following their own, personal Missions. If, for some reason, one of those people can't seek the Mission of the organization because it is in opposition to a personal Mission, I recommend that person quit and find a new job. And think about it: if you are personally against what an organization stands for, wouldn't you rather work somewhere else?

Again, your mission statement is unique to you; you will use that Mission to guide your actions as you seek the aims of the Mission of your workplace. If, for some reason, you find that your Mission and the Mission of your workplace are out of alignment, you need to find somewhere else to work. You shouldn't have to put aside your personal Mission to go to work because your Mission defines who and how you want to be. If you have to give up that definition of who and how you want to be, you are working in the wrong direction and will never become what you want to be.

The point is, you are always you, and you can't put aside or change your Mission from situation to situation or it ceases to have any effect. Your Mission needs to be firm and steady. It may evolve over time, but, once you have it established, it shouldn't need to make any sudden changes.

Illumination of Missions

To illustrate this, let me talk to you a little about sunlight.

The Sun is approximately 93 million miles away from Earth (or, more accurately, we're 93 million miles from the sun). In astronomy, that distance is actually given its own name, the astronomical unit (or AU), and other distances in the solar system are measured on that scale. The question is this: is there anything that you can do here on Earth that will affect the Sun 93 million miles away? Keep your answer in mind.

Let's say we're at a pool in the early afternoon on a beautiful, clear, summer day and I have a 10-foot pole (the kind you want to not touch things with). What happens if I take that pole and stick it down in the pool at the 5-foot depth mark? Half of the pole goes into the pool, right? And it goes *straight* in, right? But how does it *look*? Interestingly, that pole looks bent right where it touches the water. Why? Well, the sunlight travels from 93 million miles away and hits the water. When it hits the water a principle called refraction happens, making the light—or the image of the pole as illuminated by the light—appear to bend. Has the water changed the pole? No, just your perception of it. Has the water changed the Sun? Not even close. It would be impossible for the water to change the Sun. That water has, however, changed the light in this particular place.

Next, what happens if you take that same light and shine it through a prism on a table? It will split a bunch of colors (Red, Orange, Yellow, Green, Blue, Indigo, and Violet) out of the white light and scatter them across the table. This is called dispersion in physics, and it allows you to see the individual components of the white light. Interestingly, if you take another prism and have it combine the colors back together, the light will come out white again. Now, has this prism changed the Sun? Not at all. The prism has only changed the way the light shines in this particular place.

Last, what happens if you shine that same beam of light into a mirror? It bounces back and shines all over everything in the room, right? That's the principle of reflection. The mirror can actually bounce that light back on you to illuminate you. Has that mirror, in any way, changed the Sun? Nope. The sun is still 93 million miles away.

Once you have your Mission established in your heart and mind, it will act like your own, personal, inner Sun. You will shine it over any number of different situations and, depending on those situations, the light will interact in any number of different ways. But here's the point I want to make: do any of those situations change the Sun?

Now, to be clear, the Sun does change over time. *Slowly.* Likewise, your Mission can, and probably will, evolve and change *over time, slowly.* Once you establish your Mission through the upcoming activities, however, your Mission should have no reason to make sudden, drastic changes. Like the Sun, your Mission will stay constant and only the light or guidance exposed on different situations will change. Thus, you can have one Mission, but that one Mission will act a little differently from one situation to the next.

Effectiveness of Missions

And now let's address the other point about why we focus on personal mission statements instead of business ones here. As I mentioned earlier, I sometimes have clients who want to skip all the personal side of things and focus directly on the business side. They see the value in working the kinks out of their own lives, but they see more value in improving business operations. I can appreciate that thought process.

However, to me, in a lot of ways, that feels like putting the cart before the horse. To illustrate this, let me ask you a question: do you know of any businesses that are run effectively and successfully yet the owners / managers are organizational disasters? If you can name any, let me know. I need to open a business in that field.

Warren Buffett is famous for saying that he only wants to invest in companies an idiot could run because, eventually, one will. Unfortunately, if you're talking about your own company, you don't have that luxury, and the reason is that if you can't manage your own interactions and effectiveness, how can you possibly expect to be able to manage the interactions and effectiveness of your suppliers, vendors, employees, managers, customers, etc. The fact of the matter is effective businesses are run by effective people.

There is no such thing as business effectiveness if you don't first have personal effectiveness. It just doesn't work that way. As we said, you can't be one person at home and another at work. Your Mission may shine on things differently at work, but you're still you. If you can't find your own way, you aren't going to be in a position to lead others to find their way.

Consider this from another angle: if you take all the people out of a business, what are you left with? An empty building? A bunch of computers? Maybe a logo? Is that a business? I'm not sure what it is, but it's *not* a business. Without people, you don't have a business. Without *effective* people, you don't have an *effective* business.

So put away the idea that you're going to skip creating a personal mission statement and get right to creating a business one. It doesn't work that way. Effective businesses are comprised of effective people, and as the saying goes, "A chain is only as strong as its weakest link." If you can't get your life in order, you won't be able to bring order to a business.

This doesn't mean that you need to be perfect in everything; that's why you build a team—so others will have strengths where you have weaknesses. What this means is that you can't imagine that you're going to bring success to your business if you haven't prepared yourself to be successful on a personal level.

Now, with all that said, if you are an organizational leader and want to build a mission statement for that organization, you can use essentially this same process to do so. You can even involve others in the various steps along the way to create a collaborative mission statement for your organization. From here out, however, I will proceed as though you were creating and/or refining your personal mission statement.

Power Words

We talked about how certain words carry more emotion and energy than other words. These are the words that inspire you to do and be more than you have been. While the specific words will change from one person to the next, one thing stays true across everyone: if you are going to "do" or "be" these things, you are looking at actions. You are looking at verbs, not nouns.

A solid, effective Mission will inspire you to action—the right action—because it carries action and movement in the way it's written. To write your Mission, we are going to go through several steps. You will want to repeat some of these steps to further refine your Mission as we go through, but let's get started for now.

Because you need action words to frame your Mission, I would like you to choose three verbs around which to begin building. I have included a list of alphabetized verbs here and need to give credit to Laurie Beth Jones, again, as she is the first person I know of who used a list of verbs like this to help build mission statements. There are many similarities between the list I use and the list she supplies in her book *The Path*, but my list has been altered somewhat to remove a few words which, in my experience, have caused more trouble than they were worth. I have also added a few verbs, which I have found to be very motivating and powerful.

In keeping with those additions, this list is provided to help you brainstorm, not to replace your personal creative processes. If there is a verb for which you feel strongly, but which doesn't appear in this list, then add that verb and use it. Remember, this is *your* mission statement and no one else's. Feel free to add to this list or not as is appropriate for you and your situation.

You are welcome to circle the words right here in the book, if you'd like, but you'll probably need a sheet of paper or two for the next phase of the process. In any case, try to narrow things down to the most powerful, applicable three verbs. If you need to use four or five, that's okay too; just remember that mission statements are more powerful when they are short enough to memorize.

A
accomplish
acquire
adopt
advance
affect
affirm
alleviate
amplify
appreciate
ascend
associate
B
believe
bestow
brighten
build
C
call
cause
choose
claim
coach
collaborate
collect
combine
communicate
compel
complete
compliment
compose
conceive
confirm
connect
consider

construct
contact
continue
counsel
create
D
decide
delight
deliver
demonstrate
devise
direct
discover
discuss
distribute
draft
dream
drive
E
educate
elect
embrace
empower
encourage
endow
engage
engineer
enhance
enlighten
enlist
enliven
entertain
enthuse
envision
evaluate

excite
explore
express
extend
F
facilitate
forgive
foster
further
G
gather
generate
give
grant
H
heal
hold
host
I
identify
ignite
illuminate
implement
improve
improvise
inspire
integrate
involve
K
Keep
kindle
know
L
labor
launch

lead
learn
light
live
love
M
make
manifest
master
mature
measure
mediate
model
mold
motivate
move
N
navigate
nurture
O
open
organize
P
participate
pass
perform
persuade
play
possess
practice
prepare
present
praise
produce
progress

pro-GRESS	rely	stand	use
not PRO-gress	remember	summon	utilize
promise	renew	support	**V**
promote	resonate	surrender	validate
provide	respect	sustain	value
pursue	restore	**T**	venture
R	return	take	verbalize
realize	revise	tap	volunteer
receive	**S**	teach	**W**
reclaim	sacrifice	team	work
refine	safeguard	touch	worship
reflect	satisfy	trade	write
reform	save	train	**Y**
regard	seek	translate	yield
relate	serve	**U**	
relax	share	understand	
release	speak	uphold	

Have you recorded your top three choices? Good. Did any of the verbs you chose surprise you? Remember, your brain is working overtime to connect each word in this list with a set of images and emotions. If everything worked correctly, you picked the three words that brought the most powerful, positive images and feelings to your mind.

The next step is to define what these actions mean to you.

Definitions

To define these actions, don't look in the dictionary. Every single one of those verbs can be found in the Random House Dictionary or Webster's Dictionary or whatever other dictionary. That's not important to us. Are we writing a mission statement for the dictionary or for you? I want to make sure that these verbs are written in *your* dictionary. We want to see how *you* define these terms. We don't care how the world defines your verbs. The world can't write your mission statement for you, so don't let it. If, after we're "done," you want to go and look up what the dictionary says,

KIP KINT

feel free. Until then, keep all the images and emotions and thoughts in your head and save the "real" dictionary for later.

Now, on your piece of paper, in the margins of the book, or online (for those of you who have registered), record your words and write out what they mean to you. Like the Blue activity earlier, I want you to describe these things in some level of detail. Include how you feel and any appropriate specifics about the mechanics of your verbs. Tell me why these three verbs are so important to you. What is it, based on your life's experience, that draws you to these words out of all the verbs on that list (or any additions you made). Speak from your heart here and be honest with yourself. Everything else will build on this foundation, so don't be bashful now.

For example, if I chose the word "inundate" (which isn't on the foregoing list, so few, if any, of you will have picked it, which is why I can write about it here without fear of biasing anyone), I might write about how I want to flood the world with truth, fill my days with service, or overwhelm my obstacles with solutions or optimism. I might write about how the idea of inundating something makes me feel unstoppable or how the verb empowers me to think big. I might write about an experience from my childhood when I watched something get washed away by floodwaters or I might reference how the Grand Canyon, mighty as it is, was created by the slow, steady rush of water over millions of years.

You get the point. So, take a few minutes and write out what your verbs mean to you. No cheating. Write from your heart. The end product needs to resonate with *you*, after all, not your dictionary or spouse or friend or anyone else.

If you are one of those people who doesn't do definitions, never fear; I haven't forgotten about you. For those of you who prefer something a little different, I have an exercise I call "Match Game." The idea here is word association, similar to the Blue activity we did toward the start of the chapter, only, this time, I just want you to think of the first word that comes to mind. The trigger words will be your three verbs, and you need to decide on the word that "matches" each verb.

For example, if I had the verb "champion" in my list (again, not on the foregoing verb list), I might associate that with "equality." I now have the phrase "champion equality" from which to build. Someone else might take that same verb and think of the word "truth." That person now has a phrase "champion truth." You can see how those two choices bring different thoughts and feelings to your mind. If you don't want to come up with actual definitions of what your verbs mean to you, you can try Match Game instead to get your starting point. At the end of the game, you should have six words, no more. You'll have your three verbs and the three connected words you came up with.

Once you have your definitions or word pairs, ask yourself a few of the following questions about each verb. You may remember these prompts from elementary school, but don't let that deter your from really digging in to fully understand what these action verbs mean to you. And make sure to record all your thoughts and feelings in print or electronically—don't try to store all this in your head or you're likely to forget some of it.

Who?

What?

Where?

When?

Why? (And, at risk of making yourself sound like a five year-old, it can be very enlightening to ask yourself why again in response to each answer you come up with)

How?

How much?

I call this process "digging *up*" because we are digging from a level of specificity up to a level of generality and abstraction. We're really searching for the principles that drive you at this point. So be careful as you craft your Mission; you don't want focus too narrowly, or you'll exclude important parts of your life. One of the additional advantages to having a fairly short Mission is that you will, of necessity cut out the really specific parts in favor of the broader words that generate more pictures, thoughts, and emotions in your mind. In doing so, you also help your Mission to be more broadly applicable.

Refinement

Now that you have your definitions and thoughts and details about your action verbs, it's time to string them together. First, to be upfront and clear about this next step, I need you to understand that we are still just putting together your first draft. We are not going to magically create your finished, polished mission statement in the next five minutes. It will take you a week, possibly a little more, to think things over and refine what we come up with now. In fact, our goal, at this point, is just to get you 50 percent of the way there. That's all. Just halfway.

The rest of the refinement is kind of like breaking in a pair of new boots. You have to wear them around for a bit and work them for a while to get them to fit just right. We can get the sizing right together here and now, but you're going to have to keep working it to get your Mission where you really want it to be.

So here's how this next step works. I'm going to give you the first five words of your Mission. I want you to fill in the rest using your verbs and definitions. Here are your first five words:

My life's Mission is to…

Now put your three verbs and descriptions into a list. The "finished" product will likely look something along the lines of "My life's Mission is to _____, _____, (and, or, so that, for, yet) _____." If you are desperate to see an example, you can look ahead to *Appendix B*. I've included some examples there. Otherwise, read through your Mission a couple times and tweak the words so that it makes sense.

How do you feel when you read it? Does it resonate with you? You don't need to be moved to tears or fired up to the point that you're ready to go run a marathon, but your Mission should feel good on a deep level. You should be able to nod to yourself when you read it.

Now the question is whether we've hit the mark or not. Ask yourself how you feel about your Mission as it stands—and keep in mind that our goal is only a (c), if you can truthfully answer (d) you just got a bonus. Nobody, at this stage, should let themselves think for a moment that their Mission is 100 percent done. You're not. Most people are about halfway at this point, a few are further along, and a few need to go back to the drawing board and take another look at the verbs they've selected and how those verbs were defined and integrated into the Mission.

(a) Wow. That doesn't resonate with me at all.
(b) Okay. I think I see where this is going but we're still far off.
(c) Yes. That feels like it's about 50 percent of the way there.
(d) Wow. That's more than 50 percent of the way there.

If you're about 50 percent of the way to what your real Mission is (and, keep in mind, this is based on how *you* feel about it, not what anyone else says, does, or feels), then you're ready to spend some time with this shiny new Mission. Take some time to think about your Mission and how you can make it better fit who and how you want to be.

As you'll see in the homework section for this chapter, the idea is to reflect on your Mission and then refine it to better fit who and how you want to be. The target in this process is to, over time, get your Mission about 90 percent of the way there. And notice that I didn't say 100 percent.

First of all, it doesn't have to resonate 100 percent perfectly to be an actionable, ready-to-use Mission. Also, you will continue to grow and learn and evolve tomorrow and the next day and the next. Give yourself a little growing room. Besides, it's not worth the agony and stress of trying to reach that 100 percent resonance when 90 percent will serve you just as well. Finally, your level of affinity to your Mission will actually increase over time as you live it and have experiences related to it; instead of struggling to get it perfect now, let it fit naturally over time.

Once you reach that 90 percent target, you are unlikely to need any kind of major revisions anymore. That's why your Mission becomes actionable and livable. You may still tweak a word or two here or there, but the need for any kind of major changes or revisions should be past because it's close enough to perfect for you already.

As a side note, once you get your Mission to this point, don't show it off to others. There's a good chance that they'll look at it—especially if you've gotten your Mission whittled down to a single, concise sentence—and say, "I don't get it." For you, the correct response to them is, "Oh well" or "So what?"

Remember, this Mission is designed to conjure in *your* mind the critical thoughts, images, and emotions you need to be who and how you want to be. You aren't designing your Mission for someone else. You don't have to get your Mission approved by a committee. It's for you and only you. In fact, if you've gotten your Mission so precise and concise that other people no longer understand it, but it's still powerful and impactful for you, take that as an accomplishment. Remember, we all think of something different in response to the word blue too.

Once you reach 90 percent of the way there, you can ask yourself four questions to determine whether your Mission is empowering or not. If it is empowering, great. If it isn't empowering, it's not worth the paper it's written on. After all, why are you writing this mission statement in the first place if not to help you become who and how you want to be?

Question 1: Do I feel an emotional connection to my mission?

Now, to clarify this, let me point out a few things this question is *not* asking:

Do tears well up in my eyes when I read my Mission? Do I get tingles up and down my spine?

Even if you happen to feel that way the first time, you wouldn't feel that way every time you read your Mission. If you are counting on that kind of an experience each and every time you read your Mission, you're going to believe it's lost its power just when you start to get good about making decision based on it. Eventually, you'll settle into a peaceful comfort with your Mission. It'll be like a warm blanket, not like the rush of skydiving.

Eventually, your Mission will become a part of who you are, not just who you want to be, and you will actively, consciously think about it less and less. You'll become *un*consciously competent at making decisions based on your Mission. When this happens, you need to have a deeper emotional connection to your Mission, not some knee-jerk, emotionally overpowering, weepy feeling. If you start out with an overpowering feeling, that's fine; just don't expect that intensity to stay at the surface level. We're looking for a deep, emotional connection—kinship, if you will—with your Mission at this time.

It's a good thing, by the way, that your Mission can connect on a deeper, more peaceful level. How excited would you be to think about and engage your Mission for every decision if it triggered such an emotionally powerful response? What's more, how exhausting would it be to have that kind of emotional sledgehammer each and every time you thought about your Mission? It's a good thing that you can settle into a familiarity, trust, and peace with your Mission because staying in that roller coaster, extreme-emotion stage would wipe you out completely. Just think of how many decisions you make in a day. Can you imagine an emotional rush in conjunction with each of those decisions?

For those of you who are married, this next analogy will make more sense. For those of you never married, think of the most serious relationship you've been in and you'll get the picture.

There may have been fireworks the first time you went out with your then-future spouse. I certainly hope there were. However, over time, do you still have those same fireworks each and every time you see your significant other? If you say you do, you're only fooling yourself. Sure, the fireworks still go off from time to time—that's a good thing—but they don't go off every time. Instead, you settle into a deeper, more peaceful trust with one another. You gain confidence to replace the novelty. Does any of this mean that the connection is gone? That you've fallen out of love? Absolutely not. And it's the same with your Mission.

You may, or may not, feel a huge sense of relief when you first put your Mission to words. Either way, you can still feel that depth and strength of the emotion your Mission triggers. You don't have to cry or be giddy to know that you feel. We're looking for the slow, steady, rich embers of a fire, not the flashes of flame that die off almost as soon as they leap up. This Mission is supposed to fuel you, after all.

So, let me ask again, do you feel an emotional connection to your Mission?

According to the Random House Dictionary, the root for the

word "emotion" comes from the French word *esmovoir*. The etymology goes all the way back to Latin from there, but the French word means "to set in motion, to move." The idea is that emotion really means "to move the feelings." Think about the last time you heard someone say they were "moved" by an event ("moved to tears" is a frequent example).

This emotional connection will form the foundation by which your mission statement will motivate you to movement. If you don't feel that kind of connection, your mission statement won't move you, and it won't be worth the paper it's printed on.

It may look great in that mahogany frame. You may have picked the perfect font face and have the perfect watermark in the paper. People may see that Mission on the wall and gush about how profound it is and how proud you must be to have that mission statement, but if you aren't moved first in your heart and then in your actions, then it's nothing more than a pretty piece of paper—a pretty piece of paper that could have been put to any number of better uses (including making a paper airplane or shooting hoops into your garbage can).

Do you feel an emotional connection to your Mission?
(yes / no)

Question 2: Does my Mission support my significant roles?

This question really is asking two separate things. First, what are your significant roles? Second, does your Mission support them? Since you'll be able to answer the second question easily once we've explored the answer to the first question, we'll focus on the first part.

Your significant roles are those important parts you play in life. Your significant roles include things like spouse, parent, sibling, child, and friend. This set of roles also includes other aspects of your life like business owner or employee, community member, church member, or other, similar roles. And keep in mind that I use the word 'significant' intentionally. I mean roles that, if changed drastically, would change your life, on the whole, fairly dramatically too.

About once every two weeks during the spring, summer, and

fall, my role becomes lawn mower. Does my Mission support me in my role as lawn mower? Maybe. I don't really care though. Unless I work in landscaping, mowing the lawn isn't a significant role for me. If I never mowed the lawn again, I wouldn't really change as a person. If I had to mow the lawn every week, I still wouldn't really change.

Your Mission will assist in guiding you through every aspect of your life, but some of the roles you play will be small enough and unimportant enough that you won't really bother bringing the power of your Mission to bear. That would be like firing up your Ferrari to visit the next-door neighbors.

What should it look like if your Mission supports your significant roles? You should—based on your short, memorized Mission—be able to spontaneously generate how your Mission reflects off of the various facets of your life. How does your Mission apply to you as a spouse or significant other? How does your Mission apply to you as a member of a community? How does your Mission apply to you in your role as an employee or business owner?

Well, recall our analogy about how a Mission is like the Sun. The core of your Mission won't change from situation and application to situation and application, but the light will look a little different when you "shine" it around on the different roles you play in life. If your Mission just doesn't fit one of those roles at all, then we need to keep working until it does. But you don't need to worry about force-fitting your roles into your Mission because it should work in reverse. Your Mission should *support* those roles in that your Mission should help you be who and how you want to be while acting in any given role. Your Mission should help you see how to be a better spouse, sibling, friend, parent, child, employee, business owner, community member, etc. You should be better at each of those roles by virtue of what you've codified in your Mission.

This is where your Mission will need to be broad, like we've talked about before. Your Mission will serve as your bird's-eye perspective of life regarding who and how you want to be. Your Vision and your Values, which we'll get to in the next two sections, will take your Mission and apply it back to the various aspects of your life to get specifics. For now, keep your Mission broadly applicable so that it can fully support all your significant roles. If you try to apply your Mission to one of these significant roles and realize "Whoa, that's not at all who I want to be in that role," then you need to go back to the drawing board. If you apply your Mission to a role and say, "Okay, that's most of it, but I'm still missing part," then you need to go back and tweak your Mission to allow for whatever is missing. Typically, this involves being a little less specific.

And one final thing to help you expedite your ability to answer this question. Think of your closest, most intimate role in life. For those of you who are married, this is probably your role as spouse. Does your Mission support you in this closest, most personal, most intimate role?

Now think about your role in the workplace. Whether you're a manager, independent contributor, customer service rep, salesman, business owner, or something else, think about that role for a moment. Does your Mission support you in that more formal, professionally distant, results-oriented role?

If your Mission supports you in your most intimate role and also supports you in the opposite of that, which is usually your most professional role, then it follows that your Mission would support you in every role in between, because every other role is just a blend of those two in some way, shape, or form.

Take a moment to think about your significant roles in life and then answer the question.

Does your Mission support your significant roles?
(yes / no)

Question 3: Does my Mission support my role of Self? (Personal Renewal)

This is referring to your mental, spiritual, physical, and emotional self. Does your Mission support you in these facets of your life? Does your mission statement empower you to learn and grow? To meditate and ponder the deeper things of life? To take care of your physical body through exercise and proper diet? To inventory your emotions and make sure those needs are met?

Now, before you answer, I want to ask you something else: are you uncomfortable with this question? Does it make you uncomfortable to think about taking time for yourself? Does it sound a little self-ish?

Well, let's do a little role-play. We're sitting together having lunch and I ask you to pour me a cup of water from the pitcher you have. You reach out to your pitcher and find that it's empty. Unperturbed, you go ahead and pour me a glass of the contents of that pitcher...but the pitcher was empty, right? So what do I now have in my cup? That's right. Nothing. As the ancient saying goes, "You cannot pour water from an empty vessel." In other words, you can't give what you don't have.

If you're empty, what do you have to give? In Matthew 22 of the Bible, it says "Thou shalt love thy neighbour as thyself." Does that mean that you should love everyone else more than you love yourself? No. Does it mean you should love everyone else less than you love yourself? No. "As," in this instance, means "in the same way."

Contrary to the popular belief of our western, Anglo-Christian society, we aren't supposed to give up on ourselves in order to serve others. Yes, we should absolutely be serving others. That's just common, human decency and goodness. But how can you really serve others if you take no time to regenerate yourself? So you need to take the time to renew yourself and then love others in the same way that you love yourself. And let's think about that for a moment. Can you think of any people that you *wouldn't* want loving you the same way they love themselves? People who don't love themselves and, therefore, wouldn't love you either? Wouldn't you want to be loved better than that?

Let's put this into perspective with a little analogy here. Let's say your significant other, the most important relationship in your life, goes on the game show "Let's Make a Deal." And that person (your spouse, boyfriend, girlfriend, parent, child—whoever has the closest, most important relationship with you) dresses up in the most outrageous costume to get the attention of the host, Monty Hall. Well, it works.

Your significant other gets called down to the front and Monty says, "Johnny, tell this fine person what's behind Door Number 1."

And then that deep, announcer voice says, "Behind Door Number 1 is your favorite person: Mr. or Ms. Reader. Ten whole hours, just the two of you, just the way you are!"

Now, your significant other is rightly excited for this because you are a busy person, and he or she certainly doesn't get as much time as he or she would really like. And then Monty chimes in again, "And all this, Significant Other, is yours for the keeping, no questions asked…unless you'd perhaps like to see what's behind Door Number 2? Take it away, Johnny!"

And the deep voice says, "Behind Door Number 2 is . . . your favorite person again: Mr. or Ms. Reader! This time only five hours, _but_ this five hours is five hours with a rested, energized, healthy, happy, fit, and friendly Mr. or Ms. Reader!"

And back to Monty, "What do you think, Significant Other? Which will you choose?"

Just to make sure we're clear, lets deconstruct this decision. Your significant other can have ten hours with you as you are— maybe a little tired, probably ten million things going on in your head, maybe a bit overworked, possibly a little underexercised. We'll call this "so-so" you, and, let's face it, this is far more common than any of us would like to admit. A lot on the plate, not a lot of time for exercise or meditation, not a lot of time for personal renewal because life keeps coming so fast. This is the you that's going through real life, right? Still, it's ten hours of one-on-one time, no strings attached. A pretty good deal, all in all.

Well what about the "other" you? This is "awesome" you. This you is well-rested and energized, exercising properly, eating properly, taking time to meditate and learn and grow, in the moment and present, focused, relaxed, renewed, and balanced. It's only half the amount of time, but it's the awesome you and there are still no strings attached. Also a pretty good deal, all in all.

Now, to anyone reading this who honestly believes that their significant other would take ten hours of frazzled you over five hours of rested, refreshed, engaged you, think again. Unless you have starved that person for attention to an unhealthy degree, he or she would willingly live up the quantity of time for the quality of you instead. You see, when you are energized and renewed, you will be ready to have deep, quality, meaningful interactions. You'll be focused on your significant other and able to share with that person.

To be sure, if your significant other could have more time *while maintaining the level of quality*, they would take that in a heartbeat. The point, however, is that time, by itself, only means so much. If your pitcher is empty, you can hold it up until your arm falls off but you'll still never fill someone else's glass.

So stop feeling guilty about investing an appropriate amount of time into your own physical, spiritual, mental, and emotional renewal. Remember back to our discussion about the Wheel of Life; you don't need to take days to renew yourself, but if you don't spend any time to fill up the gas tank, the car can only run so long. It's better for you—and better for those with whom you interact—if you have something to give. If you're burned out and empty inside, how can you expect to bring energy or happiness or completeness to anyone else?

So throw away the idea that you're going to give something your "most." Frankly, I've become less and less impressed with what that even means over the years. It's easy to be a martyr and say things like "I gave you the most I could." You want to really show someone you care? Don't give them your "most," give them your "best." Only you can't give your best if you're not at your best. Your loved ones, clients, coworkers, etc., deserve your best, not just your most, so you owe it to them to renew yourself so that you can renew them too.

If your Mission doesn't allow for, and even encourage, self-renewal, it will push you to burnout instead. Give yourself permission to shed the guilt and spend appropriate amounts of time in personal renewal. What's appropriate will vary from person to person, but I can tell you that "none" is not appropriate.

Does your Mission support your need to renew yourself?
(yes / no)

Question 4: Do I truly desire to live this Mission?

No matter how eloquent or perfect a mission statement is, if you don't want to live it, you won't. It's that simple. When you read your Mission out loud, do you feel empowered? In part, this goes back to the emotional connection piece from Question 1. Different than that, however, is the idea that you *want* the connection, that you accept it. You can feel that deep connection and still reject it if you choose to. And if you choose to reject your Mission as it currently stands, then the only real option is to go back to the drawing board and start over.

I would only recommend, in this case, that you pause to think about why you feel unwilling to live this Mission. If you've made it this far and answered "yes" to the previous questions, what is it that makes you hesitate about accepting and embracing this Mission to guide your future? Figure that out before you go around for take two.

In the end, for your Mission to help you become who and how you want to be, you have to engage your Will. That's why we talked about Will first. If you don't want to change or don't want to live your Mission, you won't. Of course, you probably wouldn't be reading this book if you weren't interested in changing. So what you need to do in this step is make sure that your mission statement appeals to you mentally. Does this Mission describe the kind of change you want to make, or do you need to go back to the drawing board and write one that better describes what you want to live?

This isn't about waking up to fireworks in the morning. Your Mission won't be your "Eye of the Tiger" song to get you fired up like Rocky. Your Mission, if done right, will provide a quiet, confident "yes" to your mind. You already feel connected to your Mission; now you're deciding if you want to be connected to it. Does it really describe who and how you want to be.

Do you actually want to live this Mission?
(yes / no)

Once you can truthfully answer "Yes" to all four of these questions, you can move on. Until then, you need to keep repeating these Mission building steps until you get a Mission for which you *can* answer affirmatively to all four questions.

Tying It All Together

Now the time has finally come for me to reveal my own Mission to you. I have withheld it thus far in the hope that you would be better able to create your own Mission. I didn't want to bias your or muddy the waters or make you think that somehow my mission would work well as your mission. Let me dispel that myth right now in case it's still lingering for a few of you.

Your Mission is a statement of who and how you want to be. It is a clarifying, guiding, personal constitution by which you can evaluate decisions and choose behaviors that are in line with what you want to be. Ideally, your Mission is concise but powerful; it should be not only memorable but also memorizable. It should be short enough for you to recall and use in a moment of choice.

Your Mission can only be all those things if it brings to your mind all those powerful images and emotions which will drive you to be who you want to be. If you take someone else's mission statement (with or without changes), it will be *much less powerful* for you. If you don't create your own Mission, you will be less inclined to follow it.

So, you have your Mission and I want you to keep that Mission. I have some thoughts and examples and experiences I want to share with you, but I can only do so if I first share my own Mission. Please don't tell yourself it's perfect. My Mission is perfect for me; just as your Mission should be perfect for you. Here goes.

"Discover truth, embrace principles, build trust, encourage, & empower people."

So short that it almost doesn't make sense, right? Well, the list of images, thoughts, and emotions this phrase brings to my mind wouldn't fit in this book (Question 1). For me, that Mission is short enough to be easy to remember and recall when I need to make a decision, but it's also extremely adaptable to all the roles in my life (Question 2). Let me give you two examples.

First, when I shine my Mission on the relationship I have with my wife, my role as a husband, the Mission would actually read something more like this,

"My Mission is *to discover the truth* about my wife each and every day, knowing and acknowledging that she is a unique, dynamic, and ever-changing human being and that there's always new truth to discover about her; *to embrace principles* of effective communication and relationships that I may be a better husband, a better listener, and that she feels understood; *to build trust* by being, first and foremost, trustworthy, always honoring my commitments with her, that she may feel free to trust me in every way; *to encourage* her in her desires and endeavors and her goals; and *to empower her* by always seeing her as completely capable and able in every way."

Now, don't ask me to recite that one from memory. I don't have it memorized. I've never even had it written down anywhere (until now). It's too long, and more importantly, if you asked me tomorrow, I would say something slightly different anyway. The key words (the principles—in bold) would all be the same—taken straight from my actual Mission—but the way the light of my Mission reflected back from my relationship with my wife might change just a bit because I would be a little different and so would she.

For a second example, let me give you how my exact same Mission might look when shone on my opposite role as a coach,

"My Mission is *to discover truth*—truth that abounds within the coaching world, within the world of personal improvement—truth that I can search out and apply in my relationships with my clients and the truth about my clients and their desires; *to embrace principles* of effectiveness, to place myself in a position to help my clients better understand those principles and apply them in their own lives; *to build trust* with my clients by always being on time and following through on my commitments and honoring their freedoms that they may trust me in return; *to encourage* them to keep their commitments and to honor their Mission, Vision, Values, and to really go for their goals and be held accountable for those things; and *to empower them* by holding them as capable and completely whole in every way, validating their desires and their needs to accomplish."

Is that identical to how my Mission reflects back from my relationship with my wife? Nope. The relationship is different so my Mission reflects back in a different way. Has my Mission changed from the one relationship to the other though? No. It hasn't. My Mission is still just the same. Look at the key words (in bold) and you'll see that you can match them between all three versions of my Mission as included above.

And the two versions *feel* different to me. I still feel an emotional connection to each one, but we're talking about my closest, most personal, most intimate relationship for the first one, and a much more professional, formal, still important relationship for the second one. Would my wife appreciate being treated like a client? Not really. On the other hand, would my clients appreciate being treated like my wife? Can you say "awkward"? So it doesn't make sense that my Mission should inspire me to act identically in my different roles, because my different roles don't require the same actions. It does, however, make sense that the actions inspired by my Mission should be based on the same principles, regardless of my role.

Last, let's look at how my Mission would look if I pointed it back on myself (Question 3):

"My Mission is **to discover the truth** about myself, physically, mentally, emotionally, spiritually; **to embrace principles** for effective living, principles of health and fitness for my physical renewal, principles of learning and education for my mental renewal, principles related to my sense of meaning and purpose for my spiritual renewal, principles of serving others for my emotional renewal; **to build trust** with myself by making and keeping commitments to me; to not only encourage others but also **encourage** myself, to live life in my courage zone, not just my comfort zone; and to not only empower others but **to empower myself**, to see myself as capable and to live my life powerfully physically, mentally, spiritually, emotionally."

As you can see, your Mission really doesn't just point outwardly. You can shine it on yourself as well, thereby illuminating to yourself who you really are and how you are going to be.

The point is that your simple-seeming Mission can expand to illuminate additional details based on where you shine it. What may have started out seeming like a personal mission statement has become a versatile, whole-life mission statement. And the best part is that you don't need to write down seven different Missions just to have one for each major role in your life.

In fact, you shouldn't write down these applied Missions. Instead, you can just write down the core Mission, and then, on the fly, as you choose to live it (Question 4), you can see how it reflects from any given role. Let the light of your true Mission shine down like the Sun to the pool, prism, or mirror. Doing this will help you maintain principle-based stability while you retain event-based flexibility in your decision making in order to help you truly become who and how you want to be.

Mission Control

I'd like to share an experience with you that demonstrates how powerful your Mission can be for you once you get it to this point. I do this to show why having a short, memorizable mission statement is so important.

A couple months after I had trimmed down my own Mission to those nine words, I got in a bit of a disagreement with my wife. I know, I know. I hate to shatter all your illusions of my infallibility and communicative perfection, but I'm just a person too, and my wife and I got into an argument.

Now, we're not shouters or plate throwers or anything, but the tension in the room was beyond palpable. I was being very firm and unyielding in what I was saying, she was being very firm and unyielding in what she was saying. The crazy thing is that I can't even remember what we were arguing about anymore, but I clearly remember what happened because of the intensity of the emotions along the way.

This was one of those experiences where I was right, and I knew I was right. This was not one of those times when I *thought* I was right, but really wasn't, like is usually the case with men; I actually was correct, and my wife actually was wrong. In fact, if you were to ask my wife about it all these years later, she would agree with me in hindsight. Of course, in the moment of this particular disagreement, emotion was running high and there was no way either of us was going to back down.

Well, in my impatience, I'm kind of ashamed to admit that I

used my superior powers of language and my talent for articulating a point to turn the discussion just a bit and slam home my point in such a way that there could be no doubt as to the truth of my argument. I was not respectful or kind, and my agitation was clear in my voice. To top things off, in delivering my last words, my wife was forced to realize that I was right and left to feel about an inch tall. Then I spun on my heel and left the room, not even waiting for her reply.

When I got down to my home office, I flopped into my swivel chair to catch my breath. As I released the tension in my chest and let out a big sigh, I turned my chair and looked at the wall. What did I see? There, on the wall, stabbing me in the heart like a thousand knives, was my personal Mission, hanging in its beautiful frame.

I was struck to the core. As I looked at my Mission, I was pierced clean through. I was tried, convicted, and sentenced by the judge, jury, and executioner of my very own words. I knew that in the previous moment I hadn't lived a single word of my mission. I had basically done the opposite of following the principles I claimed to want governing my life.

Discover truth? I hadn't sought for truth in my wife or her feelings. I'd only sought for my own truth. Embrace principles? The only principles I had embraced were the same ones embraced by a first grade bully on the playground. I didn't embrace any principles for effective communication or respect. I hadn't tried to understand before trying to be understood. I hadn't allowed my wife the right to disagree, whether wrongly or rightly. Build Trust? If anything, I was undermining any trust that may have previously existed. I wasn't building anything by being curt and blunt and prideful. Encouraging and empowering? I was most certainly *not* being encouraging or empowering in my tone, words, or actions. I did none of the things in my Mission.

I sat there in my chair, staring at my Mission, and had a paradigm shift. It finally clicked in my head how this Mission was supposed to work. So I got up out of my chair, went back upstairs, took my wife in my arms, looked her in the eyes, and said, "Honey, I am so sorry."

Now, to her credit, in her own humility, she'd realized that I'd been right and she'd been wrong, so she tried to stop me so she could tell me that she realized I was right and then try to apologize for not seeing it sooner.

She had tears in her eyes, and I had tears in my eyes, and I said, "Honey, that's not what I'm sorry for. I'm sorry because I did not treat you with the love and respect that you deserve; I did not act in a trustworthy way; I was not encouraging; I was not empowering; I did not treat you the way that I feel about you in my heart. I did not live with you in that moment the way that I claim I want to live and be. And I am truly, truly sorry for that. Will you please forgive me?"

I don't want to make it sound like we had a difficult relationship up to that point. We didn't. Things were actually pretty good already, but we turned a corner for the better that day. *I* turned a corner for the better that day. I'm not perfect, by any means, but having that experience has helped me to see and understand just how important it is to live my Mission every minute of every day.

I've gotten even better since then. I don't make those same mistakes and then have to go back and apologize as often anymore. In fact, I'll often be talking to someone and have to pull myself up short because I realize that I'm straying from my mission. I'll stop the conversation for a moment, get my head right, and start things again. And sometimes I don't even have to think about it, I just do it second-naturally.

Good News and Bad News

Now that you've built a Mission statement, answered positively to all four of the empowering test questions, and read about some of the ways you can use your Mission and how it can help you steer your life, I have good news and bad news for you.

The good news is that, if you truthfully answered "yes" to all four questions, you are now the proud owner of a practically perfect Mission statement. Despite the fact that we only pushed it to be 90 percent of the way there, for all intents and purposes, your Mission is now perfect for you in every way that matters. Based on my experience across thousands of clients, I feel totally comfortable in saying that you have an empowering mission statement, and because your mission statement is empowering, that makes it a practically perfect Mission for you. Besides, 90 percent is, by definition, practically perfect.

So what's the bad news? Your Mission is practically perfect, but you aren't. I hope this doesn't come as a shock to you. So now comes the question: How does an imperfect person live a practically perfect Mission? Well, the answer comes from the Federal Aviation Administration.

The FAA reports that all flights, before getting approval to take off, must first file a flight plan. The flight plan will outline the place where the plane will depart, the place it will land, and any stops along the way. In addition to those broader details, the flight plan will contain specific, detailed calculations about the route, altitude, distance, and speed of the aircraft. The flight plan will be mathematically, navigationally, and geographically perfect.

A funny thing happens the moment the plane takes off though: that flight will be off course, mathematically, navigationally, and geographically, 90+ percent of the flight time (see *Appendix C* for more detail). And yet, in spite of being off course 90+ percent of the time, that plane will land within minutes of the expected arrival time (assuming it departed on time). Planes don't typically lose time in the air; flights get delayed due to issues on the ground, not generally due to issues after takeoff. So, even though all flights or actually off course 90 percent or more of the time they're in the air, nearly all flights arrive on time or even a little early—99.9+ percent of flights!

How is that even possible? How can flights be off course 90+ percent of the time and yet 99+ percent of flights arrive at the proper destination on time? The answer is Constant Course Correction. No plane is up there in the air when, three hours into the flight, the pilot suddenly realizes they've turned around completely. "Uh, Ladies and Gentlemen. Turns out we're not going to make it on time to Honolulu today because we're quite unexpectedly back where we started at San Francisco." It doesn't work like that.

We're talking being off course by fractions of degrees for seconds or less. We're talking about being a couple dozen feet too high or too low for a few seconds. We're talking about going the wrong speed for almost no time at all.

And that's exactly how you, as an imperfect person, can live a practically perfect Mission. Through Constant Course Correction, you can see yourself start to stray from your Mission and make an immediate course correction to get back on track. You don't need to wait until you've completely left the path and gotten totally lost before you refer back to your Mission and try to work back to where you want to be. Instead, you catch yourself right when you start to stray and you bring yourself back. You tap into that emotional connection with your Mission. You tap into your Will to live your Mission, and you bring yourself back into compliance. Then, the next time you start to stray a little, you do it again.

Think about the experience I shared between my wife and me. I was off course—and off by quite a bit even though not off for long—but I saw my Mission and let it impact me. I felt it in my heart, made a sincere apology to her, and got back on course. By having my Mission, I didn't have to stay off course. In fact, having your Mission will tell you what your course is, enabling you to stay on it. Without a Mission, how do you know what or where the course is to stay on it?

Since that time, I've caught myself going off course mid-communication. I'll be talking to my wife or working with a client or on the phone with a friend and realize that I'm starting to drift off course. Immediately, I can perform a little Constant Course Correction and get back on track. Sometimes I have to pause and apologize to someone, but often, I'm able to catch myself and get back on course before it even really makes any difference to the conversation.

Having your short, memorizable Mission will give you that flight plan. Beyond that, it's up to you to stay true to your Mission and Course Correct as often as needed. To give you some practice on how this works and what your destination will look like, we're going to move on to the second leg of the stool: Vision.

Homework

Spend some time in R&R with your mission statement. Don't get too excited though, I don't mean rest and relaxation, I mean

Reflection and Refinement. Read and reread your Mission several times a day, focusing on the words you've chosen and how they could be tweaked to make them more precise and more concise. Your goal in this process is to get your Mission about 90 percent of the way there. Don't stress about getting it 100 percent of the way because life's experiences require a little flexibility anyway, but you should be able to get close.

You can do this by tweaking the wording: changing out words with their synonyms and testing for how they feel, adding or removing words and phrases, or rearranging the three verbs and their attendant definitions. "Magnify others by teaching them to be effective" is not quite the same as "Teach others to be effective by magnifying them." Which order of your verbs resonates with you most powerfully?

Another thing to consider during this process is the goal of conciseness. The first, easiest thing to do to shorten your Mission is to chop off the first four or five words (My life's Mission is to...). We're talking about your mission statement. Of *course* it's your life's Mission. Unless you feel better with that introductory phrase attached, go ahead and trim it. It's useful while setting up your Mission initially, but its use is limited after the initial draft.

The next idea for shortening your Mission is that you can narrow individual phrases down to the two or three key words that trigger the same, powerful response in your mind. "Lift and inspire others to learn about their own abilities and develop confidence" can become "Inspire others to confidence," "Inspire confidence in others," or just "Inspire confidence" (leaving the "others" part as an implied object). Doing this effectively can easily cut your Mission in half or less while still maintaining all the meaning. My original Mission was well over 200 words. In it's current version, I'm down to 9 words and an ampersand (&).

So long as the original phrase and the new phrase bring the same weight and meaning and emotion and power into your mind, make the change—it'll be easier to memorize. If you still need a few more words in there to bring the full images and power to mind, *leave the additional words in.* Dropping some of the additional description and detail can be an easy way to shorten your mission statement and make it more memorizable, but *only do it if the new version still brings the same energy, images, and emotion to mind*. Remember, you're writing *your* Mission here, not mine or anyone else's. You say things just the way you want to so that they make the most impact for you.

Will you commit to spending time in R&R (reflection and refinement) with your Mission this week?

___ Yes   ___ No

If yes, how much time will you commit to spend on this refinement process per day?   _____

Vision

I see Vision as being very similar to the way Laurie Beth Jones sees it. Specifically, I see Vision as a clarified look into the future, describing the "landscape" of your life and what that life will look like if you go through life living according to your Mission. In other words, if you were to follow your Mission perfectly from here out (or near-perfectly through Constant Course Correction), your Vision is how that life would play out in the end. You Mission explains who and how you want to be; your Vision is how your life looks when you live it who and how you want to be.

Perhaps the easiest way to think of Vision is to envision it like you had a time machine. Let's say you get in this time machine and warp forward a day or a year or ten years or fifty years. What does your life look like at that point, assuming you've been living your Mission faithfully? You take in all the details and then come back to the present and write about what you saw. That's your Vision. That's the waypoint in your future that you will reach by living according to your Mission.

There are several ways to imagine your future and write your Vision. Many authors propose the idea that you should write your own eulogy. The idea, of course, is that you've now been faithful in living according to your Mission for your entire life. You fast forward to your own funeral and talk about what goes on in the ceremony. Basically, now that you've successfully reached the end of your life, what do you want other people to be able to say about you? The things you want to leave behind—your legacy—indicate the things that are important to you.

On the one hand, the eulogy approach is nice because it provides a certain amount of finality. However, I've had a couple issues with it over the years. First, I don't understand why I have to be dead for people to say and think nice things about me. Second, what if I'm only 20 years old? I'm supposed to imagine what my funeral is going to be like 60, 70, maybe even 80 years away? Sixty years ago, computers filled entire warehouses and it wasn't a law to wear your seatbelt. Things change—sometimes drastically—over timeframes like that. Besides, what 20 year-old can really think about their own death? They've still got lingering invincibility complexes from their teenage years; thinking about a funeral is too morbid and surreal.

Worst of all, with a timeframe that long, there's a tendency to think "Sure, I need to do this stuff, but I've got time. I'll worry about it in a few years." Will all young people think that way? No. But how hard is it to plan for next month? Planning for 50 years from now is even that much more detached.

So, the eulogy idea is nice, and it works for a lot of people, but I've got a slightly different approach.

How old are you? And, yes, I expect you to answer this question. You can say it in your head if you want. If you answered that you are 40 or more, go ahead and add 10 to your age and remember that number. If you are between 30 and 40 years of age, add 15 years to your age and remember that number. If you are less than 30, add 20 to your age and remember your new number.

Now take that number and round it up or down to the closest milestone birthday. This will take a little judiciousness on your part, but target that big, milestone birthday a decade or two out.

For example, if you are 23 years old, add 20 to get 43. What birthday around 43 is going to be most significant to you? For most people, this will be their 40th birthday. If you're 30 years old, you would add 15 to get 45. What birthday around 45 is going to be most significant? Your 40th? Maybe your 50th? You decide. If you are 48, add 10 to get 58. What nearby birthday will be most significant? Your 60th, maybe? You get the picture. Conveniently, in western culture, we tend to benchmark significant ages in increments of 5 (40, 45, 50, 55, 60, etc.). You should have your target birthday now.

Surprise! Happy Birthday!

Now for this birthday, we're going to imagine that your family, friends, and/or significant others are throwing you a big surprise party. I know it might seem a little strange to be writing about your own future surprise birthday party—especially since you're writing about it yourself—so you're going to have to use your imagination a bit, but hang with me and it'll come together in a minute. In any case, we're going to write about this future surprise birthday of yours.

The first thing you need to figure out is the guest list. Who's going to be there?

The way we're going to brainstorm your guest list is by listing all of the major roles in your life. I already gave you some hints when we talked about the second question to determine whether your Mission was empowering or not. To repeat those for you, think of roles like spouse, parent, child, sibling, friend, business owner/partner, employee, community member/leader, church member, and the list goes on. Make sure to list all the significant roles you play in your life.

The next step is to create the actual guest list. For each of the roles you wrote down, list the key persons with whom you would interface while operating in that role. For the role of spouse, you would put "Role Title: [husband or wife—whichever you are]" and then, underneath, name your husband or wife *by name*. You don't refer to your spouse as "spouse," so don't put them on this paper that way. My wife's name is Becky, for instance, so my list would say, "Role Title: Husband" and then, underneath, list "Key Person(s): Becky." I've actually included a sample of this whole exercise—including a template—in *Appendix D*, so you can reference it later.

For your children, you would list your role title of father or mother. Then, underneath, you would list any key person(s) for this role—namely, each of your children by name. And don't think you can escape parenthood if you happen to have children who have left the house. If you parented five children, you still have five children whether all five are at home, none are at home, or somewhere in between. And feel free to use whatever names you actually refer to your children by; there's no need to be formal here.

For the role of child, you would list whether you were a son or daughter and then name your parents—and you wouldn't list them under the name "parents." You've not called them that to their faces before so don't start now. Most people would write "Mom and Fad" or "Mother and Father" or some derivation of those names. Include stepparents, if you have them, in this role. For your siblings, put your role title of brother or sister and then use whatever nicknames you know them by, not necessarily their formal, full names. If your sister's actual name is Jennifer, all her friends call her "Jen," but you know her as "Jenny," then put down Jenny.

Continue through and do this for each group of people with whom you have a role. Whenever possible, list the individual names of each member of a given group. However, if you have a group with more than about seven or eight people in it, feel free to just write down the name of the group. For instance, naming all your clients might be a bit time consuming. Once you have named a group like this, also write down the name of a representative who could serve as spokesperson for the group—unless we're talking about your family. You need to name all your children and all your siblings, but you don't really need to name all your neighbors, for instance. You don't need to name all your coworkers. Depending on who you are and how you operate with friendships, you may not even need to name all your friends—though, if you *can't* name them all, are they *really* your friends? This spokesperson will serve as the key person for the group you named, and this is pretty common for people when they have roles where they impact a lot of people.

Once you have these roles defined with your role title and the key people involved with any given role, I want you to pick the top five roles based on their importance to you. You may have as many as a dozen or more roles, or you may only have five, but for the next step, I want you to just pick the five most important roles you have. Likely, for many people, their top five roles will be dominated by familial roles—roles like spouse, parent, sibling, and child. That's okay. Theoretically, the roles which are most important to you will also be the roles in which the key people know you the best. That will come into play in the next stage of this exercise.

This list of key people and groups will become your invitation list. These people will be those whom your significant other(s) invite to this special, milestone, surprise birthday party.

Setting the Scene

Now, before we can get into the heart of this exercise, we need to write about the setting. Where are we? When are we? And don't just arbitrarily make up the date. You know it's your 50th or 60th or 80th birthday (or whichever birthday you chose), so go to a calendar and figure out when this birthday would really occur. For example, if you were born on the 29th of February, it's unlikely that your party can happen on the 29th of February for your 50th birthday—it won't be a leap year that year. If you were born on Christmas or New Year's or the Fourth of July or some other major holiday, it might be difficult to schedule this party on your actual birthday. That's okay. Birthdays are often celebrated a few days before or a few days after the actual event. You can shift around the date of your future surprise party to make it fit everyone's schedules—just be glad you're scheduling early so you avoid a lot of those conflicts.

For instance, if my birthday was the 17th of March and my milestone birthday for this exercise put the year out in 2021, I would go and look at a calendar. It turns out that the 17th of March in 2021 is a Wednesday, so I might shift the date of this party to the 19th or 20th (the Friday or Saturday), or because there isn't another major holiday right then (St. Patrick's Day doesn't count as a major holiday for most people), I might go ahead and schedule it on the 17th.

Now that you have the date, you need to decide on the venue. Is this party in your backyard, at a local park, or at some other nearby venue? Keep in mind that there will be a lot of people invited to this event so choosing an exotic getaway for the venue will be unlikely. As much as you might like this surprise party to be in Hawaii, that's not very likely unless you already live in Hawaii (in which case it probably doesn't seem quite as exotic to you anymore anyway). For most people, the party will happen in their house or in the backyard—depending largely on the season. For some, it might be better to host the party at a nearby park. You decide where your guest list will fit because—defying the laws of party physics—everyone on your invitation list is going to show up, on time, and stay for the duration. You're that important to each and every one of them.

Now that you know when and where your party will be, describe what the party will be like. Are there games? Food? Music? Is the music coming from a stereo or a live band? What kind of food is being served? What's the weather like?

I describe my party like this,

It's August 21, 2015, it's my fiftieth birthday. It's an unusually mild, pleasant day for August in the area of the country where I live. I'm in my backyard surrounded by loved ones, friends and family. My wife and children have really surprised me with a wonderful birthday party. There's a band playing at the edge of the yard, a little combination of old-time rock and roll with some newer country music. There's a wonderful buffet table with some of my favorite foods; I see lobster (my wife really went all out—she's in big trouble later when I talk to her about it), fajitas (an amazing recipe my wife makes herself), and my favorite drink (a combination of some slushy ice with pear juice).

I'm so grateful to have my children, parents and siblings, some of my clients, and many of my professional connections all there. My wife has tables set up around the yard where all of these important people are talking and laughing with one another. I'm sitting at one of these tables, enjoying the food and conversation with my friends and family and wife when I look over and notice that she's missing. I start to look around, wondering where she's gone.

Then I hear someone tapping on the microphone, and I realize that the band has stopped playing. Turning around, I look over to see my wife standing with the microphone in hand—something she has expertly avoided much of her adult life. But there she is, voluntarily. She clears her throat and begins to thank all the people who have come to the party:

"Thank you. Thank you, all of you, for coming to Kip's 50th birthday party. Thank you for taking the time out of your busy schedules to show what your relationship with him has really meant to each of you. I am honored and I know Kip is honored too. Now, if you'll indulge me for just a moment, I'd like to talk to my husband directly.

"Kip, you have been an incredible husband to me..."

Tribute Statements

This is the beginning of a Role Tribute Statement using your future surprise birthday party as the platform. Now, I won't give you the entire tribute statement for a couple reasons. First, as usual, I don't want to bias you as you write your own tribute statements. What I want my wife to be able to say to me probably isn't quite the same as what you'd want your spouse to be able to say to you, and is certainly different from what you'd want your siblings, parents, or colleagues to say. There are likely some common themes throughout your roles, but I want your tribute to come from *your* heart, not mine.

Second, it's a bit personal to go sharing it. Unlike your Mission, these tribute statements probably should make you tear up just a bit—at least the first few times you read them. These are statements of praise, appreciation, and honor from the people closest to you in your life; if these people can't make you a little emotional, probably nothing can. These statements will be the sum of what you want that person to be able to say about you in a specific role to your face, eyeball to eyeball, in front of a crowd of other people.

That said, don't ask anyone to proofread what you're about to create. They will only be able to look at the tribute statement with their present-day eyes, but when is this surprise birthday party of your scheduled? That's right, a decade or so in the future. If you go to your brother today and have him read his tribute statement, he's likely to read it, look at you funny, and say something like, "But you're not like this." Even if you tell him to imagine that the statement is being made 10 years in the future, he's still unlikely to catch the Vision. That's because it's *your* Vision, not his. Going to someone else is just inviting unneeded criticism.

What outside parties will fail to see is that you are crafting these tribute statements based on a decade of living your Mission—a Mission you may well have created in the past couple weeks. You may not be all those things right this instant—in fact, you shouldn't be—but you will be by the time this party rolls around. So don't waste your time trying to get various key people to ratify the tribute statements you create. These statements are to help you stay on track and show you what your target is for the future. It doesn't matter whether someone would ever actually say these things about you in public. The key is to remember that you want these people *to be able* to say these things. You aren't writing a tribute statement in hopes of fishing for a complement; you're writing it so you have a better idea of where you're going so you can use your Mission to get you there.

Also keep in mind that these tribute statements should be role-based tributes. My wife, for instance, will speak to the impact I've had as a husband, not really as a father. I wasn't her father. She may speak, briefly, about how I have performed as a father for her children, but the vast majority of her tribute will be about my role as a husband. And I'm going to have her say a whole lot of wonderful things not because I want to flatter myself but because I hope to make those things come true between the reality of today's date and the future date of this surprise birthday party.

A manager or boss would speak to your role as an employee, not so much about how you build relationships with clients—the spokesperson for your clients would talk about that. And hopefully you can think of plenty of wonderful things for your boss to say and more wonderful things to hear from the spokesperson of your clients. Your children would speak to your role as a parent, not to your role as a grandparent—and they should have wonderful things to say too.

Now, don't mistake this as an opportunity for self aggrand-izement. What we're doing here is setting your Vision, your long-term targets for who and how you want to be. With that in mind, much of what you write should *not* be true yet. Let me say that again: Yet. I daresay that 50 percent or more shouldn't be true yet. These are the things you will be working toward. If you've already arrived, how can this Vision statement help to provide you movement and energy? So keep in mind that these tribute statements are designed to answer the question of what impact do you want these people *to be able to say* that you've had in their lives in conjunction with your role? This isn't about what they can say now—though some of that may be in the tribute statement too. This is about how you're going to improve in a given role over time.

By writing these things right now in the present tense, you are not lying, you are speaking the truth in advance. Because you are writing about a future date, these things can only become *un*true if you choose not to work toward making them reality. After all, you've got a time machine, remember? You've been to the future and seen these people say these things. You know you can make this a reality because you've seen it. You aren't simply "going to" do these things, after all; you Will do them. You can if you Will. So, in that light, these tribute statements are merely the fulfillment of the Vision of the person that I want to be by shining my Mission on that role and living accordingly.

Now, unlike your Mission, these tribute statements should not be particularly short. You will be writing them, not memorizing them, so don't feel constrained by the number of words. Be specific wherever possible and include as much detail as you can. You want these statements to be emotionally powerful to you. You want depth and meaning and nuance. As I said earlier, these may even make you choke up a bit. That's a good thing.

Following Your Vision

Now, because we will be using these tribute statements to help guide our futures, I always recommend that you close them in context. In other words, remember the setting of the event and close the tribute statement with "Happy Birthday!" After all, each of the attendees is there to celebrate your birthday with you. That they take turns at the microphone to thank you for all the wonderful things you've done and been in your life up to that point is just coincidence because of how grateful they are to you.

A less obvious reason to make sure we end these statements in context comes from the guilt factor. As I mentioned, the bulk of the content in these statements won't be true yet—whether because you've not made any attempt at a certain trait yet or because you haven't reached the specified level in the tribute. When you read these statements, I want you to feel honored and happy that people love and appreciate you so much, not guilty that you're falling short. Closing each statement with the "Happy Birthday" helps you to keep in mind that these are future statements. You don't need to be all these things yet. In fact, you shouldn't be. That's what you're going to work toward from now until the time of this surprise birthday a decade or two from now.

The idea is for you to be able to get up on the morning of the day of this future surprise birthday party, go to the mirror, read these tribute statements, and then look yourself in the eye and say, "I know I'm not perfect, but I believe that this person could say the majority of these things. I have consciously made an effort over the past X number of years to do the things that would allow this person to say these things about me. I don't have to hear any of this out loud to know that I have done all I could to become the [insert role title here] that I really wanted to be." *That's* the point of all this. There are any number of ways to write a Vision; I have found none more powerful than Role Tribute Statements.

These tribute statements will help you to maintain focus, or Vision, about where you're going, in order to be the kind of person you want to be. In fact, starting in the next chapter, we'll be using these statements to help guide your weekly planning. We'll be answering the question "What could I do, this week, to make this statement just a little bit more true?" Keeping the tributes in context will help you to keep them in mind as your Vision for how you will be in the future.

The goal for now is to write a tribute statement for each of the five most important roles you identified early. Ultimately, you should write tribute statements for *all* of your major roles, but, for now you can just start with the five. As a side note, when I say one tribute statement for each of your major roles, I mean it. If you have 12 major roles in life, you should end up with 12 tribute statements. If you only have five major roles in life, then you'll only have five tribute statements. Note, however, that in my experience, very few people have fewer than six or seven major roles in life—especially not successful people.

So, now armed with both your Mission and your Vision, you have your bird's-eye view of where you're going and you can see the lay of the land at your destination. The next step is to build some milestones or guideposts for yourself. These concepts will be driven by your Mission and help to support it. By living these things, you will reach your Vision. So what are these things? Your Values.

Homework

1. Brainstorm your list of significant life roles and the associated key people. Choose the top five, most important roles.

2. Write out the setting and circumstances for your surprise birthday party.

3. Write Role Tribute Statements *in context* for the five most significant roles that you identified in step one. There is an example and a template included in *Appendix D*, if you would like to reference them. Remember to identify your role title and the key person(s) involved in that role with you. Write the tribute statements as though the person(s) were really speaking to you using full sentences and ideas. Don't shortcut the process with bullet points. The goal here is completeness, depth, and detail, not conciseness.

Values

Values are the third leg of the stool—the final piece of the foundation upon which you can build a steady, balanced life. Clarified, governing Values will provide you with the guideposts along the way to help you make sure that you reach your intended destination—your Vision.

The idea for governing Values goes all the way back to Benjamin Franklin (and probably beyond that, to be fair). Benjamin Franklin had a set of 12 governing Values by which he tried to live his life and which he clarified and defined in some detail. Interestingly, at one point in the middle of Benjamin's life, a friend pointed out that Benjamin's list of Values was missing one. Probably surprised and confused, Benjamin asked which Value was missing. The friend replied that any good Christian knows that Humility is an important Value. Benjamin promptly added it to his list, making a 13th Value, and wrote about it. Even more interesting is that late in his life, Benjamin wrote about these values again—and he was back to 12 of them. Any guesses as to which Value was missing? That's right, Humility.

Was this because Humility isn't a valid or worthwhile Value? No. Humility is a great value, but for Benjamin Franklin, it wasn't one of his core Values. It didn't make his first list and it didn't make the list later in his life. He only ever added it because his friend pointed it out and made an intellectual argument to support it. To be fair, Benjamin didn't have a whole lot to be humble about—though I'm sure he still worked at it. For Benjamin, however, those other 12 Values were his true governing principles, and those are the Values that stuck with him over the years.

Benjamin Franklin's humility or lack thereof aside, he set a great example for us of a person who had a set of clarified, written, governing Values by which to live his life. In this section, we're going to spend a little time now helping you discover your own Values and how they can help guide your life. First, let's start with a definition.

Values are a series of present-tense, first-person, positive declarations detailing what matters most to you and how you demonstrate, by your actions, that you live that value. It's important to emphasize the fact that these are aspirational in nature yet still written in the present tense. Like with the tribute statements, I don't want you to think of this as lying or fooling yourself; rather, this is telling the truth in advance. If you truly value these Values, and truly live according to your Mission, these Values *will* be true at some point. So don't concern yourself about whether these things are true right this moment or not. You are planning for the future.

For example, let's say I go through the brainstorming process and decide that one of my values is physical fitness. This is a noun, it's a little abstract, and as a result, it may mean one thing to me and mean something totally different to someone else. What does it mean to me? Similar to defining our verbs for the Mission-building exercise, we need to clarify our Values before we can really use them. To do this, you need to describe what it means to live it— and how that looks in some detail.

Brainstorming Your Values

To start with, you need to brainstorm your list of Values. This list can be whatever length you deem appropriate, but most people end up with between 5 and 12. If you have too few, your Values won't provide enough clarity and guidance to maximize their worth. If you have too many, it will become difficult to remember them all and account for all of them as you make decisions and plan for the future.

I'm going to give you a list (similar to the list of verbs I provided with the Mission exercise), but first I want to point out two things. One, you are welcome to add to this list. To attempt to build an exhaustive list of possible Values would be nearly impossible. Instead, I am providing a list of Values I've seen consistently over the years. If there's something you see as a Value but you don't see it on this list, please add it for yourself. Just like with Benjamin Franklin, no one else can tell you what your Values are. Your friends (including me) can give you thoughts and suggestions, but only you can make the decisions.

Additionally, I need to explain what it means to brainstorm. Brainstorming is a creative process by which you generate the maximum number of ideas that you possibly can in the shortest period of time. Now, we're not as concerned with the time constraint as we are with getting this right, so we won't worry about that. It's best to brainstorm in a single, big chunk of time (to avoid needing to get your creative juices flowing time and again), but this can be done over a series of smaller sessions, if need be.

The other key, critical, crucial, vital element to brainstorming is that you cannot, under any circumstances edit your list of ideas as you write it. Creativity stems from the figurative right hemisphere of the brain (current neuroscience research actually kind of debunks this, but that's a discussion for another day), but editing and logic stem from the figurative left hemisphere. You cannot physically, mentally do both tasks at the same time. The moment you begin editing your list, you shut off your creativity and end the brainstorming session. So, for the duration of your brainstorming, you need to just focus on listing more items, not crossing off anything. We'll take time to edit later—after you have a solid list.

Just to be clear, you are brainstorming possible Values right now. Your Values are, quite simply, the things you Value. As you'll see in the following list, most of these are nouns—thought-based concepts, really—not verbs like with your Mission. In order for you to really Value some*thing*, it kind of has to be a *thing*.

A few questions to consider are these:

- What are my highest priorities?
- What are the principles (natural law or fundamental truth) that I want to focus on in my interactions with others?
- What gives me the most joy in my life?
- What principles help me to be the most effective?
- What would I spend my time doing if I had no other time constraints?

So spend at least 15 minutes brainstorming ideas for what your Values are. We'll narrow down the list after that.

Here's a list of ideas to kick start your brainstorming:

Business

Experience

Commitment

Communication

Emotional Stability

Experience

Family Unity

Fidelity

Financial Independence/Freedom

Friendship

Fun

Generosity

Happy Marriage

Honor

Humility

Integrity

Intellectual Growth

Intelligence

Love

Organization

Physical Fitness

Relationship with God

Self-Reliance

Service

Spiritual Growth

Trust

Wisdom

ability to work with others

adaptability

analytical ability

artistic talent

business sense

caring nature

cheerful attitude

collaboration

confidence

courage

creativity

decisiveness

dedication

dependability

determination

endurance

enthusiasm

experience

fairness

faith

fearlessness

flexibility

forgiving nature

friendliness

generosity

global expertise

good character

good judgment

gratitude

honesty

industriousness

intelligence

intuition

kindness

knowledge

leadership

learning quickly	sense of adventure
motivation	sense of humor
negotiation	service to others
nurturing	social interaction
organization	spirituality
patience	teachableness
persistence	teaching ability
personal drive	thoughtfulness
persuasion	thrift
positive attitude	tolerance
problem-solving	trustworthiness
relationship-building	understanding
resourcefulness	vision
respectfulness	willingness
responsibility	work ethic

Prioritizing Your Values

Now that you have your long list of Values (and for some people these can be *very* long lists), you are ready for the next step: prioritizing. I sometimes have clients ask why they should need to prioritize their list of Values, and my simple response is that it's better to be aware than ignorant. Before we do this, let me just point out that most people don't want to prioritize their Values because all their Values are important to them. Who wants to choose between one good thing and another, right? Don't we want to accept all the good we can—and then look for more?

Sometimes difficult decisions arise in life—decisions that pit the things we value most against one another. Thankfully, this doesn't happen often, but it can happen, and I want you to be ready so you aren't paralyzed if that time ever comes. For instance, let's say you value financial independence and family. Those two things typically work hand in hand. Research indicates that stable, nuclear families provide all sorts of financial benefits for the members of that family. But what happens when your youngest child gets sick? The doctors have a good chance of saving her, but it's going to wipe out your savings and you'll probably have to refinance your house in order to afford the treatment. Suddenly your family and your financial independence are at odds. What will you do? You don't need to answer that question right now if you don't want to, but you might want to think it over.

The first thing to do at this point is to go through the list you've brainstormed and cross off anything that doesn't really resonate with you. You did a great job of not editing yourself while you were writing. Now you can take the time to go ahead and edit your list. Once you've "narrowed down" your list to only Values you actually feel a connection to (Benjamin Franklin would have removed Humility at this point), it's time to put them in order.

To help you better prioritize your Values, I have a series of activities.

The first is easy and fairly simple. Imagine that your values were actually in competition with one another for your time. Which ones would win? Sort your Values into a rough order. If you're not exactly sure which of two Values would win out in a competition, go ahead and leave them tied for now. You're just trying to get your Values into a loose priority order at this point; we'll refine the order with the next two activities.

The I-Beam Exercise

The next activity is going to take just a little explanation. Those of you familiar with construction will know what an I-beam is. For the rest of you, an I-beam is the piece of steel they use to frame big buildings. In your home, they typically use a wooden 2x4. In office high-rises, however, the stresses and weights borne by the building are far greater, requiring a far stronger building material. Your typical I-beam is shaped like an I or H when you look at a cross-section of the beam, depending on whether you've set it upright or on its side. They vary widely in width, height and length, but, for the purposes of our exercise, we'll say our I-beam is about 16 inches wide. Now, for an I-beam this wide, it's probably also 20-30 inches tall.

As it so happens, I happen to have an I-beam just like this sitting in the mall parking lot near my house. The beam is about

120 feet long, and I'll give you $10 if you hop up on one end and walk to the other. Easy, right? The top of the beam is more than a foot wide. You don't even need to put your arms out to balance. Besides, if you fall, it's only about two feet to the ground. There's no real danger.

Now, what happens if I put that beam five feet in the air and set up a pair of stepladders so you can get up? Will you still walk it for $10? How about for $100? I mean, it's going to hurt if you fall off, but the thing is still 16 inches wide across the top. That's five inches wider than a standard sheet of paper; this is not some tightrope here. Okay, I understand. There's a minuscule chance that you'll get caught in a sneezing fit halfway across and fall, so I'll up the ante to $1,000; that'll cover the cost of a broken wrist.

So let's make this really interesting. In Malaysia, there are twin buildings called the Petronas Towers. These towers are the tallest twin buildings in the world and until 2004, were actually the tallest towers at all.[11] These towers are 1,483 feet tall; that's nearly a third of a mile. Of course, that's only if you include the spire. I couldn't get permission to put my I-beam across the spire, but I did get permission to stretch it from the top floor of one tower to the top floor of the other, a mere 1230 feet up (approximately a quarter of a mile).

My question is, would you walk across that I-beam now? If I was standing at the other end shouting to you and waving that $1,000, would you walk across and get it? No? Why not? How about $10,000? $100,000? Okay, fine, I'll make it an even million—$1,000,000.

As an aside, I often have clients hesitate at this point, particularly clients at the very beginning or very end of their financial rope. That said, like you, most of my clients still won't walk across that I-beam—even for a million dollars. I can up the ante to a Billion dollars and still not have many takers. With a billion dollars, you could essentially live the rest of your life without working ever again—and live it in comfort. So why won't

[11] "Petronas Towers." *Wikipedia: The Free Encyclopedia.* Wikimedia Foundation. Last Updated 3 May 2013. Accessed 8 May 2013. http://en.wikipedia.org/wiki/Petronas_Towers

people walk across that I-beam? Because no matter how high the upside potential might be, what's the downside? You have to walk, not shimmy, and there is no safety harness, no safety net. If you fall, it will take you less than ten seconds to hit the ground.

Now, with the downside in mind, take the top Value on your list. Let's say that Value is a person and a terrorist has just abducted that Value and escaped across the I-beam. Now you're in the tower on one side and the terrorist—with your Value—is in the tower on the other end of the I-beam. He turns around and says, "If you come over here, I'll give your Value back." What are you going to do?

This isn't *really* any different from the I-beam when it was down in the parking lot, right? Just because the weight of the beam will cause it to sag a little in the middle shouldn't stop you; it's still 16 inches wide along the top. You might be high enough that the wind is blowing and gusting a bit, but you're sure of your balance, aren't you?

For which of your Values would you be able to bring yourself to walk across that I-beam a quarter mile above the ground with no safety harness? What I'm really asking is for you to decide for which of your Values you would risk death. Would you risk your life for Integrity? Financial Independence? Physical Fitness? Family? Remember, this is totally anonymous so be totally truthful in your answers.

What you'll find is that unless you are a daredevil by nature, you end up with a very short list of Values for which you'd risk walking across that I-beam and a much longer list of Values for which you wouldn't be willing. Does that mean that the second list isn't important to you? Not at all. It just means you see more value in Life itself than in those particular Values.

The Titanic Exercise

The next exercise doesn't put your life at risk, so you can relax a bit. So far, you've gotten your Values into a rough priority order and sorted the ones you would die for from the ones that are still important but not worth dying for. This next activity will help you refine the priority of your Values, giving you more clarity for making decisions in the future.

Imagine now that you're on a beautiful cruise ship. It's state-of-the-art in every way. It's the biggest, fastest vessel around and has every luxury and amenity you could possibly dream of. You have brought along, as guests, all your Values, and, together, you're having a great time. You're having a great time, that is, until the watchman calls out that he's sighted an iceberg. The next thing you know, the whole ship lurches violently, throwing you and your guests off your feet. A few moments later, you manage to collect yourselves and get back up. Then the Captain bursts through the doors.

"Reader, we've just hit an iceberg and the engineers tell me the ship is going to sink. I've got a place for you in a lifeboat, but you can only bring five of your guests."

Now it's up to you. When the ship goes down, any Values you left behind will undoubtedly be drowned and lost. Which of your five Values will you save? And don't try to be creative and say that you'll give up your seat to save a six Value; it doesn't work that way. Take a moment to decide which five of your Values you are going to save before you continue reading.

Good. You bid a tearful goodbye to your remaining values and start toward the lifeboat. You've scarcely left your room when the first mate runs up and says, "Captain, Reader, I've got bad news. We miscounted the occupants of the lifeboat. Reader, we've only got space for you and *four* of your guests."

Which of your five Values will you send back to the room? Which four will you keep with you?

Well, the captain and the first mate rush off to find other passengers and make sure that everyone is taken care of, leaving you to find your way to the lifeboats. You rush through the halls, twisting and turning until you come to a bulkhead door that's already sealed shut. There's an override switch, but it's broken and only works if someone stands there and holds it open. There's no time to go back and get one of your other Values to hold the door; you'll have to leave one of your four Values behind to hold the door so you and the other three Values can escape to safety.

Which Value will you leave behind? Which Value will you sacrifice to hold the door, and which three will you bring with you?

You and your remaining three values continue through the hall until you reach the deck. You can see the lifeboat waiting for you some distance up the deck so you start running. Then, without warning, a huge wave breaks against the side of the ship, nearly washing you overboard. As you struggle back to your feet on the slippery deck, you realize that your Values are gone. A quick look around reveals that they have been washed over the railing. All three are clinging to the wrong side of the railing and slipping fast. You've only got two arms. Whichever Value you don't grab is going to fall off the boat into the icy water below.

Which two will you save? As much as it hurts, which value will you let fall?

You pull your two Values back on board and rush up to the lifeboat. When you finally reach it, with your last two values in tow, you see a young mother, clutching an infant child, just climbing in ahead of you. You do a quick count and realize that there are now only two spots left. In spite of everything that's already happened, you're going to have to leave behind one of your last two Values.

Which Value will you keep and which will you leave on the deck?

Okay, I know that wasn't easy. Take a moment and breathe; it was just a thought exercise. I'm sorry to put you through that, but it serves a very valuable purpose. If you took the exercise seriously, you now know, in priority order, your top five Values. If you think about it for a moment, the five you chose to go with you are the most important five. How many came from the list you would walk the I-beam to save? I would guess that your entire I-beam list were selected as your first five Values—unless your I-beam list was longer than five, that is.

The priority order is just the reverse order of when Values got left behind. The Value that made it into the boat with you is the single most important Value on your list. The one left standing on deck as the lifeboat was lowered to the water is your second most important Value. The one that washed over the railing was your third most important Value. And so on from there. To test that, go back and compare your top priority to your second priority, then compare your second to your third, then third to fourth, etc.

I mentioned this briefly before, but I'll say it again now: life is very unlikely to ever force you to choose between your Values like this. In most cases, your Values will actually work together in a synergistic manner to make you better and stronger than you otherwise would have been. Still, rare times come up for some people in which those people do have to choose. Maybe you'll have to give up financial freedom for your child's health and wellbeing. Maybe you'll have to give up your own health to care for your spouse. Maybe you'll have to let go of a sibling or business partner to save your integrity—or maybe you'd give up your integrity to save that sibling or business partner. Or it could be something as simple as tax time and needing to finalize your business return on the same night as your daughter's little-league baseball game. You can only do one of the two, which will it be? Wouldn't it be good to know before that time comes so you don't have to agonize over it in the moment?

Thankfully, these situations are extremely rare. I just want you to be ready, safe, and confident *just in case*. When we talked about Mission, we talked about how one of the purposes was to prevent the need to make decisions in the urgency, expediency, or indifference of the moment. Knowing the priority order of your Values will help you be ready so you can't be blindsided by these more difficult situations and end up making a decision in a way you'll regret.

Going forward, you just need that prioritized list of your top five Values. If you want to repeat the next steps later with additional Values, that's fine (Benjamin Franklin had 12, after all), but for now, just stick with the five you have identified.

Creating Value Statements

Now that you have your Values narrowed down, let's take a moment to look at them again. In all likelihood, your values are nouns right now. That's how I gave them to you in the list and that's how concepts typically come across. Unfortunately, a noun can't really serve as a guiding Value because it's too distant from you. So, in order to make these Values stick to you, we're going to first turn them into statements of declaration. In doing this, remember that we are going to put them in first person ("I...") and in present tense—even though the statements themselves might not actually be entirely true right at this moment.

For instance, if I have the Value of Physical Fitness in my top five, it doesn't really mean anything until I change it slightly to say, "I am physically fit." Now let me point out a couple things. First, this will mean something completely different for each person who says it; that's why we'll create clarifying statements for each of your Value statements in just a moment. Second, this is a statement of affirmation. It's true insomuch as you choose to make it true going forward. There is, however, no power in saying, "I will be physically fit." Stating an affirmation in the future tense is really just dreaming. There's no commitment to it.

Creating these affirmation statements is really quite easy. You simply take the Value and combine it with one of the following three introductions: "I am...," "I can...," or "I have...." Whenever possible, it's better to use the first two options there. Saying "I am a loving parent" is far more powerful than saying, "I have love for my family" or even, "I have a loving family." You want these statements to be empowering in the same way that your Mission is.

Once you have turned your five Values into effective, empowering statements of affirmation, you are ready to move to the next step.

Clarifying Statements

Clarifying statements serve to support and explain our Values. These are written in much the same way that Values are written: positive, present tense, and first person. The reason we need these clarifying statements is because any number of people can all have the same Value, and yet each of them can see that Value differently and be influenced in a different way. Think back to my example of physical fitness.

"I am physically fit" means very different things to different people. To some people, being physically fit means they can bench-press twice their own weight. To another it might mean being able to run a half marathon just for fun. To still others it might mean just being able to climb the stairs to their apartment when the elevator is out without needing to pause for a rest on every landing. What really matters is what does being physically fit mean to you. What would you need to do to be able to feel comfortable saying you were physically fit?

These clarifying statements provide the additional depth, detail, and specificity necessary for you to fully explain what you mean in the Value statement.

For me, "I am physically fit" would be followed by clarifying statements like these:

- I maintain a body fat percentage of 18 percent or less.
- I exercise six days a week; three days, 30 minutes for cardiovascular endurance, and three days, 45 minutes for muscular strength
- I eat a healthy, well-balanced, nutritious diet
- I get plenty of sleep and rest; at least eight hours every night
- I lead a vigorous lifestyle

Someone else with a different personal definition of physical fitness would have different clarifying statements, but, for me, those statements explain what I mean when I say "I am physically fit" (for more examples, see *Appendix E*). The idea here is to remove the ambiguity so I can know exactly what I'm trying to accomplish. Rather than saying that I'm physically fit and then struggling to decide on what that means from day to day, I have a list of specific, actionable statements that if complied with, will tell me that I'm succeeding at living the Value. Do you see why the clarifying statements make your Values so much more powerful and relevant?

So, to recap everything in this chapter, your Mission serves to answer the question of who and how you want to be from the big picture. Your Vision is a reflection of who and how you want to be in the long term, including the impact you want to have in the various roles of your life. Your Values, to finish the picture, are the details of how you will go about doing these other things. Now that you know where you are, where you're going, and what to look for along the way, it's time to plan your journey.

Homework

1. Brainstorm your list of Values.

2. Prioritize your list of Values and select the top five most important.

3. Turn your Values into Value affirmations.

4. Add clarifying statements with sufficient detail to explain to yourself what you mean by the original value statement.

You Can If You Do

A long time ago, in a galaxy far, far away, a very wise, albeit very small little creature counseled his apprentice: "You must unlearn what you have learned." The young man, in a tone that demonstrated his lack of belief and conviction, replied, "Alright, I'll give it a try." The master was quick with his rebuke, "No! Try not! Do, or do not, there is no try."

Though only a movie character, the wisdom of Yoda has been invoked by millions of others over the last 30+ years. Why? Because it's based on principle, and a principle is a natural law, or fundamental truth.

Let's try a little experiment. It's most powerful if you actually do it, but if you aren't in a position to act then at least imagine it as vividly as you can. Take a pen and place it on a flat surface. Now, when I say go, try to pick up the pen. Ready, Set, "Go."

What happened? Did you pick up the pen? If you did then you did not understand my instructions very well. I said to "try" to pick up the pen. Let's do it again. Ready, Set, "Go."

What happened this time? If you still picked up the pen then we have bigger problems to address than understanding the nature of "try." However, if this time you did *not* pick up the pen, then I would ask if you at least touched it. Or, if you really tried hard, did you grasp the pen as hard as you could, with your hand shaking, a grimace on your face, and a good audible grunt demonstrating the level of your effort? No? You didn't do that? Why not? I did say to "try." Of course, to give a full physical effort like the one I'm describing and not actually pick up the pen would feel pretty ridiculous, and the reason is simple:

When you are perfectly able to do a thing, you can no longer "try" to do that thing. You either choose to do it, or you choose not to. You cannot "try" to do that which you are perfectly able to do.

Picking up the pen would be one example of this principle. Calling someone on the phone would be another. Meeting a friend at the mall, mowing the lawn, or going to bed on time would be some others.

So, is there such a thing as try? Sure, try to pick up a car by yourself. Try to fly to the moon by only flapping your arms. Seriously though, there are some things that would constitute a true "try" scenario.

Imagine that you have just had a lesson on how to shoot an arrow from a bow. By the end of your one-hour lesson you have become fairly adept at placing the notch of the arrow on the string, drawing it back, and letting it fly in the general direction of your target. Let's say you have proven you can fire the arrow 20 times in a row. Can you now "try" to fire the arrow? No. You are completely able to perform that action. You cannot try. However, based on experience, distance to target, and wind conditions, hitting the bull's-eye is still a true "try." You may hit it, or you may not, but it's not as simple as choosing to. In effect, the only time you can "try" to do something is when you can put your full force of will behind an action and still be uncertain of having success.

So when it comes to following through on the majority of commitments we might make, to others or to ourselves, most of the time there is no try, only do or do not. Remember that the next time someone says to you, "Will you call me tomorrow?" and you say, "I'll try." Seriously? Is the phone going to all of a sudden become too heavy to hold or the numbers too difficult to dial? Or, do you really mean to say, "I don't want to commit, but I don't want to tell you that so I'm saying, 'I'll try' instead, knowing full well that I'm probably not going to do it."

"Will you send me a proposal this week?"

"I'll try."

"Will you be honest with me?"

"I'll try."

"Will you be nice?"

"I'll try."

You would be well served to remove the word "try" from your vocabulary, since there are so few situations that call for a true "try" rather than a simple commitment and follow through. I suggest you drop the "try" and separate the contraction of "I'll" which leaves you with "I Will" and empowers you to actually do. Otherwise, just be honest and say, "I won't." Oh, and if you're wondering if there is any time in life where a "try" is good, the answer is yes... rugby (good for 5 points).

Stinky Wishes

I tell that little story as a preface because we're about to get into a pair of topics that everybody is willing to "try," yet so few actually "do." Specifically, we're going to talk about goal setting and planning.

Consider two sayings: "a goal not written is only a wish" and "if wishes were fishes, the world would really stink."

The idea here is that everyone has a long list of the things they "wish" they had or they "wish" would happen. If all those wishes turned to fish, the world would be carpeted in fish. So, instead of doing what comes naturally and just "wishing" for things, you need to take charge and make a habit of doing the things that failures don't like to do. You need write those "wishes" down in goal format and then work toward them. A key to remember is that, if you don't write down that goal, it's just a wish. You need to give clear boundaries for what your goal includes—and excludes—and delineate the steps you need to take in order to accomplish the goal. Anything less that that is just another wish to add to the pile of rotten seafood.

It really comes down to the fact that when you wish, all you're really doing is saying that you want some other force to magically make your dreams come true without you needing to put in any of the required work. You want Bill Gates to sweep in and give you a million dollars so you don't have to do the work and earn that million. Wishing is, at its core, a lottery mentality.

Alternatively, you can go and create a business plan, buy your business license, and start building your business. The Bureau of Labor Statistics tells us that something like half of all small business fail in the first 3-5 years. That sounds pretty rough, right? You'll put in all that time and effort and only come out with a 50-50 chance of success? But compare that to the lottery ticket. How many thousands of people spend millions of dollars on lottery tickets—and how many win?

Which percentage would you rather gamble on? Winning the lottery would be big, but most lottery winners have lost everything within a few years anyway. Entrepreneurs—workers—may experience some setbacks, but the odds are in their favor.

So, though you may have read plenty of literature on goal setting in the past, we're going to cover the topic in terms of small goals and then large goals. Once we've done that, we'll talk about the final key of setting goals: planning how to accomplish them.

Goal Setting 101

Have you ever set a New Year's Resolution and given up after a while? Why? Do you remember what that resolution was? The exact wording? Many people set a goal like, "I'm going to lose 20 pounds this year" or "I'm going to focus and work harder in my job" or "I'm going to get in shape" or "I'm going to spend more time with my family" or "I'm going to keep my office organized."

I don't want to give you the impression that any of these are unworthy, but most of them are unobtainable. Why are they unobtainable? Because you don't know what the goal actually is. Losing 20 pounds in a year is a clear goal; focusing and working harder in your job isn't. And what does it mean to "get in shape" or "spend more time with family"? You see, no matter the emotional connection these goals may have, they are too unclear to really be actionable. In order for you to really follow through and keep this kind of a commitment to yourself, you have to know what you're doing. For that, I recommend SMART goals.

We've probably all heard the acronym before, but how many of us can remember what each of the five letters stands for?

Specific: Your goal needs to be specific enough that you know what your actual target is. Losing 20 pounds is good; you can weigh yourself now and then daily or once a week or whatever until you see that you've lost the 20 pounds. Spending more time with family, however, is not such a specific goal. How much time? How do you know when you've arrived? Focusing and working harder in your job is about as vague as you can get. Which aspect(s) of your job? What does this new focus look like?

Measurable: Having appropriate specificity leads right in to measurability. This refers to the metric by which you will measure your progress and success. For losing 20 pounds, the measurement is obvious. What measurement do you use to decide whether you are spending more time with your family? Time, probably, but we've already discussed the fact that time is insufficient if your pitcher is empty. Perhaps you should measure in terms of quality, renewed, energized time instead. How will you measure your "in-shape-ness"? Your office organization level? You need to have metrics in order to track your goals; you can't have a specific goal without some sort of metric along which to measure.

Attainable: This plays in with your level of specificity and measurability. In setting this goal, can you really, actually achieve the goal? Losing 20 pounds is the basis of a great goal for many people. What if you only weigh 100 pounds as a full-grown adult. You don't have 20 pounds to lose. Keeping your office organized is a nice idea, but what if you share it with three other people and all of them are complete slobs? How much of your time will you expend trying to make up for their sloppiness and disorganization? Or what if you have a medical condition such that your doctor has restricted you from the kind of activity necessary to get you "in shape." Make sure that you can take the actions necessary to achieve the goal and that the target mark is within reach. A couch potato can train up and run a marathon, but he'd better leave himself enough time to do all the training—the first guy to ever run a marathon died of exhaustion at the end.

Relevant: What's the point in setting the goal if you don't really care about the outcome? By relevant, we mean relevant to your Mission, Vision, and Values. Does this goal promote who and/or how you want to be? If not, why would you waste time on it? Don't you want to focus on the things that really matter? So, when you go to set a goal, make sure you actually care about the outcome, otherwise it will become a back-burner item until you can convince yourself to forget about it entirely.

Time-bound: Without a deadline or timeframe, there is no accountability. You may have a "goal" but you're so much less likely to have the drive to see it through unless you have some form of end date. By what date are you going to organize your office? How long will you spend getting in shape each day?

So, for my clients, I recommend that they set their goals in SMART format by following this template:

I Will _____ by
_____.

The specificity, measurability, attainability, and relevance go in the first blank. The second blank holds the timeframe. For an example, "I Will clean out and organize my garage by June 30." Now, sometimes, you'll reread that goal and realize that there isn't enough specificity the way you initially write it. A goal like, "I Will lose 20 pounds by the end of the year" suffers from a similar problem. Many of our goals do, but, because we think we've followed the SMART format, we don't see the problem. This sets us up for failure.

The missing specificity is often related to the measurement of success or the method for success. To include some of the method, take a moment to clearly visualize your ideal outcome, like you did with your Role Tribute Statements. Then take that detail and add a little more to your goal: "I will clean out and organize my garage—meaning everything will be off the floor, shelving units will be installed, and the car will fit inside again—by June 30." Now you know exactly what needs to happen, what it looks like, and by when you need to be done.

Of course, that's only an example for a project-based goal. I call these checkmark goals because, once you complete them, you can check them off. What about goals like getting in shape? You'll never complete that goal because, even once you get in shape, you'll have to constantly work to maintain your fitness.

For process-based goals, like getting in shape, we alter the template slightly:

I Will _____ beginning
_____.

So, for this kind of goal, you might put something like "I Will maintain my fitness by working out hard enough to sweat three times a week for 30 minutes per session beginning June 1."

Now you know exactly what you need to do to comply with that goal—and notice there is no end date. Rather than a deadline for the end, there's a deadline for the beginning. You can start sooner than June 1, but by June 1 you need to be breaking a sweat during three workouts per week. You could even take this goal a step further and identify the exact days a week on which you will work. Remember, the more specific you are, the easier it will be to comply with the goal.

Now, notice that for both of these templates, we capitalize Will. This is done intentionally. We're not simply saying we're "going to do something," we're saying that we Will this thing to happen. You can if you Will, and we want you to make it reality.

The Wheel of Life, Take 2

Now that we've talked about goal-setting, let's go back to your Wheel of Life (I told you we'd come back to it).

With your understanding of Will and your foundation in Mission, Vision, and Values, you're ready to work on rounding out your Wheel, bringing balance to your personal effectiveness. Look at each of the eight different aspects of the Wheel of life. For each category, what is one thing you could do in the next 12 months to bring yourself closer to a performance level 10 in that category? Write out that thing as a SMART goal.

For example, if you're working in a job you don't like and you've always wanted to start your own business, you could set a goal to get all the necessary registration paperwork done to start your business. Maybe you need a little more time for recreation; you could set a goal to spend an hour or two each week doing something you love. Maybe you've been a bit of an absentee parent, and you want to start spending more time—more *quality* time—with your children; set a goal to improve yourself as a parent.

When you're done, you should have eight, clear goals time-bounded somewhere in the next 12 months. Were some of the goals harder to come up with than others? Typically, if you have a low satisfaction score—regardless of your performance score—it's easy to come up with a goal. On the other hand, when you are fairly satisfied with your performance—regardless again of how you rate that performance—it gets a little harder to think of a way to improve. Why is that? And what might be the effect on your future performance?

Burning Platforms

If you have a low performance number with a high satisfaction number, that might be okay. Certainly it's good to not add stress to an already less-than-ideal situation. However, let me pose to you a question: How likely are you to make any real headway on the category in question?

For example, let's say I'm 50 pounds overweight, I don't exercise, and although I do an okay job of eating right for meals, I eat a lot of junk food in between. I might rate myself fairly low in Health/Fitness. Let's say a three. However, no one seems to mind that I'm overweight. I haven't experienced any of the health problems for which I'm putting myself at risk, so I'm pretty comfortable with the *status quo*. We'll call me an eight on satisfaction. When we add the two and divide, I have a 5.5 out of 10 (8 + 3 = 11 / 2 = 5.5). But how likely am I to change? What are the chances I'm going to stick with a program to do anything differently?

In change literature, there is a concept often referred to as "the Burning Platform." The idea is that for each facet of life, you are standing out on a floating platform over the Grand Canyon. Nearby is another platform—but you'll have to take the risk of jumping to reach it. How many of you would jump? Remember, the price of failure is free fall without a parachute. Unless you are one of the few risk-seekers out there, you are probably going to stay put. There's nothing unsafe about the platform whereon you are already standing. It's not falling apart or anything else. This is the idea that, "If it ain't broke, don't fix it." Why take the risk, right?

What if, however, that comfortable platform is made of wood and someone on the edge of the canyon shoots a burning arrow into it? Now your platform has caught fire. Who is going to try jumping to the other platform now? With this change in circumstances, so too change the numbers. While there will be a few who would rather go down with the ship than take the chance, most people will take the risk and make the jump.

So the first step to making a change is to recognize that something is "broke." If I want to lose that 50 pounds, I first have to feel less satisfied with the fact that I weigh 50 pounds more than I want to. I have to be less satisfied with the *status quo*. This is why it's sometimes hard to write a goal to improve an area in which we're already satisfied—even if we recognize that we have low performance in that area.

If my office is a disorganized, black hole of a nightmare, but I'm satisfied with that, I'm unlikely to motivate myself to expend the effort to organize my surroundings. Until I recognize the negative effect of all that clutter on my productivity (and maybe not even then), I won't care enough to change.

This is where Mission, Vision, and Values come in. Organization may not be a natural thing for you, but how would it support and promote your Mission, Vision, and Values? Being 50 pounds overweight may not really bother you, but does it support your Mission? Does it reflect your Values? If not, what would?

Your Mission, Vision, and Values become the catalyst for you to plan change into your life and your Will become the fuel by which you push for that change. SMART goals, then, are the roadmap that takes you from where you are to the Vision you've created of where you want to be.

But what about those really big goals—like losing 50 pounds or organizing your office? We talked about the need to be specific and, when I introduced the goal template to you, I mentioned that sometimes you have to add a little more detail. So what do you do with a goal that's important to you, but, written out in that template, doesn't feel very specific or attainable? What do you do if some of your goals, especially the longer-term ones, get to be a bit large?

Tackling Large Goals

Forgive me as I answer a question with another question:

Think, for a moment, about goals you've set in the past.

Okay, now think about projects you've had in the past.

Good.

Which, between the two (goals and projects), tends to be more personal in nature? Which tends to be more related to business?

So which do you think gets accomplished at a higher percentage? Personal goals or business projects?

Now, I agree with you, but why do you think people accomplish more projects in the workplace than goals in their personal lives? That's right: accountability. There's a lot more obvious reward in the workplace. There are also a lot of severe punishments and risks around failure to complete projects in business, right? It seems like there's a lot more at stake for a business project.

Now let me ask another question: Between the two, personal goals and work projects, which do you think tends to be more broken down into the detailed component pieces? Which is more structured?

I would submit that this is the very reason why more business projects are completed compared to personal goals. By their very nature, projects are clearer, more defined, and more supported by accountability. Personal goals tend to be more vague, general, and pie in the sky. Which ones are typically written down? That's right, projects again. Many projects have detailed action plans to explain the accountability. Many people keep their goals in their heads (and we've already talked about how I feel about that).

Thanks for playing along with me. I'll get to the point now: Do you know what the difference between goals and projects really is?

You might need to sit down for this one. *Nothing*. Semantics.

The only differences are the ones we imagine for ourselves. When you really think about them both, projects and goals are just some delineated future objective. There is absolutely *zero* difference between a goal and a project beyond the differences in how we unconsciously treat them. We tend to give more time, attention, focus, effort, and energy to projects, but there is no inherent reason why that should be the case.

Would you like to accomplish a higher percentage of your personal goals? Turn them into projects, just like any work project, and give them that kind of effort, focus, and energy. So how do you do that?

Let me explain the answer to that question by first laying out some facts for you.

Fact: The elephant is the largest land animal on earth today.

Fact: Male African elephants can grow to be as much as 13 feet tall.

Fact: Those same elephants can weigh as much as a school bus—10,000-14,000 pounds.

Did you know all that about elephants? Okay, then let's bring it a little closer to home.

Fact: The average height and weight for an adult man is 5' 9" and 180 pounds. The average height and weight for an adult woman is 5' 4" and 145 pounds.

Fact: The average healthy adult consumes between 1.5 and 3 pounds of food per day depending on height, weight, and metabolism.

Fact: The average human does *not* consume elephant as a normal part of their diet.

Fact: …They could if they wanted to…

So how *does* one go about eating an elephant?

How many of you said, "One bite at a time"? Right?

We all know that. But what does that really mean? Have you ever sat down to figure it out? I have.

If you started eating a 10,000 pound elephant today, at an average rate of 2 pounds per day, it would take you about 13 years, 8 months, and 10 days—and you'll still have some leftovers for the better part of the next day. Guess you'd better start eating. Now, the next time someone asks you how to eat an elephant, don't just tell them "one bite at a time," actually break it down and let them know that, if they give you a little time, you can tell them exactly when you'll be finished.

Most people don't break it down though. We can all recite the cliché, but so few of us actually sit down to run the calculations and start planning everything out. If you really want to know how to eat an elephant, you need to break that beast down into hunks, chunks, and bites and plan out which parts you are going to eat on which days. It's not enough to say you'll eat one bite at a time; you need to know which bite is next, or you'll get lost in the enormity of the task. Just to eat the trunk, for example, would take 114 days (trunks can weigh as much as 400 pounds); that's just shy of 4 months.

And let's break it down another way. Because you can only eat one bite at a time, how much can you eat in one bite? One pound is 16 ounces, so let's say you can eat 1 ounce per bite. That means you could eat a quarter-pounder hamburger in four bites, but keep in mind that we're only talking about the patty inside, not the bun and lettuce and everything else. So it will take 16 bites to eat each pound of elephant. That's 32 bites of elephant per day (16 x 2 = 32). If each bite takes a minute to chew and swallow, you'd better plan on spending half an hour per day for the next 13+ years eating that elephant—and we didn't even include the time required to properly cook your two pounds each day. Daunting, isn't it?

And this is the other reason that so many people give up on their goals. They set goals that are in line with their Mission, Vision, and Values; they are motivated and ready to go; they engage their Will to accomplish the task; and then they fail. Why? Because the task was just too big. They weren't pacing themselves. Did you know that one of the most frequently cited causes for abandoning a new exercise routine is that people start out too intense? They push themselves so hard coming out of the gate that they can't keep up. It hurts too much and makes them feel too weak and bad, so they give up. In their enthusiasm, they over-extend themselves.

Project Management

What are *your* elephants? Some may be huge, 10,000 pound adult African male elephants and some may be baby elephants. Do you want to make a million dollars? Lose 50 pounds? Make it to every little league game your child plays this season? Finally start that business idea you've been tinkering with? Organize your home?

Conveniently, all elephants, regardless of size, are "eaten" the same way: one bite at a time. But you can't stop there. You have to have a system for how to get through so much meat. Have you broken your goals down into the major hunks? Have you then broken those hunks into manageable chunks? Have you further broken down those chunks into individual steps? Do you know the order of the steps? Do you know what you need to work on now? Do you know what comes next? There's more to eating an elephant than simply rushing out to start eating. That will only make you sick, and then you run the risk of giving up early. If you can't figure out the pacing, you're in serious danger of failing.

So, just like with your Value statements you had clarifying statements, for your bigger goals, you need component goals. Let's look at the example of cleaning out the garage. I actually already named the hunks when I added some specificity: everything off the floor, shelving units installed, the car inside.

But even those hunks are a bit large, so let's break them down into smaller pieces—chunks. For the shelving units, as an example, the first step is to plan the location for the shelves. Next, I need to build the shelves. Last I need to install them.

Now we're sounding more manageable, but I can break these chunks down still further—into bites. In planning the location for the shelves, I need to measure the floor space in the garage, decide where I want the shelves, and clear that area. To build the shelves, I have to first buy them and get them home. Then I can build them and, last, I can move them into place and use any necessary mounting hardware to secure them.

Depending on how you count them, I have as many as 8 little bite-sized goals now. Notice how none of them are particularly large or intimidating? Some of you may even be thinking that I've broken things down a level too far just to drive home a point. I haven't. You don't want to start eating and then find out that your bites are so big that you choke on them. By making the bites as small as possible, you make them that much easier to plan for and accomplish.

Additionally, the act of breaking things down will reveal any holes in your planning. As you break the process down, you'll see if there were steps or pieces that you were forgetting about. If you were to leave the hunks or chunks in full size, you might not realize just what you were getting into. By breaking it down, you can actually see clearly. You can also put things in chronological order (so you don't get ahead of yourself) and figure out which parts of the process can be run in parallel (simultaneously). I could, for instance, order the shelving units to be delivered to my house before I finished clearing where they go. Then, while the shelves are being shipped, I can increase the priority on getting that area cleared so that the garage is ready when the units arrive.

Basically, now these bites can be written out as SMART goals, and the goals can be listed out in project management format just like you would for your job. Because you know exactly what's required, what order to complete things, and how long each of the components will take, you are far more likely to follow through.

Additionally, these bite-sized goals are now the right size to be used in our planning process, so let's take a look at that process and how it works.

Weekly Planning

A lot of people plan big events far in advance. You know you've got a family reunion coming up this summer, so you block that out in your calendar and stop thinking about it. Of course, how often do we get right up to that kind of event and realize that we've subsequently double-booked ourselves with another activity or two?

I compare planning to the act of driving down the highway to a place you've never been. Hopefully, you've had that experience before, but, if not, just try to imagine it.

You're driving to a distant destination. You've got good, clear directions, but those directions only really help if you can connect

164

them to the signs on the freeway. It doesn't do you much good to know you need to get off the highway at Exit 273 if none of the exits are marked—or if you're not looking at the signs. You can still sometimes get close to your destination, but it's tough to find the right way without wasting time on lots of wrong ways.

I compare planning to your efforts in looking at the signs. Monthly and yearly planning, for instance, is like that moment when you first see the big green sign a mile or two up the road. You know it's coming, and you know you might need to get off on the exit, but you can't quite read the words yet to be sure if this is your exit or if you need the next one. Still, even though you can't be totally sure of the exit, you can get a great field of vision. You're far enough back that you've got plenty of time to change lanes and get in the right place. You are also far enough back that you can look around to appreciate the lay of the land down the exit ramp and check your mirrors for other cars.

Have you ever had that experience, though, where you're driving up the freeway and almost out of the corner of your eye, you see your exit—right as you're driving past? You end up going up another exit and turning around to come back? Daily planning is like being so close to the sign that you can see it clearly, but you're too late to react. If you're in the exit lane, you're taking the exit—whether it's the right one or not. If you're still over in the left lane, you're not going to make it without hitting someone else in the attempt, so you better hope it wasn't your exit. The problem with daily planning, on its own, is that a daily plan is, by nature, somewhat reactionary. A daily plan is merely the fine-tuned execution of plans you've already made and put into play. So what if there were no other plans?

Or what if the only plans you made were back in the big picture of monthly and annual planning? You couldn't actually read the signs then, so how could you properly prepare to merge over or not? You wouldn't even know if you needed to.

Now, don't get me wrong, there is value in monthly planning, yearly planning, and even daily planning. However, using only those forms of planning omits the most crucial, powerful, valuable form of planning: weekly planning.

Weekly planning puts you a quarter mile from the exit. You're close enough to read the sign, most importantly, but still far enough out that you can negotiate the traffic and change lanes, if necessary. Weekly planning doesn't give you the same lay of the land as monthly planning or the same quick reaction as daily planning, but it gives you more control—more accurate control—than either of the other two methods.

Lots of people plan annually. Many of them also plan monthly. A number of people take a few minutes in the morning to plan their day too. But did you know that *everyone* plans weekly? That's right everyone plans weekly. Don't scowl at the book, point your finger at yourself, and shake your head. You do too plan weekly. You just might not spell it the right way.

You see, in my experience, you either plan weekly, or you plan weakly. Monthly planning is great for the big picture, daily planning is good for rearranging things and putting out the inevitable "fires" of life, but weekly planning brings the two together and helps you be effective. If you decide to forego weekly planning, then you are weakening your planning process.

The problem is well described by Thomas Monson when he said, "When the time for decision arrives, the time for preparation has passed." The point is, once you're in the heat of the moment, you've used up all your time to plan. If all you ever do is daily planning, then all you ever do is too much like waiting for the last moment, and you're unlikely to have any effective plans. It's too late to orchestrate any kind of efficient, effective strategy, so you'll end up on fire detail instead—rushing from emergency to emergency, always putting out fires and never feeling like you're getting anywhere.

Weekly planning is, therefore, the best form of planning. Daily, monthly, and yearly planning all play a role, but that role supplements weekly planning; it doesn't supplant.

The Fifteen Game

To demonstrate how weekly planning works, I like to reference one of those little brainteaser games called the 15 Game. In this game, you are given a board with sixteen empty slots, arranged in a 4x4 grid, containing fifteen numbered tiles. The object of the game is to move the numbered tiles into the single empty space in order to rearrange the tiles into the proper order. A sample image is included below to give you a visual of what the board looks like when jumbled. The black space is the empty one.

What would happen, hypothetically, if you jammed a sixteenth tile into the board? Would you be able to move the tiles around anymore? No. If you completely filled the board, it would be locked in place, and if it wasn't already in order, you'd never be able to get it in order. It would be locked up and you'd have to just throw it out.

Alternatively, wouldn't it be nice to play the 15 game with somewhere between 8 and 12 tiles? That would give you a few extra spaces and make it a *lot* easier to get everything in order. Too few tiles and everything just starts to fall apart, but between 8 and 12 tiles would hold together while also giving you plenty of space in which to operate.

Interestingly, each and every day has 24 hours in it. If you're supposed to be sleeping eight hours a day (the requirement for a truly healthy lifestyle), how many hours does that leave for everything else in your life? That's right, 16. Just like the game we were discussing. Now, you already know what I'm going to ask, but I'm going to ask it anyway: What happens if you fill up all sixteen of those hours in your day with activity?

In project management, there is a concept referred to as slack, or float, which is the idea that a task needs to get done but it can have a buffer before and after in case things change and the timing needs to shift a little. If you fill all 16 hours of your day, do you have any slack left? Another way to think of slack is in terms of flexibility. What happens when you've successfully scheduled all 16 hours of your day, you're ready for maximum efficiency and effectiveness, and then the doctor's office is running late and it puts you back half an hour? Now you've got to look through your schedule and cancel something else so you can get back on track—and let's hope you don't run your schedule like this every day or you won't be able to reschedule what you're canceling now.

If there is sufficient slack, or float, in your schedule, then it can absorb these kinds of setbacks without breaking apart. In my experience (and I gave a not-so-subtle hint of this earlier), a normal schedule should be planned for between 50 and 75 percent of the waking hours; i.e., between 8 and 12 hours of structured planned activities each day. Any more than that and the schedule begins to get too rigid and fragile. Any less than that and there's too much free time. Have you ever heard the phrase, "If you want something done, give it to the busy person"? There's some truth to that saying. If you have too much unplanned time, there's too much temptation to procrastinate because there's "plenty of time" to do it later.

This means that on the very busiest of days—even accountants on April 14 and 15—you should still never have more than 12 hours of structured activity planned. Now, this doesn't mean you can't work more than 12 hours in a day—sometimes there are deadlines to meet—but it means you shouldn't be scheduling more than 12 hours of your day. You can still get work done in the unplanned portions of the day, and leaving some open space will give you room to fit your schedule around those things that inevitably "come up."

Speaking for myself, I'm not sure I've ever had a week go by perfectly according to plan. Usually the surprises are small and easily managed—sometimes less so. In a normal week, though, I'd say I probably have between 10 and 20 percent of my planned activities get shuffled around a bit. This could be as simple as a team member getting caught in traffic and needing to push a staff meeting back an hour or as drastic as catching the flu and being out of commission for two days. Regardless of the why, having flexibility in my schedule allows me to adapt to situations as they come without losing control over everything.

You need to leave some space for life to happen or you'll find that life passes you by. You don't want to have to delete important things—or just miss them and hope there's no fallout. Give yourself permission to maintain some flexibility in your schedule instead. Then, rather than missing or deleting an event, you can shuffle it around to later in the day, or the next day or week, and still get it done while also being able to respond to the immediate event that has cropped up. Because, let's face it, no matter how well you plan, urgent, important things will still spring up from time to time.

So leave a little space. Shuffle things around as needed; that's not failure. Of course, to know what to shuffle around and how to give precedence to one thing over another, we need to talk about two words I used in the last paragraph: urgency and importance.

Urgency *vs.* Importance

Planning, and in particular weekly planning, is the answer to one of the more common problems faced by people today. That problem is the emotional response to urgent problems. Before we get any deeper into this topic, however, we need to take a very brief step back and visit Stephen Covey's importance *vs.* urgency matrix. Those of you who have read *The 7 Habits of Highly Effective People* will recognize this; for the rest of you, I'd recommend you go out and pick up a copy of the book because my explanation here will be much less thorough.

Before we get into the particulars, I want to make sure we're on the same page with regard to the definitions. Importance refers to activities about which you can clearly articulate how they relate to and promote your Mission, Vision, and Values or other goals, roles, and responsibilities. In other words, you need to be able to explain why the activity or event matters, and you need to be able to do so without hesitation, confusion, or inconsistency. If you can't quickly, accurately, completely state why something matters to who and how you want to be, then it's not important *to you*. That thing may be important to someone else, but it's not important for you.

Urgency, on the other hand, is largely an emotional response. Essentially, it's a question of whether or not you feel like the activity or event requires immediate attention. And, because this is an emotional response, it needs to be connected to reality in any way. Immediate action may, or may not, actually be required. All that matters for this designation is how you feel about it.

The difference between the two is that determining whether something is important or not takes time and careful thought. You have to be able to call up your Mission (see why it's good to keep it short and memorizable?) and compare the event to determine whether the two align. You don't have to do anything for urgency. You'll either feel it or you won't, but, if you feel it, you'll feel it immediately. Because it's an emotional response, it travels at the speed of the electrical impulses in your brain—no conscious thought required.

I take the time to point this out because if both of these things are present in the same moment, which will you recognize first? That's right, Urgency. Urgency is an emotional impulse and manifests almost instantly. Deciding if something is important or not takes focus and thought and effort—all of which take time. And, interestingly, many people don't, or can't, differentiate between the two well enough, so, the moment they feel a little urgency, they immediately believe that the activity must be important.

Stephen Covey did a wonderful job of explaining the relationship of how these two characteristics overlap to describe every event in our lives. At the core of his explanation is a 2x2 matrix, similar to the Worth-Difficulty Matrix from earlier in the book. For simplicity's sake, I'll describe the quadrants briefly here, but again, I'd recommend you go out and get *7 Habits* and read the appropriate section (in fact, it's one of the bonus homework assignments at the end of this chapter).

Quadrant 1 is comprised of tasks and events, which are both urgent and important. Whatever this thing is—a crisis, surprise meeting, phone call from a stranded child—it's going to *feel* urgent. And that feeling will come first. Additionally, if I took the time to try, I would be able to clearly articulate how acting on this event supports my Mission, Vision, and Values. Because this quadrant is both urgent and important, it has actually earned the nickname of the Quadrant of Necessity. Whatever it is needs to get done and it needs to get done *now*.

To be sure, urgency is never a fun thing, but all the same, this quadrant is not "the bad guy" because it's still filled with important things that support your Mission, Vision, and Values. If something supports those inner, core principles, it can't really be "bad." It might be inconvenient—and often it is—but it's still important to get it done. So get it done.

Quadrant 3, on the other hand, is events that are urgent but not important. The problem here is that items in quadrants 1 and 3 *feel* just the same initially but Quadrant 3 is *not* important; it does *not* contribute to your Mission, Vision, or Values. But it does *feel* the same at the onset, and, because of that feeling, the Quadrant is known as the Quadrant of Deception.

It has earned this name because, if you don't stop to evaluate whether the activity supports your Mission, you will *feel* the urgency implying importance—feigning importance. Unfortunately, importance can't be felt, it must be discerned by reason, so we often misinterpret urgency as importance. If it needs to get done now, it must be important to get it done, right? Believe it or not, the average person spends 50+ percent of his time in Quadrant 3, but he will self-assess that they spend 10 percent or less. That's the power and deception of urgency.

Quadrant 4 is everything that is neither urgent nor important. It's called the Quadrant of Waste and Default. Default comes first because this is the quadrant to which you will go if you aren't operating in any of the other quadrants. That sounds a little simplistic and obvious, so allow me to explain. If there is nothing urgent going on, you can't be operating in either of quadrants 1 or 3, and, if you have nothing important going on, you can't be in quadrants 1 or 2. In other words, whenever you are doing some-thing just to pass the time, you're in Quadrant 4—that's why it has the second name of Waste.

The way this often works is that you spend so much time

bouncing back and forth between quadrants 1 and 3, going from one urgent task to another, that you end up burned out. When you are burned out, you won't have the energy necessary to follow through on something important, so you're likely to default to the low road and waste your time: excessive TV, endless video games, Spider Solitaire, Angry Birds, Words with Friends, I Love Lucy marathons, etc. Now, just to be clear, these activities in and of themselves are not inherently Quadrant 4. Where we came from, why we went there, and how much time we spent there determine whether or not it was Quadrant 4.

Quadrant 2 contains items that are important but not urgent. Because these are important items that are completed proactively, rather than reactively, Quadrant 2 is called the Quadrant of Leadership. This isn't Leadership by title, obviously; it's Leadership by example. This is true leadership—the ability to make plans and follow through with them to accomplish difficult things. The Triple P—Planning, Preparation, Prevention—lives and breathes in this quadrant. Relationship building; personal development; goal setting; connecting your Mission, Vision, and Values; service; and any number of other forward-thinking things like them are all part of Quadrant 2.

This is where you want to spend the bulk of your time because this is where you really create value. When things are urgent, they are typically in a crisis situation and rather than creating value, you are typically preserving it. When you plan ahead and make things happen, you create value. Because of this, I would argue that you want to be in this quadrant 75 percent of the time. In a perfect world, we'd like to be here 100 percent of the time, but we don't live in a perfect world. Crises still come up, which are also important, and we do have to spend some time in Quadrant 1.

The Urgency Response Flowchart

Stephen Covey built an excellent framework for us to understand the demands on our time. Now I want to take things a step further and show you how you can use these principles more effectively in your own life. I believe—having lived and used these quadrants for years—that there are two keys to harnessing the power of the Urgency Importance Matrix. The first lies in distinguishing between quadrants 1 and 3. The second is in shifting items from Quadrant 1 to Quadrant 2.

Here's the context: something happens which triggers an urgency response in your mind. What is the natural response to this stimulus? That's right, the natural response is "GO!!" This feels urgent; it feels like it needs to get done right now.; and most people will listen to this emotion every time.

What I propose is that you take the opposite approach. Remember, successful people form habits to do the things that other people don't do. When you feel that urgency response—your pulse starts to quicken, your hair stands up, your feel rushed—I'm going to tell you to "STOP!!"

You don't need to stop for long, but I want you to stop just long enough to try to articulate how this fits in with your Mission, Vision, and Values. If you can, it won't take more than a couple seconds. If you can't, then I have a brief process I want you to follow; I call it the Urgency Response Flowchart, at the top of the next page.

As you can see, the first step is to try to articulate whether or not the event is important. If you can, then ACT. It's that simple.

If you can't articulate how the event supports your mission—you're drawing a blank instead—then consider that it *might* be Quadrant 3 (Deception). We don't know yet—we could just be having a hard time finding the right words—but start considering that possibility in your mind.

So here's the backup question, ask yourself if there is any consequence from *not* acting which you can't live with. Can you live with the consequences of inaction or not? If you can't, it doesn't mean that this is a Quadrant 1 event, but go back to the previous question and with this added clarity, try to decide if the activity supports your Mission, Vision, or Values. Continue in this loop until you either can articulate why the event is important and aligned or you decide you can live with the consequences of ignoring the event.

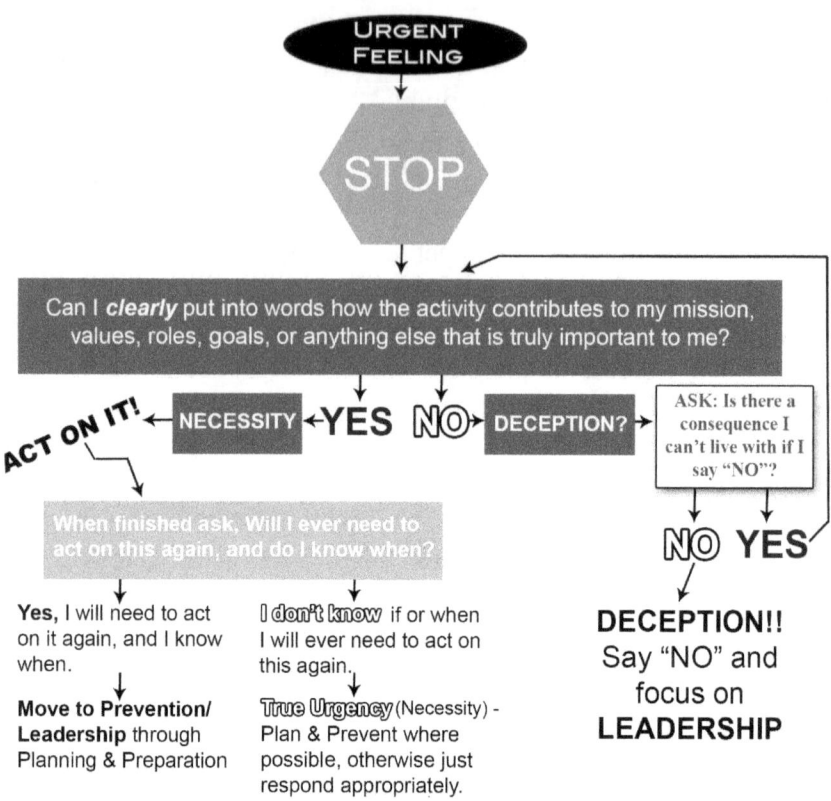

If you can live with any foreseeable consequences, then the event is most likely Quadrant 3, and you should just ignore it. Focus on something in Quadrant 2 instead and live with the consequences. Don't get sucked into doing something unimportant just because it feels urgent. Keep your focus on the important things.

Now, for simplicity's sake, I haven't fully covered one branch of the flowchart yet. When you ask yourself whether an urgent event aligns with your Mission, Vision, or Values and you answer "yes," you should act. We covered that part. What I didn't cover was what comes next. After you perform the action and the crisis is averted, are you done?

No. You are *not* done. Now it's time for R&R (Reflect and Refine). You were just caught up in a necessity. In all likelihood, it disrupted your day a bit. It might have thrown off your rhythm for the day or forced you to reschedule other important tasks. Do you like rescheduling things? Do you like having crises arise in your life? If you don't, then you need to ask yourself a question:

"Will I ever need to do this thing again?"

If the answer is no, you're done. Move on.

If the answer is maybe or yes, then ask yourself this follow-up question:

"Do I know *when* I'll need to do this again?"

If the answer is no, you've experienced a true crisis—something that exists by nature in Quadrant 1—and all you can do is keep yourself prepared for the future.

If you answered yes, however, then you can prevent this crisis in the future by effectively planning for it. Through planning, preparation, and prevention, you can move the event from Quadrant 1 to Quadrant 2 in the future. Allow me to illustrate with a pair of short stories.

When are individual taxes due in the United States? That's right, April 15. Does that day change from year to year? Not really (there are occasional shifts of a day or so to account for Sunday), tax day falls on April 15 pretty much every year. Do people feel pretty urgent about their tax returns on April 15? Yes. Why? I don't know! They've known about the deadline all year! Yet April 15 is the busiest day at the Post Office for sending in returns. In fact, in many areas, the Federal Government panders to our inner procrastinator by keeping the Post Office opened until midnight to take returns and empower procrastination!

For argument's sake, let's say you wake up on April 15 and your head pops off the pillow in dread. You say to yourself, "Oh no. It's April 15 and I have procrastinated my taxes." Do you feel a sense of urgency? Yes. Now stop! Can you clearly articulate how filing your taxes today supports your Mission, Vision, and Values? Sure. It's hard to be effective when the IRS is slapping you with tax liens, garnishing your wages, or even charging you with tax evasion. There are some definite advantages to filing your taxes properly and on time.

So this is a Quadrant 1 crisis. You shuffle your schedule to make room, get your return all filled out, and get it postmarked by

11:55pm. Phew! But are you done?

No. Now you are going to ask yourself a question: "Will I ever need to file my taxes again?"

The answer is yes.

"Do I know when I will need to file my taxes again?"

Yes. April 15 next year.

Now the stage is set. Through planning, preparation, and prevention, you can do your taxes in Quadrant 2 next year instead of letting them pop up in Quadrant 1. You should have all the necessary documents by the end of January. Set an appointment with your accountant for the first week in February to go through everything. Finalize your documentation by February 15, two full months ahead of time. If you owe anything and you don't want to pay your taxes early, you will have your return ready to go, your check cut, and you can drop it in the mail at your convenience on the morning of April 15—no urgency required. If you're getting a refund, maybe you drop the return in the mail right away—February 15—and stop worrying about it.

However you want to do it is fine. The point is that the urgency was no longer necessary because we planned, prepared, and prevented. And that works for more than just your taxes. That urgent call from your daughter because no one is there to pick her up from swim practice? You can plan that one away too. The vendor who calls because no one was there to receive the early-morning shipment? Planned for, Prepared for, Prevented. Your wedding anniversary? Yup. That one too.

But there are situations you *can't* plan out of Quadrant 1. A second story.

We're out to lunch together, you and I. We're having a nice little conversation about how much more empowered you are now that you have your Mission to live by. It's a nice steakhouse and the food is hot and delicious. You're looking around at some of the decor on the walls when you realize that I've gotten suddenly quiet.

When you look back at me, there is a panicked look in my eyes, I'm grasping my throat, and my face is starting to look a little blue. Does this situation give you a sense of urgency? I hope so—my life depends on it. Now stop (but not for very long, please). Would saving my life support your Mission, Vision, or Values? We're friends, so I hope you can (quickly) answer yes. That means this is a Quadrant 1 activity.

Inspired by necessity, you jump up, step around the table and administer the Heimlich Maneuver. A piece of steak goes flying across the room, and I collapse back into my chair, thanking you profusely. Crisis averted. But are you done? No.

Will you ever have to administer the Heimlich Maneuver to me (or anyone else) ever again?

Who knows? Maybe?

Okay, even if you did know, would you know *when* you'll need to administer the Heimlich next?

No. This was a true Quadrant 1 event, so what do you do? All you can do is prepare for the possibility and brush up on you Heimlich technique. You might encourage me to take smaller bites and chew more effectively, but you can't really plan for or truly prevent someone else from choking.

Interestingly, if all the Quadrant 1 crises in your life truly were Quadrant 1—not Quadrant 1 because you didn't plan, prepare, or prevent (*i.e.,* you procrastinated)—then you would really have very few Quadrant 1 events. By far, the majority of the emergencies in our lives arise out of a lack of planning. Still, we can never quite eliminate all the crises from our lives, so no matter how well you plan, you'll also need to stay flexible and be always ready for those true Quadrant 1 events.

Detours and Surprises

As we've gone through these concepts, you may have been thinking, "If flexibility is so essential and my week is never going to go fully according to plan anyway, then why bother with the weekly plan at all? Why not just make a list of tasks and work through them."

Let me give you an analogy and then relate a couple of experiences with my clients that I think will clarify this point for you.

Think back to when we were driving on the highway at the beginning of this chapter. You had your directions, but you'd never been to your destination. Now let's imagine that you see one of the diamond-shaped orange signs ahead. It says, "Road Closure Ahead: Begin Detour" and gives you an arrow to follow. What are you going to do? Drive to the end of the road and have to turn around or take the detour?

You take the exit for the detour and start driving again. Half an hour later you realize that you haven't seen a single other sign indicating the detour or where to go. You're now well off the route provided in your directions, and you have no idea where you are in order to get back to the right course. Have you ever experienced a detour like this? I call it a bad detour.

Now, rewind a moment to where you see the detour sign. Of course, you don't have any other real option, so you take the detour. This time, however, there is another sign telling you to turn right as you get off the highway. You turn right and drive for a bit when you come upon another detour sign with an arrow pointing up, indicating that you're on the right course. You drive a while farther and you see a detour sign with a left arrow, so you turn left.

Then you continue for quite some time, passing several more detour signs with up arrows at even intervals. Finally, you reach another sign that says to turn left, so you do. A little way farther down there is another detour sign to tell you to keep going. Finally, there is another highway onramp and a detour sign turning you to the right. As you head back onto the freeway, a sign tells you "End Detour." I call this a good detour.

Which detour would you rather encounter? It's not so much that we *like* encountering detours—good or bad—but they aren't always things we can prevent. If there's a rockslide across the highway, you're going to be detoured. If a HAZMAT tanker truck jackknifes and spills across the highway, you're going to be detoured. If your child crashes his bike on the way home from school and you need to take him to the ER, you're going to be "detoured" from your weekly plan. If a client calls with an emergency, you're going to be "detoured" from the plan.

Planning can help prevent a lot of detours, like the example of planning ahead for tax time we discussed earlier, but planning can't prevent *all* detours. Wouldn't you rather have a good detour? Wouldn't you rather know the next steps to get back on track?

I had an experience with this a few years back (I've had lots of experiences with this since too, but this experience stands out to me as a particularly good example). I was just finishing up a morning meeting over breakfast with a client when I had another client call in an absolute panic. This second client was having a problem with an employee that could potentially cost his firm tens of thousands of dollars.

Could I have planned for this event? No. Begin Detour.

I looked at my schedule and saw that I had a little self time scheduled for the next hour—I was going to get a massage—so I called and rescheduled the appointment to the next evening. The next thing in my plan was to get my car washed. I was the only one involved there so I just moved the "appointment" over to the following Saturday. By the way, I actually moved both of these appointments in my actual calendar right on my Smartphone.

Now, that gave me a decent chunk of time open to work with this client, but I knew his issue could potentially take more time than what I had so far set aside. I had a lunch appointment scheduled with a friend that day (I subscribe to the philosophy of never eating alone), but I wasn't sure whether I'd be able to make it or not now, so I checked my calendar. I had an opening the following Monday, so I called my friend to see if we could reschedule. He agreed, and we moved the lunch appointment to the following Monday.

I already had some "open" time to get some different, smaller tasks done for the early afternoon, but then I had a meeting with a company client. To reschedule that meeting would involve coordinating nine different schedules (including my own), which was something I didn't want to do. So I didn't touch that appointment; I left it in place. Then I called back this panicked client and we started working through his problem. When we were done, I knew right where I was supposed to be next because I could refer back to my weekly plan. I made the call with my company client later that afternoon and was right back on track. End of Detour.

In retrospect, I probably could have made the lunch appointment with my friend, but I didn't want to risk canceling at the last minute. I looked at my directions, plotted the detour, and moved forward. Was it a failure to take that detour or reschedule those appointments? Not at all. It was a conscious, Mission-based and Values-based decision that was appropriate for the circumstances. Because of the float I'd left in my schedule, I was able to move—not cancel—the three appointments to make room for the emergency. Without that weekly plan, I would likely have forgotten one of the appointments I had and been left to cancel at the last minute—or forget entirely, and miss the appointment without warning anyone, impacting my credibility and my relationships.

So now you see why having that list of activities to come back to was helpful. I had an emergency come up, and rather than losing the whole day to it, I was able to address the situation and then get immediately back on track. But some of you might be thinking, "I could do that with a task list too. I'll just make a big list of everything I need to do and then come back to the list when the emergency is over," and you'd be right . . . sort of.

Task Lists

To me, when people say that it sounds an awful lot like a pilot saying, "If I'm just going to be off course 90 percent of the time, why file a flight plan?" Would you want to fly with that pilot? Now, don't get me wrong, I love a good list. I love the euphoric effect of checking things off. I love having a place I can go to see what miscellaneous things I need to get done. But I have some strict guidelines for myself when it comes to task lists, and there's a reason why.

The problem that I have with task lists is best demonstrated by the second client experience I wanted to share. This particular client was a business leader from back east. We'll call him John. John was an intelligent man, but he didn't like the idea of a full-on calendar. He preferred to use a task list—a checklist of what he needed to accomplish.

One day, we were talking about prioritized daily task lists and he confessed to me that he just felt overwhelmed by everything he had going on.

So I said, "How are you doing with prioritizing your daily task list?"

He replied, "Oh, I'm a total list maker. It's perfect."

I said, "You know, a prioritized, daily task list is just that. The things on the list are all intended to be done *today*. You shouldn't have anything on your task list that you don't really believe you can do today."

"I know, I know. And that's how I do it."

"Oh, okay. That's interesting. So, tell me, how many items do you have on your list *right now*?"

Keep in mind that we were meeting at about ten o'clock in the morning, so there was still quite a bit of day ahead.

After a little pause, John said, "Um . . . 40."

"Wow, John. That's a lot of stuff. Okay. And these are all things you're going to get done today, right?"

"Oh, yeah. Absolutely. I have to get them done today."

So I said, "Do you *normally* get them all done every day?"

"Well...huh...no...but these are the ones that I've got to get done today, so I put them all on the list."

"Okay. Interesting. Tell me, how many do you have done so far today?"

Without hesitation—and maybe with just a little pride—he said, "Four. I got four done before talking to you this morning."

I thought about that for a moment. "Okay. Let's look at the first one then. Not the first one on the list but the first one you actually did this morning."

"Okay. I've got it right here. It was a phone call to a vendor."

"Alright. And how long did that take?

"About five minutes."

"And you checked it off the list?"

"Yup."

"Okay. What about the next one you did? How long did it take?"

"Oh, not long either. Another phone call to a different vendor. Maybe three or four minutes. It was pretty quick."

"What about the third one?"

"That? It was an email I needed to send out to my team."

"And how long did it take?"

"Eh, about seven minutes."

"And the fourth one?"

"Another email. This one was to an association I belong to. It took a little longer—maybe 10 minutes."

"Okay. Great. So you've gotten four things done and they were basically 5 minutes, 4 minutes, 7 minutes, and 10 minutes, right?"

"That's right."

"Are we seeing a theme here? Out of curiosity, let's look at the remainder of your list. Why don't you tell me about the next thing on your list. How long do you think it's going to take you? And not some pie-in-the-sky, best-case time, give me the worst case scenario."

He looked at it a minute and then said, "It's anywhere from 10-20 minutes, depending on how things go. So, by what you're telling me, I would say 20 minutes."

And I wrote that down before saying, "And the next one?"

"About 20-30 minutes."

"Next one."

"Oh, 20 to potentially an hour."

And so on and so forth for the rest of his list. Now, he didn't know it (we were on the phone), but I was sitting there writing down the times as he gave them to me. Finally, we got to the end and I had all 40 items listed out with best-case and worst-case times.

And before I even said anything he said, "Whoa."

So I asked, "How much time do you think it would take you to do all this?"

"Way longer than I thought it would. This is like 18 hours worth of stuff that I'm claiming I want to get done today."

"John, *37 hours and 15 minutes*. This is your *daily* task list? Thirty-seven hours and 15 minutes, if they all take the worst-case scenario. But what do you think are the chances that they'll all take the best-case scenario?"

"Well, not very good because they don't usually take the best-case scenario."

"Would it even matter? Even in the best-case scenario, you've still got 22 hours of stuff scheduled for today."

No wonder he was feeling a bit overwhelmed. And this is why I don't like using just a task list.

But I kept going with him. "John, tell me something. Why do you think you chose to do this first item first?"

"Well, I don't know. Maybe, somewhere deep down, I knew that it was going to be quick and easy."

"The statistics do seem to show. The first four things you did each took 10 minutes or less. Let's look at some of the stuff you've got down at the bottom of that list. Four hours; two hours; two and a half hours. That's a whole day's work right there. And you look at this, this four-hour item; turn to yesterday's task list. Is it there?"

He looked and said, "Yup."

"What about the day before that?"

"...Yup."

"John, how long has it been on your task list?"

He had to turn back *three and a half weeks* to see the first time it had gotten on his list. He'd been rolling it forward all that time because he didn't have four hours to do it—even though he hadn't actually written out that it would take four hours. His subconscious still knew that it would take all that time, so he just kept rolling it forward from one day to the next.

Instant Checkmark Gratification

As it turns out, he was doing the same thing that most people do when they "prioritize" a task list—he was prioritizing based on how quickly he could get it done, not on how important it was to get it done. Of course, that was happening at a subconscious level. He'd fallen victim to what I call Instant Checkmark Gratification.

And here's why that happens. If I have 40 things on my list, visually, they all have the same value. No item looks more or less important than any other. Now, if I want to be productive and show that I've accomplished a lot of things, my mind is going to naturally gravitate to those things that subconsciously I know I can do quickly. After all, the goal, by putting everything in a list like this, must be to shorten the list as much as possible. So if something takes four hours, I'm going to save it for the end because I might be able to get six or seven other things done in that time—and it doesn't actually matter to me which one is the most important.

As you go through the course of a day, instant checkmark gratification might sound something like this: "Check, check, check, check, check, check, check, check..., check...., check......, check..........., check...................., ch..e...c...k...................., c...h...e...c...k...." Essentially, at the start of the day, you're able to check off a lot of things really quickly. As the time goes on, however, the tasks get longer and longer, and those checks get fewer and further between, until, by the middle of the afternoon you're looking at your checklist and thinking to yourself, "I am beat, but look at all the stuff I've done. I got 30 out of the 40 done. I think I've earned a break." Never mind that the 10 you left behind were actually the most important. Because of checkmark gratification, you end up leaving the longer, often more-important tasks for another day.

So here's my philosophy on task lists. If you *truly* prioritize your task list and *actually* rank things by how important they are, not just how quickly you can get them done, and all you got done in an entire day was *one*—the Number 1 most important thing on that list—leaving the other 39 undone, then you were more successful than if you'd gotten the 39 done but left that most important item undone. And I firmly believe that until you adopt that kind of a paradigm, you will always be swayed by quantity over quality—by the total number instead of the total impact.

So let me take a moment now to make you a promise. I offer this with a 100 percent money-back guarantee. Every night from now for the rest of your life, you'll be able to lay your head down on your pillow and, in all honesty, think to yourself, "I did *not* get it all done." You will. I promise. Every night. Even after reading and applying every principle in this book. Even if you become perfect at everything I'm teaching you here, you'll still be able to tell yourself that you didn't get it all done. And here's why: what is "it all"?

"It all," of course, is *everything*. Every thing. Each and every individual thing that you can think of that you need to do. You'll never be able to do that much. Ever. The human imagination is far too creative, and we are far too critical of ourselves, to ever be able to do everything that we can dream up. That will always be the case.

However, this doesn't mean you're doomed to failure for the rest of your life. Instead, lay your head down on your pillow, confess that you didn't get "it all" done, and then see if you can follow up with this statement: "But at least what I got done was more important than what I didn't get done." If you can say that, you have every right to sleep peacefully. And that's why we don't measure our success based on whether or not we got "it all" done; measure your success by whether you got the right things done.

Interestingly, as you start to live this principle, you will find that you accomplish a lot more in terms of what matters, but you will likely notice an overall decrease in the quantity of "it all" that you do. This is because you will be prioritizing to accomplish what really matters instead of spinning your wheels with the things that don't. In fact, I'm going to go out on a limb and tell you that if you fully embrace these principles, you'll find that you do less than you have ever done in your life—but it will be because you've eliminated all the stuff that doesn't matter as much.

Until you can let go of the quantity paradigm and truly operate by priorities, you'll always be busy, yet also always be at risk to, as John Wooden said, "mistake activity for achievement." Or, in the words of Goethe, "Things that matter most must never be at the mercy of things that matter least."

In exchange, you'll be focused on what are often referred to as the "big rocks" of life. And to explain that, I'm going to tell you a story for which the original author is unknown.

Big Rocks or Little Gravel

One day, an expert in time management was speaking to a group of business students and, to drive home a point, used an illustration those students will never forget.

As he stood in front of the group of high-powered overachievers, he said, "Okay, time for a quiz."

He then pulled out a one-gallon, wide-mouth Mason jar and set it on the table in front of him. Then he produced about a dozen fist-sized rocks and carefully placed them, one by one, into the jar. When the jar was filled to the top and no more rocks would fit inside, he asked, "Is this jar full?"

Everyone in the class said, "Yes."

Then he said, "Really?"

He reached under the table and pulled out a bucket of gravel. Then he dumped some gravel in and shook the jar, causing pieces of gravel to work themselves down into the space between the big rocks.

Then he asked the group once more, "Is this jar full?"

By this time the class was on to him. "Probably not," one of them answered.

"Good," he replied. He reached under the table and brought out a bucket of sand. He started dumping the sand in the jar and it went into all of the spaces left between the rocks and the gravel.

Once more he asked the question, "Is this jar full?"

"No," the class shouted.

Once again, he said, "Good." Then he grabbed a pitcher of water and began to pour it in until the jar was filled to the brim. Then the expert in time-management looked at the class and asked, "What is the point of this illustration?"

One eager beaver raised his hand and said, "The point is, no matter how full your schedule is, if you try really hard you can always fit some more things in it."

"No," the speaker replied, "That's not the point. The truth this illustration teaches us is this: If you don't put the big rocks in first, you'll never get them in at all."

"What are the big rocks in your life?"

"Your children?"

"Your loved ones?"

"Your education?"

"Your dreams?"

"A worthy cause?"

"Teaching or mentoring others?"

"Doing things that you love?"

"Time for yourself?"

"Your health?"

"Your spouse?"

"Remember to put these BIG ROCKS in first, or you'll never get them in at all."

"If you sweat the small stuff (*i.e.* the gravel, the sand) then you'll fill your life with little things you worry about that don't really matter, and you'll never have the real quality time you need to spend on the big, important stuff (the big rocks)."

"So, tonight, or in the morning, when you are reflecting on this short story, ask yourself this question: 'What are the 'big rocks' in my life?' Then, put those in your jar first."

Calendaring the Big Rocks

So how do we identify these big rocks? The first step is to actually prioritize all those tasks on your list. The easiest way to do this is to assign each of them a time block long enough to accomplish the entire task—for tasks too large to complete in a single day, break them down into subset pieces and assign those pieces instead (we'll talk about this more in a bit). Like in the 15 game, each of these tasks becomes like a little tile in your week. Some tiles might be quite large, others will be much smaller.

This will naturally start to introduce priority to your tasks. After all, you can't pretend that a three-minute phone call "costs" as much as a four-hour project. The moment that you take the tasks off your list and put them into a calendar and block out the time, you will see the staggering difference in cost. You won't treat each task as equal with each other task because you'll be able to see the difference.

My personal rule of thumb for a task list (to-do list, honey-do list, etc.) is that there should be nothing on it that will take you longer than 10-15 minutes. If it's 15 minutes or less, then go ahead and throw it on a list because that's a tiny little block to put on your calendar. A three-minute phone call? Don't put that on your calendar—unless you've committed to a specific time to make that call, in which case you do need to schedule it.

If an activity will take longer than 15 minutes, however—and especially if it will take 30 minutes or more—then it has no business being on a list that doesn't clarify the amount of time required to accomplish the task. Besides, how often have you ever finished something up and said, "Oh, I've got half an hour free all of a sudden, why not tackle that big task off my to-do list?" No. If you had that half hour open up, you'd use it to do half a dozen of the little items off your list, leaving the longer items for larger windows of time. So, if a task is more than 15 minutes, put it on your calendar and block it out, giving yourself enough time to accomplish the task even if it doesn't go according to the best case.

If my business client had done this, his calendar would have been completely full before he'd made it a third of the way through his 40 items. Then, seeing all that blocked out with the necessary time investment, he could have stopped "buying his own bull" about how he was going to get all 40 items done in a single day.

And here's another piece of advice: Let's say you have four items on your list and each will take 15 minutes. How much time would it take for you to complete all those tasks? Why not block out an hour on your calendar and label it "Work on Task List" or something similar? Now you know you can get to those items because you've blocked out and reserved time to do so. You won't have to push them from one day to the next in search of time to get them done. After all, none of us is a time magician that can just pull an extra hour out of thin air. When your task list starts to get a little long, block out time in your calendar to just focus on those items and get them done.

Finances of Time

Calendaring—weekly planning—is a lot like budgeting for your finances. You only have so much money each day/week/month/year, and you need to see where it's going if you want to manage it properly. I've got news for you, the phrase "time is money" is a little too literal for me, but it makes a good point. You only have

24 hours in a day, 168 in a week, and 8,760 in a year. And that's before you account for sleeping a third of those hours.

The catch is, time is even more precious than money because of some key differences between the two. First of all, time is limited; money is not. If you think to disagree with me on that point, keep in mind that you can go and cut your neighbor's lawn and earn an extra $10 if you need to. What activity can you perform to earn yourself more time?

You may invest both time and money, but money will return you more (or less) of the same. When you invest time, you never earn back more time; the earnings come in other forms (like improved relationships, financial success, etc.). So the question becomes whether or not you will invest your time wisely. A task list doesn't show you how you're investing. When you calendar, you can clearly see where and how you are investing your time. Are you doing so in accordance with your Mission, Vision, and Values? Are you investing in the best, most powerful, most impactful things possible? Or are you frittering it away on a large quantity of low quality things?

And, let's face it, if you're reading this book, it's because you're already doing pretty well and you're trying to figure out how to reach a higher level. When you're at that point, you're not really choosing between investing your time in good, noble pursuits or squandering it in waste. You're probably choosing between two good things. Which will you choose?

That's up to you and your Mission, Vision, and Values. But if you don't plan ahead on a weekly basis and calendar out your activities, you're just that much more likely to default to the wrong good thing. It won't be a total loss, but you'll miss the opportunity to do what would have meant more to you. True power in decision-making isn't choosing the good over the bad, it's choosing the best over the rest. The rest being, of course, all the other really good things you could have been doing.

I already shared with you the quote from Goethe about priorities. At this point I'd like to give you a slight variant: "Things that matter most must never be at the mercy of things that matter less than the most."

For example, what happens when it's March 1, with the

business tax deadline on March 15, and you've got some accounting work building up in your office? You've been so busy with everything else that you've let the paperwork slide a little, but now it's tax time and it's a do-or-die situation. Would it be a good thing to put in a couple extra hours tonight and get caught up so you can get everything over to your accountant for your taxes? I think it's fair to say yes.

But what if tonight also happens to be your son's regional championship game for his basketball team? You can do the work and get your business caught up, or you can go to your son's game, but you can't do both. Which do you choose? I can't give you the answer. It comes down to your personal Mission, Vision, and Values. When you did the I-beam exercise, what were you willing to walk the span for? When you did the Titanic exercise, where did your business, financial freedom, and family rank in comparison to one another?

Arguably, either choice is a good one. Which choice is best is up to you.

Now, the solution to this situation is, of course, to better plan out your week so you can see potential conflict like this in advance. How do you do that? Anything more than 15 minutes goes on the calendar and don't fill your week 100 percent. Leave yourself some room for flexibility.

Six-Step Planning Process

When it comes to the actual planning process, the one I teach is very similar to the one Stephen Covey recommends. Over the years, I've made some alterations and improvements, but much of the core is the same. The process itself goes in six steps, which we'll get to in a moment.

First, as I mentioned earlier, you can't start planning when you're already supposed to be executing from the plan. It just doesn't work. So, for a weekly plan, if you're trying to plan it after the week has already begun, you've missed the window. I guess the next question is, "when does the week begin?"

Well, in our western culture, many of the calendars you find will begin on Sunday. This doesn't really make sense to me though because Sunday is quite clearly referred to as part of the week*end*. For planning purposes, therefore, the week begins on Monday and ends on Sunday.

As an aside, many calendaring programs give you the option of switching the layout to put Sunday as the 7th day of the week, rather than the first (iCal, Google Calendar, Microsoft Outlook, etc.). Doing this may help you better visualize the week.

I recommend that you plan out your upcoming week no later than Sunday and no earlier than Friday. Why? Before Friday (and really before Friday afternoon) is really too early to know all your obligations will be in the coming week. A lot can happen on a Friday, or even a Saturday or Sunday, which will change what you plan. So I recommend waiting until the week has "ended" (i.e., Saturday or Sunday) before planning the next week.

If you wait until after Sunday, you've missed your chance. The week is already on you and you won't be able to plan effectively anymore because you'll already be responding to emergencies.

If you will, think back with me to the story about the big rocks and the little gravel. Consider that your week is like that big, gallon-sized Mason jar. There's a lot of space in there at first. Scattered around on the table are any number of fist-sized rocks. These rocks represent all the most-important things in your life. Now, there's not really room in that jar to fit *all* those big rocks at the same time, but you can fit a bunch of them.

Above the jar is a faucet of sorts. However, instead of a spigot handle to turn it on, there is a timer, counting down. The timer is counting down to Monday at some point in the wee hours of the morning. When the timer expires, the faucet will open up and begin pouring little gravel—like the kind you use in a fish tank— into your mason jar until the jar is full. Then, automatically, it will shut off.

The faucet doesn't care how much gravel it gets to pour into your jar; it will pour just enough to completely fill the jar, leaving no extra room but not spilling either. If some of those big rocks are in the jar first, great. If they aren't, the faucet will make sure that room isn't wasted.

As you may have gathered, the faucet is life. When life starts on Monday, it immediately begins packing everything it can into your schedule—whether those items are important or not. If you try to add important things—the big rocks—to your schedule after life has already begun filling your week, you'll be too late. You'll find that life has already filled up all your time.

So it's up to you to place your big rocks in the jar first. As you do so, remember what those big rocks represent; they represent the most important things to you in your life. I have seen people plan out their week and place those important, big rocks in their schedule. Then, to my amazement and dismay, when the little gravel started pouring in and filling their jar, they were so conditioned to grasp at quantity, rather than quality, that they actually pulled the big rocks out of the jar to make room for more little gravel.

In other words, placing your big rocks and giving them precedence is important and may initially be difficult (until it becomes second nature), but your job isn't over once you've taken that step. When life starts to fill your jar with an endless wave of little gravel, you have to stay disciplined—stay true to your Mission, Vision, and Values—and exert your Will to resist the urge to make room for more of the stuff that isn't so important because it comes at the expense of the stuff that *is* so important.

We've all heard the expression that "less is more." In this case though, "more is less." Remember that it is the *quality* of your life that matters, not the quantity. Why do "more" when you will be happier with "enough"?

Now let's take a moment to talk through the six steps that I have found to be the best way to get those big rocks in before the little gravel starts to fall.

Step 1 – Connect With Your Mission
5 minutes

The actual first part of your weekly planning session will be Step 6 from the previous week—Reflect and Refine—but we'll operate here with the understanding that you've already moved through that step, closed out your previous week, and readied yourself to plan for the coming week.

First, you need to realign with your guiding star. Spend at least five minutes with your Mission. Now, I give this five-minute requirement deliberately. For the Mission we designed together, you could probably read or recite the entire thing in ten seconds or less; however, it's not about just reading your Mission.

The purpose of this time is to really step outside of life and into your Mission. I want you to reconnect on that deep, emotional level. I want you to think about your actions and how they align with your Mission—and how they could *better* align with your Mission. Remember, you're trying to mentally, emotionally prepare yourself to plan for the coming week. What do you want to have as your overarching thought as you begin that planning process?

Spend five minutes really pondering your Mission before you move on.

Step 2 – Review Your Vision and Values
10 minutes

Now take some time and review your Role Tribute Statements. Who do you want to be in your various roles? Realign with your Vision. Remind yourself of what's most important. What qualities do you want to exhibit in your roles?

I also recommend that you review your Values at this point and remind yourself of why you chose them. Realign with those priorities so you're ready to plan according to your clarifying statements.

Once you are fully connected, review your roles and select the ones for which you will set specific goals over this coming week. Consider which roles you've been working on recently and which roles might need a little more attention. Also take into account which roles require more time and attention. For example, one role that I will not make optional for you is the role of "Self."

You should be working on yourself every single week. Which aspect of yourself you choose to work on may change from week to week, but you need to do something to fill your pitcher, remember? You must take at least a little time to renew (physically, mentally, emotionally, spiritually) yourself. Even if you took a vacation all by yourself to the middle of nowhere without a single soul—no friends, spouse, children, family, anybody—you are still bringing your *self* with you. So, every week, you need to renew, or you will simply burn out and find yourself in the Quadrant of Default and Waste.

Other roles should also make your list very frequently. The role of spouse, for instance, should be on your list nearly every week of the year. Unless you or your spouse is out of town with limited contact for the week, you should probably be working on that role (it *is* the most important relationship in your life, after all).

If you're a parent, that role should be on your list far more often than not—in excess of 80 percent of the time if you have any kids at home (40+ weeks per year). When your children are all grown and gone, that number may drop a little—but only a little. They're still your kids and you'll still be involved with them far more often than not. This doesn't mean that you'll target each child each week, but rotating between them will require weekly planning even more than just trying to reach out to each of them every week.

Your role as a child will probably make the list half the time or more. This doesn't mean that you need to be visiting your parents half of the weeks in the year, a phone call will do in most cases, but you should be keeping in touch with them.

You'll probably find that you need to focus on your role as a sibling fairly frequently too. It's easy to grow up, move away, and drift apart. If you want to avoid those awkward Holiday conversations when you realize you don't know anything about the people you grew up around, spend a little time making sure you still know them. Again, a phone call or a letter can meet the requirement here.

Your role as a business leader or employee will probably be on the list nearly as often as your own children. Work requires a lot from us, and achieving success takes time and effort. Unless you're on vacation, your work role is probably on the list—which means an excess of 40-45 weeks out of the year for most of us.

Basically, you can look at how frequently you act in a given role. You should be working on those individual roles in approximately the same proportion that you act in them. The more often you act in a role, the more often you should be working to improve that role.

Think of it like bridge repair. The more frequently traffic passes over a bridge, the more frequently it will need repair. If no one ever—or hardly ever—drives across a bridge, it'll last a very long time. And your roles are, essentially, bridges between you and other people.

Now, to avoid overextending yourself, I recommend a maximum of 7 roles in a week (8 if you include the automatic, required role focus on self). And don't feel the need to max out either. Commonly, my clients (or even myself) list 4 or 5 roles to focus on (plus one for the self).

Step 3 – Set Your Weekly Role Goals

15 minutes

Now it's time to actually set your goals for the week. The way this begins is by identifying the goal you want to set for each of the roles you identified in Step 2. Based on your review of your Tribute statements, what can you do this week to make yourself fill the role that person is describing?

These goals should be important but cannot be urgent. You want to set a goal for something that is a priority but not something that is going to demand your attention. In particular, you want to set a goal to do something that you probably wouldn't do if it weren't for this goal you're setting.

These goals don't have to be out-of-this-world extreme or anything. They can be simple. Let's say, for example, that I chose my roles of Husband, Father, Business Owner, Coach, and Friend. Just so you can see the range of what goals could be like, I'll give a few samples here.

Husband: My goal will be to take my wife to Las Vegas for an overnight stay (we live just a couple hours away anyway, so it's not that far of a drive). We'll have a nice dinner, catch a show, and eat a buffet breakfast in the morning. Maybe we'll even get a chance to lounge around the pool a while before we come home. It'll just be a little 24-hour thing, but that's my goal in this role this week.

Father: I've got a number of children, but *this* week, I'm just going to focus on one of them: my eight year old. I'll take her out to a movie—a matinee, of course—and then we'll go and get ice cream afterward. Neither she nor I have anything scheduled for Thursdays, so I'll plan on then.

Business Owner: I'm going to spend two full workdays on getting this book ready.

Coach: I've got one client in particular that I'm a little worried about. In addition to our normal coaching session this week, I'm going to text him at least three additional times to just check up and see how he's doing.

Friend: It's been a while since I last spoke to a good friend of mine—the best man at my wedding, in fact—so I'm going to give him a call this week and catch up.

As you can see, some of these goals are a little more involved than others. But you can also see how each is a SMART goal like we talked about before (they're all bound by the timeframe of the week if no other time was specified). I also want to point out that these aren't my *only* goals this week; these just happen to be the goals related to the things in my life, which I find to be the most important. I will plan and execute other things for the coming week, but everything else will fit around these goals.

Before we move on, I wanted to share with you one last thought. So often in goal setting, we focus on doing this or doing that. This is a good thing, and it helps us to move toward specific objectives, but there is an important principle you need to recognize: you are a human *being*, not a human doing. Remember the power of habit and second nature. In goal setting, we tend to emphasize the step-by-step process of moving from one stage of a goal to the next—the doing goals.

Once in a while, consider setting a "being" goal for yourself; something like "be kind" or "be helpful" or "be confident." You can still set metrics for yourself to make the goal measurable, but not everything in life is about accomplishing a task. If you really want to become a better person, you need to set some goals around bettering yourself as a person.

These *being* goals shouldn't replace your *doing* goals—those are still important—but supplement them. In addition to "doing" the things we deem important, we should spend some effort on "being" who we want to be.

Now, take a few minutes to craft SMART goals for each of the roles on which you plan to focus this week.

Step 4 – Organize Your Activities

20 minutes

In this step, you will actually need your calendar. Start by adding the role-based goals you identified in Step 3 where appropriate. These are the goals related to your most important priorities in life, so give them priority here. And remember, if a task will take more than 15 minutes, it should be blocked in on your calendar. If a goal will take less than 15 minutes, you can put it on a task list instead.

For example, taking my wife to Vegas or my daughter to the movies would need to be blocked in. Working on this book would also need to be blocked in. When I call my friend, we'll probably talk for more than 15 minutes, so I'll block that in too—even though it might change to another time that works better for him. Texting my struggling client won't take very long though, so I'll just put that on my task list.

Next, there are likely already appointments and items on your calendar from previous weeks and any monthly and yearly planning you've done. Consider those things as additional big rocks and check to see if there is any necessary planning or preparation for any of these things. Be sure to schedule those items as well.

For instance, if I'm scheduled to teach a seminar on Tuesday evening, I might need to block in half an hour extra ahead of the seminar for travel time and/or setup. If you promised to call someone back on Wednesday, either block out the time for it or, if the call is expected to be short enough, you can put it on your task list. I personally prefer to schedule out anything I can, recognizing that the timing of the events may shift around slightly. Otherwise I run the risk of overloading my task list and then finding out the hard way that there isn't enough time in the day to do everything I intended to do.

Now consider any long-term goals you may have (elephants you are eating) and add the appropriate bites to your weekly schedule.

What are the next steps from your project plans to move you along toward completion of your goals? By putting these items in now, instead of scrambling to add them during the week, you make sure that you have time and room to get your long-term goals into your calendar. If you wait, these things will suffer the same fate that your big rocks would have suffered.

At this point, you may also do well to remember that no day should be filled more than 75 percent—that means no more than 12 hours of scheduled, defined events—and you should only have 12-hour days during your very busiest times.

Last, look at the various tasks you have for the week. These are your to-do items that will take less than 15 minutes. Rather than building a master list, rolling it from day to day, and being overwhelmed by it, choose the appropriate day for each task and put items on the respective task lists for those days. Include a projected time requirement for each task and *prioritize them according to importance*. Also make sure to keep in mind just how much you can accomplish in any given day. If your task list starts to look a little long, consider blocking out some time specifically to work through your list on that particular day.

Step 5 – Execute

167 hours

Now comes the hard part. A week is 168 hours. If you spend 1 hour planning each week, that leaves the other 167 hours to execute the plan. In essence, no part of your life is not part of this plan. It's just that 99.4 percent of the plan is living it, not planning it. The idea here is to practice keeping commitments to yourself. You've set your goals for the week, and you've put everything into your calendar. Now it's time to stick to it.

It's time to do what you planned to do when you planned to do it—as long as the plan is still the most important thing to do. There is some truth to the quote by Helmuth von Moltke, "No plan survives contact with the enemy." You will need to shift things around as your week progresses, but if you planned properly, it won't ruin your plan. Remember to set good detours and remember to be flexible, but don't fall prey to the Quadrant of Deception. If you can't articulate the importance of something urgent when it pops up, don't pretend it's important just because of the powerful, emotional response of urgency. And whatever you do, *don't take out the big rocks to make room for more little gravel!*

Stay true to your Mission, Vision, and Values.

Step 6 – R & R

10 minutes

This is called Step 6, but it's actually the first thing you'll do each time you restart this process. Step 6 is actually the beginning of your planning session for next week. You'll Reflect on what happened in the previous week and Refine yourself going forward. Doing it this way helps you to finalize the week and move on. In the words of Emerson, "Finish each day and be done with it. You have done what you could. Some blunders and absurdities no doubt crept in, forget them as soon as you can. Tomorrow is a new day, you shall begin it well and serenely...."

In our case, we would apply that to the week level. So take the first ten or so minutes of your weekly planning session to review your previous week. What mistakes did you make? How can you plan to avoid those mistakes again in the future? What successes did you have? Did you record them in your Victory Journal? How can you achieve additional, similar successes in the future? How effective were you at honoring your big rocks and focusing on what was important? How often did you have to shuffle what you planned in order to put out a fire? How many of those fires were actually important?

Treat your week just like we treated your Mission when you were first creating it. You want to spend time to Reflect and Refine. You are the best case study for your own life; don't pass up this chance to learn from yourself, apply the principles, and move on.

After your first planning session, the order of the steps will go 6, 1, 2, 3, 4, and then 5. This may seem a little strange, but consider a face clock. It seems a little strange that 12 should precede 1, doesn't it? In both cases, we are dealing with a circle of time. In the case of the clock, it comes back around every twelve hours. In the case of your weekly planning, it will come around again every six steps.

It's important not to skip or forget the sixth step. Having it will bring closure to your past week before you begin planning out the next week. In effect, it gives you the chance to sign off on a week and file it away, rather than having an unlimited number of open weeks stretching back for years and years.

I just want to say again that this is the most effective method for planning that I've ever encountered. But I'm not going to ask you to live it forever, just every week for the rest of your mortal existence. It's not necessarily a "fun" way to plan; it's certainly not a natural way to plan. In fact, at first, I didn't like planning this way. It was hard because it took time and focus. Since that time, however, I have come to appreciate the value and turned this method into my second nature. That's why I'm only committing you to live this planning method for the rest of your mortal life. After that, you can choose to continue living it or not. See? I'm not so hard to work with.

Don't give up just because this doesn't feel "natural." Remember, those who are methods-focused will only ever get the results that come from pleasing methods. Have your results been sufficiently pleasing so far? Or do you want to elevate your time management and effectiveness by focusing on the results in spite of the methods? It's your choice. You can use this planning method, if you Will.

Systems for Effectiveness

We've talked about setting goals and breaking them into manageable bites, and we've talked about the best planning process I've ever found. Now it's time to talk about where these principles derive their power.

The answer is systems. A system is a group of related pieces or components that work together to perform a task which none of those components could do on their own. For instance, the steering in a car is a system of different shafts, gears, and even computers, which interpret the rotation of the steering wheel into a change of angle in the drive wheels. Perhaps a more familiar example is that of a computer system: a group of capacitors, silicon board, chips, switches, and other peripheral devices that work together to store, retrieve, and compute data.

So, based on that definition, is a paper airplane a system?

Believe it or not, the answer is yes. In this case, however, it is a system of folds and creases in a sheet of paper that, when applied correctly, will enable a normal sheet of paper to fly. It's a very simple system; I agree. But, if there was no system—no method and arrangement of the folds to allow them to work together—you would essentially be balling up that paper and chucking it.

Admittedly, an airplane built like this can only go so far and so fast. The world record distance for a paper airplane is 226 feet, 10 inches. The plane was built by John Collins and thrown by Football Quarterback Joe Ayoob. The longest a paper airplane has stayed in the air, to date, is 27.9 seconds. This plane was built and thrown by Takua Toda. Both of those world records are from the Guinness Book. Another "paper" airplane (really made of a cardboard material) was launch over the Arizona desert and hit 100 mph before crashing down. It also happened to be 45 feet long.

All of this sounds really impressive because what is the purpose of a paper airplane? To fly, right? And to get so much out of paper is surprising. However, what's the purpose of the space shuttle? Also to fly, right?

Did you know that the Space Shuttle goes about 17,500 miles per hour while orbiting the earth?[12] Believe it or not, that's faster than a speeding bullet. The fastest bullets in the world only travel at about 2,700. The shuttle crew is actually going so fast that they can see a sunrise or sunset every 45 minutes. Each of the Space Shuttles—except for Challenger—traveled farther than the distance from the earth to the sun (remember? 93 million miles?). The Shuttle also stays "airborne" for as much as two weeks at a time.

So why is it that the paper airplane is so outclassed by the space shuttle? Both are manmade—and paper airplanes have been built a

---

[12] Norton, Lily. "8 Surprising Space Shuttle Facts." Space.com. Last Updated 30 June 2011. Accessed 10 May 2013.
http://www.space.com/12127-8-surprising-space-shuttle-facts.html

lot longer than shuttles. The answer is based on the complexity and relationship between the various systems.

What systems does a paper airplane employ? Just a series of folds and creases. What systems does the space shuttle employ? Navigation, propulsion, life support, fuel systems, monitoring systems, computers of all sorts and sizes, plumbing, refrigeration, heating, waste management, telemetry, and the list goes on.

As an aside, what's the most complex, most sophisticated system of all on that shuttle?

That's right, the people. The human system is a system of systems. You've got the digestive system, the pulmonary system, the endocrine system, the skeletal system, the muscular system, the nervous system, the circulatory system, the lymphatic system, and so on and so forth. And each crewmember becomes a system of systems in the greater network of systems within systems in the space shuttle. It is only through the interaction and synergy of those systems that the space shuttle can achieve such amazing results. It takes all these systems to enable the space shuttle to go so much farther so much faster than the paper airplane.

And here's why this matters to you: When you have the right systems, you can go farther faster too. Which would you rather be? A space shuttle that soars with the stars or a paper airplane that is doomed to crash-land every time?

If you're tired of underachieving what you know you could be doing, and you've always avoided employing systems like project management and weekly planning, consider the space shuttle. If you've been waiting for the "perfect method for you" to give you results, maybe it's time to stop focusing on the methods—the natural thing to do—and start focusing on the results—the successful thing to do.

Weekly planning is one of the systems that will help you rise to a new level, and you can use it…if you will.

Homework

Will you begin utilizing the 6 Step Weekly Planning Method and continue to use it for the rest of your mortal life? You don't need to use it any longer than that (though you are welcome to), but I expect you to use it for the rest of your mortal life.

___ Yes   ___ No

You Can; Will You?

I once knew a young man, a salesman, of no small ability. He was talented, sure, but the more important thing was that he was quick to learn what was expected of him and act on it. And, no, I'm not talking about myself. The young man was consistently at the top of the charts at work. He was always earning the top achiever—consistently exceeds expectations box on his performance review. His boss and coworkers had only good things to say about this young man.

He was consistently in the top earners for his position and tenure because of his performance, and he typically got the top bonuses too. In fact, he was just plain awesome at what he did. He knew what was required of him because it had been clearly spelled out and he acted on it, day in and day out. But over time he grew a little unhappy with the situation. As so often happens when a person achieves such consistent success, he wanted something more.

Eventually, this desire to be more and do more grew in his heart until he decided to leave the company where he'd had so much success and start out on his own. After all, if he'd performed so well within the confines of the corporate structure, wouldn't he do even better without all that extra red tape? Wouldn't he do so much better without all that stifling accountability and all those hoops?

As it turns out, he didn't. He still had all the talent, skills and abilities to do what he had decided to do, but he struggled tremendously. His follow-through dropped. His structure and organizational skills evaporated. Why?

Well, it turns out that, like so many other people, this young man didn't have the same structure within himself that he'd experienced back in his old company. All of the accountability and commitment and structure that had been "imposed" upon him in the past—and which had shown him how to flourish—was gone. He no longer had to report to anyone but himself, and losing that chain of command had crippled his drive.

We all need structure and commitment. We have to take ownership for our actions and those things over which we have control. If these things are not created for us by the organization where we work, then we must create it for ourselves. Believe it or not, this is a much harder path.

Contrary to popular belief, entrepreneurship is not freedom from responsibility and goals and targets and ownership and structure. In fact, for those of you who think owning your own business is easier than working for a company, think again. In most cases, it's harder because you have to take ownership and enforce responsibility and commitment and structure on yourself; there's no one there to enforce it for you.

One of the major reasons so many entrepreneurs fail is because they mistakenly believe that they don't need to have structure and organization anymore. That's why they left whatever job the previously had, right? To escape being under the thumb of "the man"? But that thought process is a serious, fatal mistake.

Think about it for a moment. Why do great companies have all that structure? They have it because they know it will make them great companies. If they didn't think it would make them into better companies, do you really think they would create all those rules and metrics? It takes a lot of time and money to create those kinds of performance monitoring systems. And if they *did* create stuff like that just for the fun of it, throwing away all the money to do so, do you think those companies would last long in the face of more nimble, less-encumbered competition?

For those of you who want to be successful entrepreneurs, I have a recommendation for you. Do you remember that employee handbook from your last job? Someone spent hours and days creating that thing. Why? To make the business more effective. Do you have an employee handbook? Do you have performance reviews? Sure, you'll be reviewing yourself, but doesn't everyone believe that they are their own toughest critic? I would recommend that you create your performance metrics; what does it take to "consistently exceed expectations"? What about "meets expectations"? "Beneath expectations"? Do you need to use all the legalese and be "PC"? No. You can write it in shorthand. But you need to write it all out and keep it where you can reference and update it as your company evolves.

Ask yourself, what does it take to succeed in your business? Are you monitoring yourself along those metrics? You should be. You should be tracking those metrics just like you would if your boss could call you up to the office and grill you at any moment. And why should you do all this? To take control of your course, of course; to take ownership of where you are going and what you are going to do. Because the alternative is to leave it up to what comes naturally—and we all know where that will lead.

Taking Ownership

There's an interesting point about ownership. It is: you cannot be truly responsible and truly take ownership while also being a victim. You can't claim to control your life and claim to be a victim at the same time. It just doesn't work. Taking ownership is being in charge; being a victim is saying that someone else is in charge of you. You can't have it both ways.

Put away the idea that your company is out to get you or anything else like that. Instead, focus on the idea that you are a company of one; you. No matter where you are, no matter who writes the check for your salary, you are a company of you, and your responsibility as that company is to provide award-winning service and quality to all your clients. Those clients may be actual clients, if you own your own business, or they may be your boss and coworkers, if you are employed in a larger organization. The point is, you are the master of your fate. Life is an empty box; it's only worth as much as you put in.

So you can sit back and draw a paycheck and hope no one catches on—playing the victim role—or you can step up and take charge of you and your individual company, making great things happen. Can I tell you a secret? You've never known a great person who was a victim. Then may have suffered through unmentionable atrocities, but they were never a victim because they never surrendered ownership of their self to anyone else.

According to Victor Frankl, "Those of us who were in concentration camps can remember the men and women who went around from hut to hut encouraging others, even giving away their last piece of bread. They may have been few in number, but they offer sufficient proof that everything can be taken away from a man but one thing, the last of human freedoms: the ability to choose one's attitude in any given set of circumstances—the ability to choose one's own way."

There was a point in my life, shortly after I started at Franklin Covey, where I was feeling pretty down. I was working hard, but I didn't feel like I was being rewarded commensurate with my efforts. Of course, at the same time, I was being immersed in wonderful principles like the ones I've been sharing with you. I was learning so much with which to improve my life. Still, in the face of the difficulties I faced, I was having more than my fair share of pity parties about a number of different aspects of my life at the time. It was at this time that I discovered that quote by Frankl.

I had an immediate paradigm shift that day. In fact, I memorized the quote just so I could repeat it to myself any time I got tempted to start saying, "Woe is me" about anything. Do yourself a favor some time and take a few minutes to think about what it would have been like to be in a concentration camp: your family torn from you and split apart—possibly dead or alive—very little food or water, forced labor with a painful death as the punishment for poor performance, etc. Yet, in the face of those conditions, there were some who maintained the Will to move forward and lift others. *That* is the power of ownership. That is the power of choosing your own course and sticking with it.

When I read that quote, I felt about an inch tall. I knew that my troubles were nothing in comparison to what Frankl and his people faced. I gained immediate perspective about what I had and how I *wasn't* a victim. In all the years since, maintaining an attitude of ownership has helped me avoid getting bogged down into thinking I'm a victim. Maintaining that attitude has helped me to stay at the wheel and drive my own life.

Be Great or Don't Suck

Another tool that will help you avoid a victimized mindset is the power of positive thinking. In essence, this is looking for the best, most empowering way to say things. One way to think of it is to always focus on what you *can* do, rather than what you can't. In some respects, this may feel like semantics; however, semantics have real power in the subconscious.

To help you understand the power of this concept, let me tell you about a study conducted some years ago. The researchers took several hundred people out to a golf course, to the putting green, specifically. They then split the group in half to give them different instructions.

Keep in mind that these two groups were of equivalent skill. Everyone participating in the study had the same handicap (or level of golfing ability).

To the one group, the researchers had them focus on the idea "Don't miss the putt." To the other group, the researchers said to focus on the idea "Make the putt." This may be a dumb question, but what do you think was the outcome of that experiment? That's right, to a statistically significant degree, the golfers in the second group were more likely to make the putt.

Why did it work out this way? Don't "Make the putt" and "don't miss the putt" mean the same thing? Not exactly. The human mind is too good at imagining things—but how do you imagine *not* doing something? The second group was able to clearly visualize themselves making the putt; this was empowering. For the first group, however, the image was that of missing the putt with some kind of voice-over that said, "don't do this." But, of course, what were they picturing? No matter how clear the voice-over was, they were still imagining missing the putt.

Consider this: Would you rather "be great" or "don't suck"?

So, instead of focusing on the negative side of what you can't do, focus on the positive side and acknowledge what you can do. This will empower you and help you to take ownership, rather than being a victim.

Establishing Patterns

For the next tool to help you take ownership and keep commitments to yourself, I'm going to share with you a little riddle. It comes from so long ago that the author has been lost to time, but the riddle itself is powerful all the same:

I am your constant companion.

I am your greatest helper or your heaviest burden.

I will push you onward or drag you down to failure.

I am completely at your command.

Half the things you do, you might as well turn over to me and I will be able to do them quickly and correctly.

I am easily managed.

You must merely be firm with me.

Show me exactly how you want something done and, after a few lessons, I will do it, automatically.

I am the servant of all great men and, alas, of all failures as well.

Those who are great, I have made great.

Those who are failures, I have made failures.

I am not a machine, though I work with the precision of a machine plus the intelligence of man.

You may run me for profit or run me for ruin.

It makes no difference to me.

Take me, train me, be firm with me, and I will place the world at your feet.

Be easy with me and I will destroy you.

Who am I?

I am HABIT

I have always loved this poem for the power it represents. If you think back to unconscious competence vs. incompetence, that is the realm of habit. On the one hand, you have the habits that will destroy you and bring you down—unconscious incompetence—and on the other hand you've trained yourself to have the habits that will launch you for success—unconscious competence. But habit doesn't care if you use it at level 1 or level 4. It doesn't really exist at levels 2 and 3, because that's consciousness and habit doesn't exist in the conscious mind.

In the words of Aristotle, "We are what we repeatedly do. Excellence then is not an act, it's a habit." Have you ever known someone who had the world, metaphorically at least, placed at his or her feet because of great habits? And they don't have to be famous to qualify. Now, what about the reverse? Do you know anyone who lost everything to a habit that got out of control?

Sadly, I know more of the latter than the former. As John Dryden said, "We first make our habits, then our habits make us." We get to pick and choose our habits, if we want to. We build them in the realm of consciousness and then let them work in us for good or ill. We are the habits we make. Don't be easy on your habits because they won't be easy on you. Build the habits for success, in spite of the fact that they are hard to build, and those habits will launch you like the space shuttle. Or build "natural" habits by defaulting to a methods-preference. If you choose that road, however, you are choosing your own condemnation—and no one or nothing will be able to shake you from the path you choose.

So what habits do you want to make? How about some habits of excellence? How about the habit of making and keeping commitments to yourself? We've talked about how hard that can be, but making and keeping commitments to yourself is the key to success.

True Commitment

Now I have a trick question for you: is it harder to make a commitment, or to keep it?

Think about that one for a moment.

If you're like many of my clients, your experience with goals and New Year's Resolutions in the past may incline you to believe that keeping commitments is harder than making them.

I'm going to respectfully disagree, and here's why: What does it look like to make a commitment? Is it enough to just say "I'm gonna…"? Even if I *really* mean it, is it enough?

Let me put it to you this way. You've just bought a house. It's a nice house—granite countertops, heated tile floors in the bathrooms, basketball hoop in the driveway—and you are going to the bank to take care of the loan documents. When you arrive, your mortgage broker smiles and waves you over. You walk up to him and say, "I'm gonna pay this all back over time," he gives you the check, and you leave. Raise your hand if you believe that would happen.

I don't see any hands.

Why don't I see any hands? Because that's not enough commitment in the bank's view. So what is your mortgage broker really going to have you do? You're going to sit down and go through about a thousand pages of legal nonsense, signing half of them. Did you know that one of the federally required documents is actually an acknowledgment of your right to change your mind and *not* take out the loan—for up to three days *after* you've signed all those documents agreeing to take out the loan?

From a legal standpoint, your commitment to repay that mortgage doesn't become a real commitment until four days after you've signed the paperwork. The bank won't give out the money to the title company until then. And why is that? Because now the bank has a signed, sealed, legal document stating your agreement and explaining their method of recourse if you break that agreement. *That's* a commitment. Up until that point, that very same mortgage is just another "I'm gonna…."

A commitment becomes a real commitment when we write it down and sign our name to it. This is because at the point where we sign something, we put ourselves on the line. We potentially expose ourselves to what I believe is the second biggest fear in humanity (which, interestingly enough, is the motivating factor behind the first biggest fear): public failure. People are absolutely terrified of public failure and the associated shame, so they will do anything in their power to not be caught failing publicly—and that means avoiding writing down commitments that they might later not keep. So, if you want to be better about keeping your commitments to yourself, start writing them down. I would even recommend that you add a little line where you can commit yourself by your signature.

Let's take a moment and examine commitments together. Obviously, there are different kinds of commitments and different levels of commitment associated with them.

I'm going to list a few phrases, and I want you to play a little game. You've got $100 for each phrase, and the odds are double or nothing for any portion you bet. It I follow through with the commitment, you get double whatever portion you bet. If I don't follow through, you lose whatever portion you bet. Remember, you get $100 to bet all, some, or none, and you get a new $100 for each phrase, but you can't roll over the money from one phrase to the next.

Here goes:

"You know, I think I might kinda like to maybe think about possibly sorta running. It sounds kinda cool. Maybe I'll think about doing a bit sometime this weekend. Maybe."

How much will you bet? _____

"You know, I'd really like to go running this Saturday. That sounds fun. I think I'd like to go do that."

How much will you bet? _____

"Um…yeah. I'll go running this Saturday."

How much will you bet? _____

"I am going to go running. This Saturday."

How much will you bet? _____

"Reader, do I have your complete attention? I need your complete attention now because I'm about to share something with you that's very important to me. Do I have your complete and undivided attention? Good.

"Reader, *hear me now*. With God as my witness, I am going running at 10 am this Saturday come hell or high water. Death alone will prevent me from running at 10 o'clo—! Reader, are you hearing me? Do you get what I'm telling you? Is there any doubt in your mind whether or not I will do it?"

How much will you bet? _____

How many of you, after being hesitant the whole time, bet it all on that last one? That's called a "Hear me now..." commitment, and it doesn't get much stronger than that. It may sound a little old-fashioned, but anything you say to another person that starts with those three words has just had the level of commitment upped substantially.

When a person starts a commitment in that manner, you know they have no fear of being accountable for the result. And, honestly, if you're serious enough about something to make a commitment, you shouldn't ever fear the accountability to that commitment. In fact, you shouldn't really fear accountability at all. Ever.

Accountability is a Four-Letter Word

You may have capability, sensibility, adaptability, amicability, and even be filled with possibility, but if you don't have accountability, you won't accept responsibility, and thus have little probability of happiness and success. Accountability and Responsibility are the greatest abilities one can possess. Accountability is, by definition, your ability to account for something for which you were responsible. It's really that simple. You had a task; how did you do on it?

Unfortunately, in society we've turned accountability into something of a swear word. My original subtitle for this book was "Achieving Success Through Commitment and Accountability." Then, as I thought about it, I realized that a subtitle like that might drive away the very people who needed this information the most. So I changed it to the current subtitle.

Why has accountability gotten such a bad rap? Let me ask you two questions. Have you ever done something really well—I mean so well that you wanted to tell the whole world about it—but no one knew it? And, when you tried to tell people about this great thing you'd done, you couldn't really describe it in all its amazing grandeur? That is a serious disappointment, isn't it?

Now my second question; Have you ever done something dumb and gotten caught for it? Been publicly shamed for a mistake you made—whether or not you fixed the error?

The reason people are so afraid of "accountability" is because society's perception is all wrong. When you do something, and do it well, you're accountable for it. It just also happens that if you do something wrong, you're accountable for that too. Interestingly, as humans we often push our memories to capture the negative things in life in the most detail. This is one of the reasons I encouraged you to start keeping a victory journal.

So we remember and share all the negative things but keep the good ones to ourselves. Want proof? When's the last time you were standing with a friend and they smelled something nice? What did they do? Sniff it again? How long was it before they let you take a smell? Did you have to ask before they remembered to share?

What about the last time they smelled something bad? Instantly their arms are out away from their face as they shove the rancid whatever under your nose, right?

So accountability has gotten an unfair bad rap because people only share the experiences where they were caught on the wrong side of accountability. Go back to the definition: the ability to account for something. Would you say you do more right or wrong in a day? If all your acts were put on one of those old-fashioned scales like the scales of justice, would the good in your day outweigh the bad? You do realize that you're accountable for all that good too, right? So relax a little. Accountability isn't a bad thing.

And here's why you need accountability. Picture that it's Thursday. You just went out to diner with your spouse or some friends or a business client. Toward the end of the meal, you decided to visit the restroom. As you were buttoning your pants again, the button popped off. Now, to be fair, the thread was probably a bit worn—these are your favorite pants, after all—and you had eaten a lot of food, but how do you feel as you stare at that button on the floor? Maybe a little rounder than you did a moment before? So you do what any sensible person would do and decide to go running that following Saturday morning.

But now Saturday morning rolls around. Your alarm goes off to wake you up and you roll over and look out the window. You had a rough night and you're tired. To top things off, the thunderstorm that kept you up half the night has lingered and you can see a very light rain drizzling outside your window. The light is gray and gloomy and it looks so wet. Are you going to get up and go running now?

Most people would say no. I know that some of you would get up and go; I don't want you to think I'm underestimating you or anything. I'm just saying that, statistically speaking, most people would roll over and go back to sleep. And why is it so easy to roll over and go back to sleep? Because there's no external accountability in this situation.

We talked about how when we make a commitment to someone else, most of us are extremely good at following through and keeping that commitment, right? But what about when the only person involved in the commitment is the self? Why are we so much worse at keeping commitments to ourselves?

For one, it's easy to rationalize away our deficiency when no one else is there to poke holes in the argument. How many times have you dissuaded yourself from doing something hard by using an excuse you would never even have considered using on your boss or friend or spouse?

To me, this is backwards. Who is the one person that as long as you live and no matter what else happen, you will have to live with? If you answered anyone but your self, you need to guess again. You are the only person that you are guaranteed to live with for your entire life, so why consider yourself less important that everyone else? Why value commitments to yourself less than commitments to anyone else?

Developing Self-Accountability

I said this once before but it bears repeating: if you can keep commitments to yourself, it will be second nature to keep commitments to everyone else. And, let's face it, if you're going to do the hard, "unnatural" things necessary to achieve success, the person that will be able to best hold you accountable is your self. Train yourself to keep commitments to yourself—build that habit—and you will find that you can, and will, do anything you set your mind to.

So don't run from accountability thinking it only entails the negative. Remember that you want to think and speak positively. That starts by embracing accountability—and both the good and bad that it represents. In reality, your ability to make and keep commitments to yourself—to be accountable to yourself—is a strong reflection of your true, innermost character.

So what do you do if you're not so good at keeping commitments to yourself? Let me tell you a little story about a rehabilitation facility in California called Delancey Street. This place takes the absolute worst of society—con men, druggies, and thieves—and turns them into law-abiding citizens with hope for a real future. How? By making them responsible for one another. In effect, each of the convicts becomes an accountability partner for each of the convicts.

I only share this example to demonstrate the power of accountability to you. If those people did their time and were released back on the street, most would be back in jail within a week. At Delancey Street, 90 percent or so go on to live real, normal, upstanding lives—without serving more jail time. They become successful business owners and contributing members of society.

Why, though? Why give these people an accountability partner? Why not just let them be accountable for themselves? That hasn't worked out too well so far. So what about you? Are you having the success you want to have? Why can't you just be accountable to yourself? Well, maybe that hasn't worked out too well so far.

So you need to really introspect and decide for yourself. Do you understand these concepts well enough now to apply them faithfully? Or would it be better to get a little outside help in the form of an accountability partner?

If you find that your ability to hold yourself accountable needs a little more practice, don't just settle for the results you can achieve through those pleasing methods; get someone else involved for a while. Ideally, this person is someone who knows you and loves you but won't let you off the hook for failure. Sometimes a spouse can fill this role, but often not, because they often love us so much that they are too soft on us. In any case, it needs to be someone who has your best interest at heart and will not be a naysayer for you. You can't afford to enlist an accountability partner only to have them doubt your ability to keep commitments. Life is hard enough without inviting more difficulty.

Always remember the goal, however, of working toward being able to hold yourself accountable. Your partner can help you out initially, but in the end, you are who you are, and decisions will arise in which you need to act in the absence of outside help. So use a partner if you need to, but focus on developing your Will until you can keep commitments to yourself. Remember, you have the ability within you. You might need to dig it up and clean it off, but it's there. If it wasn't there, you wouldn't have opened this book.

Parting Words

In our journey through these concepts together, I've tried to share with you the truths that have helped me and helped my clients to overcome challenges, find direction, and achieve success. We've talked about the various roles you fill and the facets of your life that need attention in order for you to find balance. We've talked about your Will and how what you choose to do and become is what you will become. You can ignore the decisions that life presents and pretend that they don't happen, but that's just choosing by default.

We talked about the natural, default course of action and how it doesn't bring success. If it did, everyone would be successful and I wouldn't be writing this book. We talked about being motivated by results instead of methods. We talked about establishing a foundation of the principles that form your core, and we talked about how to bring those Mission, Vision, and Values to life.

Last, we talked about the process of setting goals and planning your life in order to take control and shape yourself into the person you want to become. We talked about being positive and creating habits to carry you through the difficult times. We also talked about making yourself accountable to you.

A very famous ancient philosopher named Anonymous once said,

"Commitment is what transforms a promise into reality. It is the words that speak boldly of your intentions and the actions that speak louder than words. It is making time when there is none. Coming through time after time after time, year after year after year. Commitment is the stuff character is made of: the power to change the face of things. It is the daily triumph of integrity over skepticism."

In our time together, I've given you the fundamental tools to direct your life down a successful road, but it's up to you to use them. During our discussion of Mr. Gray's "Common Denominator of Success," I shared with you that being able to make *and keep* commitments to yourself was the true "secret" to success in life. I reiterate that point again now. If you can keep your promises to yourself, all your other promises will come easily.

If you are reading this book, you are fully capable of adopting all of the principles I've shared, but it's up to you to have the commitment to do it. You can do all the things we've talked about so far, if you Will.

You can. Will you?

Appendices

Appendix A
The Common Denominator of Success

By Albert E.N. Gray
Reprinted June, 1992

This inspiring message by Mr. Gray, a timeless piece of life insurance literature, first appeared as an address at a 1940 NALU (National Association of Life Underwriters) annual convention. Mr. Gray was known throughout the country as a writer and speaker on life insurance subjects. You will notice as you read that the principles discussed are not merely related to the selling of life insurance.

SEVERAL YEARS AGO I was brought face to face with the disturbing realization that I was trying to supervise and direct the efforts of a large number of men who were trying to achieve success, without knowing myself what the secret of success really was. And that, naturally, brought me face to face with the further realization that regardless of what other knowledge I might have brought to my job, I was definitely lacking in the most important knowledge of all.

Of course, like most of us, I had been brought up on the popular belief that the secret of success is hard work, but I had seen so many men work hard without succeeding and so many men succeed without working hard that I had become convinced that hard work was not the real secret even though in most cases it might be one of the requirements.

And so I set out on a voyage of discovery which carried me

through biographies and autobiographies and all sorts of dissertations on success and the lives of successful men until I finally reached a point at which I realized that the secret I was trying to discover lay not only in what men did, but also in what made them do it.

I realized further that the secret for which I was searching must not only apply to every definition of success, but since it must apply to everyone to whom it was offered, it must also apply to everyone who had ever been successful. In short, I was looking for the common denominator of success.

And because that is exactly what I was looking for, that is exactly what I found.

But this common denominator of success is so big, so powerful, and so vitally important to your future and mine that I'm not going to make a speech about it. I'm just going to "lay it on the line" in words of one syllable, so simple that everyone can understand them.

The common denominator of success – the secret of success of every man who has ever been successful – lies in the fact that he formed the habit of doing things that failures don't like to do.

It's just as true as it sounds and it's just as simple as it seems. You can hold it up to the light, you can put it to the acid test, and you can kick it around until it's worn out, but when you are all through with it, it will still be the common denominator of success, whether you like it or not.

It will still explain why men have come into this business of ours with every apparent qualification for success and given us our most disappointing failures, while others have come in and achieved outstanding success in spite of many obvious and discouraging handicaps.

And since it will also explain your future, it would seem to be a mighty good idea for you to use it in determining just what sort of a future you are going to have. In other words, let's take this big, all-embracing secret and boil it down to fit the individual you.

If the secret of success lies in forming the habit of doing things that failures don't like to do, let's start the boiling-down

process by determining what are the things that failures don't like to do.

The things that failures don't like to do are the very things that you and I and other human beings, including successful men, *naturally* don't like to do. In other words, we've got to realize right from the start that success is something which is achieved by the minority of men, and is therefore *unnatural* and not to be achieved by following our *natural* likes and dislikes nor by being guided by our *natural* preferences and prejudices.

The things that failures don't like to do, in general, are too obvious for us to discuss them here, and so, since our success is to be achieved in the sale of life insurance, let us move on to a discussion of the things that we as life insurance men don't like to do. Here, too, the things we don't like to do are too many to permit specific discussion, but I think they can all be disposed of by saying that they all emanate from one basic dislike peculiar to our type of selling. We don't like to call on people who don't want to see us and talk to them about something they don't want to talk about. Any reluctance to follow a definite prospecting program, to use prepared sales talks, to organize time and to organize effort are all caused by this one basic dislike.

Perhaps you have wondered what is behind this peculiar lack of welcome on the part of our prospective buyers. Isn't it due to the fact that our prospects are human too? And isn't it true that the average human being is not big enough to buy life insurance of his own accord and is therefore prone to escape our efforts to make him bigger or persuade him to do something he doesn't want to do by striking at the most important weakness we possess: namely, our desire to be appreciated?

Perhaps you have been discouraged by a feeling that you were born subject to certain dislikes peculiar to you, with which the successful men in our business are not afflicted. Perhaps you have wondered why it is that our biggest producers seem to like to do the things that you don't like to do.

They don't! And I think this is the most encouraging statement I have ever offered to a group of life insurance salesmen.

But if they don't like to do these things, then why do they do them? Because by doing the things they don't like to do, they can accomplish the things they want to accomplish. **Successful men are influenced by the desire for pleasing results. Those who experience failure are influenced by the desire for pleasing methods and are inclined to be satisfied with such results as can be obtained by doing things they like to do.**

Why are successful men able to do things they don't like to do while failures are not? Because successful men have a purpose strong enough to make them form the habit of doing things they don't like to do in order to accomplish the purpose they want to accomplish.

Sometimes even our best producers get into a slump. **When a man goes into a slump, it simply means that he has reached a point at which, for the time being, the things he doesn't like to do have become more important than his reasons for doing them.** And may I pause to suggest to you managers and general agents that when one of your good producers goes into a slump, the less you talk about his production and the more you talk about his purpose, the sooner you will pull him out of his slump?

Many men with whom I have discussed this common denominator of success have said at this point, "But I have a family to support and I have to have a living for my family and myself. Isn't that enough of a purpose?" No, it isn't. It isn't a sufficiently strong purpose to make you form the habit of doing the things you don't like to do for the very simple reasons that it is easier to adjust ourselves to the hardships of a poor living than it is to adjust ourselves to the hardships of making a better one. If you doubt me, just think of all the things you are willing to go without in order to avoid doing the things you don't like to do.

All of which seems to prove that the strength which holds you to your purpose is not your own strength but the strength of the purpose itself.

Now let's see why habit belongs so importantly in this common denominator of success.

Men are creatures of habit just as machines are creatures of momentum, for habit is nothing more or less than momentum translated from the concrete into the abstract.

Can you picture the problem that would face our mechanical engineers if there were no such thing as momentum? Speed would be impossible because the highest speed at which any vehicle could be moved would be the first speed at which it could be broken away from a standstill.

Elevators could not be made to rise, airplanes could not be made to fly, and the entire world of mechanics would find itself in a total state of helplessness. Then who are you and I to think that we can do with our own human nature what the finest engineers in the world could not do with the finest machinery that was ever built?

Every qualification for success is acquired through habit. Men form habits and habits form futures. If you do not deliberately form good habits, then unconsciously you will form bad ones. You are the kind of person you are because you have formed the habit of being that kind of person, and the only way you can change is through habit.

The success habits in selling are divided into four main groups:

1. Prospecting habits
2. Calling habits
3. Selling habits
4. Working habits

Let's discuss these habit groups in their order.

Any successful life insurance salesman will tell you that it is easier to sell life insurance to people who don't want it than it is to find people who do want it, but if you have not deliberately formed the habit of prospecting for needs, regardless of wants, then unconsciously you have formed the habit of limiting your prospecting to people who want life insurance and therein lies the one and only real reason for lack of prospects.

As to calling habits, unless you have deliberately formed the habit of calling on people who are able to buy but unwilling to listen, then unconsciously you have formed the habit of calling on people who are willing to listen but unable to buy.

As to selling habits, unless you have deliberately formed the habit of calling on prospects determined to make them see their reasons for buying life insurance, then unconsciously you have formed the habit of calling on prospects in a state of mind in which you are willing to let them make you see their reasons for not buying it.

As to working habits, if you will take care of the other three groups, the working habits will generally take care of themselves because under working habits are included study and preparation, organization of time and efforts, records, analyses, etc. Certainly you're not going to take the trouble to learn interest-arousing approaches and sales talks unless you're going to use them. **You're not going to plan your day's work when you know in your heart that you're not going to carry out your plans. And you're certainly not going to keep an honest record of things you haven't done or of results you haven't achieved.**

So let's not worry so much about the fourth group of success habits, for if you are taking care of the first three groups, most of the working habits will take care of themselves and you'll be able to afford a secretary to take care of the rest of them for you.

But before you decide to adopt these success habits, let me warn you of the importance of habit to your decision. I have attended many sales meetings and sales congresses during the past ten years and have often wondered why, in spite of the fact that there is so much good in them, so many men seem to get so little lasting good out of them. Perhaps you have attended sales meetings in the past and have left determined to do the things that would make you successful or more successful only to find your decision or determination waning at just the time when it should be put into effect or practice.

Here's the answer. **Any resolution or decision you make is simply a promise to yourself, which isn't worth a tinker's dam unless you have formed the habit of making it and keeping it. And you won't form the habit of making it and keeping it unless right at the start you link it with a definite purpose that can be accomplished by keeping it.**

Any resolution or decision you make today has to be made again tomorrow. In other words, any resolution or decision you make today has to be made again tomorrow, and the next day, and the next, and the next, and so on. And it not only has to be made each day, but it has to be kept each day, for if you miss one day in the making or keeping of it, you've got to go back and begin all over again. But if you continue the process of making it each morning and keeping it each day, you will finally wake up some morning a

different person in a different world, and you will wonder what has happened to you and the world you used to live in.

Here's what has happened. Your resolution or decision has become a habit and you don't have to make it on this particular morning. And the reason for your seeming like a different person living in a different world lies in the fact that for the first time in your life, you have become master of yourself and master of your likes and dislikes by surrendering to your purpose in life. That is why behind every success there must be a purpose and that is what makes purpose so important to your future. For in the last analysis, your future is not going to depend on economic conditions or outside influences of circumstances over which you have no control. **Your future is going to depend on your purpose in life**. So let's talk about purpose.

First of all, your purpose must be practical and not visionary. Some time ago, I talked with a man who thought he had a purpose which was more important to him than income. He was interested in the sufferings of his fellow man, and he wanted to be placed in a position to alleviate that suffering. But when he analyzed his real feeling, we discovered, and he admitted it, that what he really wanted was a real nice job dispensing charity with other people's money and being well paid for it, along with the appreciation and feeling of importance that would naturally go with such a job.

But in making your purpose practical, be careful not to make it logical. Make it a purpose of the sentimental or emotional type. Remember needs are logical while wants and desires are sentimental and emotional. Your needs will push you just so far, but when your needs are satisfied, they will stop pushing you. If, however, your purpose is in terms of wants and desires, then your wants and desires will keep pushing you long after your needs are satisfied and until your wants and desires are fulfilled.

Recently I was talking with a young man who long ago discovered the common denominator of success without identifying his discovery. He had a definite purpose in life and it was definitely a sentimental or emotional purpose. He wanted his boy to go through college without having to work his way through as he had done. He wanted to avoid for his little girl the hardships which his own sister had had to face in her childhood. And he wanted his wife and the mother of his children to enjoy the luxuries and comforts, and even necessities, which had been denied his own mother. And he was willing to form the habit of doing things he didn't like to do in order to accomplish this purpose.

Not to discourage him, but rather to have him encourage me, I said to him, "Aren't you going a little too far with this thing? There's no logical reason why your son shouldn't be willing and able to work his way through college just as his father did. Of course he'll miss many of the things that you missed in your college life and he'll probably have heartaches and disappointments. But if he's any good, he'll come through in the end just as you did. And there's no logical reason why you should slave in order that your daughter may have things which your own sister wasn't able to have, or in order that your wife can enjoy comforts and luxuries that she wasn't used to before she married you."

He looked at me with rather a pitying look and said, "But Mr. Gray, there's no inspiration in logic. There's no courage in logic. There's not even happiness in logic. There's only satisfaction. The only place logic has in my life is in the realization that the more I am willing to do for my wife and children, the more I shall be able to do for myself."

You will never succeed beyond the purpose to which you are willing to surrender.

Imagine, after hearing that story, you won't have to be told how to find your purpose or how to identify it or how to surrender to it. If it's a big purpose, you will be big in its accomplishment. If it's an unselfish purpose, you will be unselfish in accomplishing it. And if it's an honest purpose, you will be honest and honorable in the accomplishment of it.

But as long as you live, don't ever forget that while you may succeed beyond your fondest hopes and your greatest expectations, you will never succeed beyond the purpose to which you are willing to surrender. Furthermore, your surrender will not be complete until you have formed the habit of doing the things that failures don't like to do.

Appendix B
Sample Mission Statements

From Franklin Covey's *7 Habits of Highly Effective People*, *7 Habits of Highly Effective Families*, *First Things First*, *The 4 Roles of Leadership Participant Workbook*, *What Matters Most Participant Workbook* and *7 Habits of Highly Effective People Participant Workbook*.

Here are some examples of mission statements. Yours does not have to look like any of the examples. We provide them simply to give you ideas for your own mission statement.

Personal Mission Statements:

My mission is to live with integrity and to make a different in the lives of others.

To fulfill this mission:

I have charity: I seek out and love the one—each one—regardless of his situation.

I sacrifice: I devote my time, talents, and resources to my mission.

I inspire: I teach by example that we are all children of a loving Heavenly Father and that every Goliath can be overcome.

I am impactful: What I do makes a difference in the lives of others.

These roles take priority in achieving my mission:

Husband—my partner is the most important person in my life. Together we contribute the fruits of harmony, industry, charity, and thrift.

Father—I help my children experience progressively greater joy in their lives.

Son/Brother—I am frequently "there" for support and love.

Christian—God can count on me to keep my covenants and to serve his other children.

Neighbor—The love of Christ is visible through my actions toward others.

Change Agent—I am a catalyst for developing high performance in large organizations.

Scholar—I learn important new things every day.

My Mission:

To live my life ever aware that who I am is as much what others see as it is what I believe.

To live my life without excessive indulgences, aware that my mind and my body are my true assets.

To love my family with many indulgences, aware that they are my only treasures.

To deal with others with honesty and integrity, tolerance and compassion, evenness and consideration.

To dedicate my remaining years to helping others find purpose in their lives, ensuring that my influence on others is consistent with my values and principles.

To teach others that which I believe to be right in both the personal and professional stream, yet never presume that my way is the only way.

To live my life on purpose and with purpose and use up all my potential.

My mission is to create, nurture, and maintain an environment of growth, challenge, and unlimited potential for all those around me.

My mission is to explore and wonder, as a child with my playmates, discovering eternity in the beauty of the world and the potential in our souls.

To inhale every sunrise, and look under every rock for the joy life has to offer.

To uphold, discover, and support trust, honesty, and integrity in all relationships.

To recognize, promote, and inspire the divine connection in myself and others. –Laurie Beth Jones

To live the days gifted to me gratefully with discipline, purpose and as an adventure.

To discover and accept what is really me using and stretching my strengths with confidence and joy.

To treasure my family.

To enrich my life and the lives of all who cross my path or share my hearth, by caring, by affirming their unique worth in love, by giving what I have to give and accepting what they have to give me, and if they so wish, by teaching them what I know and learning what I can from them, and by helping them to discover and pursue their way.

To protect and promote the ethos of South Africa and the community in which I live and also the environment upon which I depend.

To recognize and accept that I am not an owner of anything, but a steward in trust, and that rights are much less important than obligations.

To seek my God constantly and understand my way to Him.

I cultivate growth and refinement by listening with an open heart and nurturing self-discovery.

While keeping an eye single to the glory of God, to make the world a better place in which to live by empowering people to live more meaningful lives.

Starting first with my family and then expanding my circle of influence:

To live true to the principles I hold dear (charity, fidelity, self-sufficiency, honesty, integrity, proactivity, giving, trust . . .).

To make the burden a little lighter and the way a little brighter for everyone I have regular contact with.

To not take myself too seriously and to keep everything within its proper context.

To live and let live, to learn and teach, to give and receive, to love and be loved, to understand and be understood.

To act in a manner that brings out the best in me and those important to me—especially when it might be justifiable to act otherwise.

To be the person my children look to with pride when they say, "This is my dad."

To be the one my children come to for love, comfort, and understanding.

To be the friend known as caring and always willing to listen empathically to their concerns.

To be a person not willing to win at the cost of another's spirit.

To be a person who can feel pain and not want to hurt another.

To be the person who speaks for the one that cannot, to listen for the one that cannot hear, see for the one without sight, and have the ability to say, "You did that, not I."

To have my deeds always match my words through the grace of God.

Family Mission Statements:

The mission of our family is to create a nurturing place of order, love, happiness, and relaxation, and to provide opportunities for each person to become responsibly independent and effectively interdependent, in order to achieve worthwhile purposes.

Our family mission:
To always be kind, respectful, and supportive of each other,
To be honest and open with each other,
To keep a spiritual feeling in the home,
To love each other unconditionally,

To be responsible to live a happy, healthy, and fulfilling life,
To make this house a place we want to come home to.

The mission of our family is to create a nurturing place of faith, order, truth, love, happiness, and relaxation, and to provide opportunity for each individual to become responsibly independent, and effectively interdependent, in order to serve worth purposes in society. -Covey Family Mission

Our family mission is to:

Value honesty with ourselves and others.

Create an environment where each of us can find support and encouragement in achieving our life's goals.

Respect and accept each person's unique personality and talents.

Promote a loving, kind, and happy atmosphere.

Support family endeavors that better society.

Maintain patience through understanding.

Always resolve conflicts with each other rather than harboring anger.

Promote the realization of life's treasures.

No empty chairs.

Corporate Mission Statements:

Franklin Covey Company

We inspire change by igniting the power of proven principles so that people and organizations achieve what matters most.

Ritz-Carlton

The Ritz-Carlton is a place where the genuine care and comfort of our guests is our highest mission.

We pledge to provide the finest personal service and facilities for our guests who will always enjoy a warm, relaxed yet refined ambiance.

The Ritz-Carlton experience enlivens the senses, instills well-being, and fulfills even the unexpressed wishes and needs of our guests.

Appendix C
By Raymond Jones

If you were to take a long trip, say from San Francisco to Hawaii, aboard a 747 with several other people, you might be appalled if you knew who was flying the airplane. It is not the pilots; it is a couple of guys named Fred and George.

Fred and George are two black boxes, and they really are referred to as Fred and George. Fred is a gizmo called an Inertial Navigation System. Fred knows at every moment exactly where the airplane is and where it is supposed to be. In the old days a human navigator took a look at his instruments and did some figuring, and by the time he had the position worked out the plane was long from that spot. Fred knows now where the plane is.

George is the autopilot. He moves the controls to guide the airplane this way and that, speed it up or slow it down. He and Fred talk to each other constantly. If their conversation were in English, it would sound something like this: Fred will say, "George, we're off course two degrees to starboard. And George will say, O.K. Fred, I'll fix it."

"George, we're off course three degrees to port."

"O.K. Fred, I'll fix it."

"George, we're forty knots below our airspeed."

"O.K. Fred, I'll fix it."

"George, we're three hundred feet too low."

"O.K. Fred, I'll fix it."

This conversation continues all the way to Hawaii, and George and Fred bring the giant plane within a thousand yards of the runway in Honolulu within five minutes of the scheduled time of arrival.

The incredible thing is not so much the accuracy of Fred and George, but the fact that the airplane has been in error 90% of the time of its flight. In error 90% of the time and still it lands on target and on schedule!

The secret is that George made thousands of errors in driving the airplane, but for each error Fred called out a correction and George corrected. The flight line was made up of thousands of small jogs that crisscrossed the ideal straight flight line and still put the airplane at its destination when it was suppose to be there. A rocket to the moon travels in exactly the same way.

If we human beings could see that we can get a 747 to Honolulu or a rocket to the moon even having been in error 90% of the time, we might be a little less uptight about being in error ourselves.

There's nothing that kills performance like fear of failure, fear of being foolish, fear of being caught in error. We are particularly prone to this fear.

The secret to the success of Fred and George is correction. They work as a perfect team. Fred spots an error. George corrects it immediately. Some human beings work that way. Most don't.

To be in life means we are constantly off course. What is important is not that we are off course, but whether or not we make the corrections that need to be made. Human beings differ from Fred and George in one important and often fatal respect - the desire to protect one's position.

Suppose Fred and George were human and Fred had just pointed out for the fiftieth time that George was wrong. George, the human George, would likely reply, "Will you leave me alone! I'm doing the best that I can. If you think you can do any better, come and fly this thing yourself.""

Fred and George, the machines, don't do that. They work together and get the job done. Human beings don't like correction. They prefer to protect the position they have taken. But, in reality, any response that takes offense to correction is inappropriate. If the person who gives you correction is a fool, to be upset by a fool is to make yourself an even greater fool. If the input is of value, then to not consider it places you once again in the position of a fool.

Most people don't make the necessary corrections because they are too busy being concerned with protection. Most people's failures in life are a product of protecting themselves when they should have been correcting themselves.

It is almost as if people drive down the highway of life and suddenly notice that the gas gauge is nearly empty. Instead of correcting, pulling into a gas station, they cover up the gauge and pretend it isn't there, hoping that when they wake up in the morning, an elf, Santa Claus or the Easter Bunny will have filled up the gas tank.

The unwillingness to be in error and correct it is the source of most failures. Somehow the notion persists that you can get away from failure, that we can succeed enough to never fail again. That possibility just doesn't exist. It is like trying to eat once and for all.

Successful people, like the 747 airplane, are willing to live in error and are willing to correct. They are people who are busily doing what they don't know for sure how to do. They recognize that life is not a riskless process.

"George, you aren't going in the right direction!"

"O.K. Fred, I'll fix it."

Appendix D
Role Tribute Statement Exercise

1. **Identify your roles.** Roles are your key relationships and responsibilities.

You may have several roles in your life. Some common **Role Titles** include:

Husband/Wife
Father/Mother
Son/Daughter
Brother/Sister
Business or Community Leader
Business Professional
Friend
...and many others

Roles provide a natural framework for living your mission, and also for evaluating balance in your life and planning effectively.

2. Create a vision of effectiveness in each role by creating **Role Tribute Statements.** Role tribute statements help you capture a vision of the difference you can make with your life if you carry out your most important roles with excellence over time.

• Begin by visualizing a significant future birthday celebration in your honor. It should be approximately 10 years or more in the future at an age that you might consider a milestone in your life. Attending the celebration are the key people from each important role you play in your life. Identify the key person that is most affected by each role. Some roles may have several or even many key people. It may be helpful to identify the names of the key groups first, and then the name of one individual who would serve as the "spokesperson" for the group on this special occasion.

• Second, write a detailed statement describing how you would like the designated person in each role to perceive you and what tribute you hope they would give you (write it as if they are saying it **to** you). What do you hope these people say? What contributions do you hope they mention? What difference do you want to have made in their lives? These statements should be long enough to do justice to the occasion. They should be written in such a manner that, if it were really your birthday and you really heard these words spoken to you, you know you would be moved by it. Be sure to close each tribute the way a real tribute would be closed: with the person wishing you Happy Birthday!

• Complete tribute statements for each role (approximately 5 – 7 roles). If you are working on your mission statement, watch for common themes, as this is a good sign you are on the right track.

Sample Role Tribute Statement

Role Title: Husband
Key Person(s): Susan (my wife)
Role Tribute Statement:
It is May 19, 2018. Today is my 60th birthday. I am down the street at my neighborhood park with dozens of friends, family members, colleagues and former clients. My wife and children have surprised me with the most wonderful party. It is pleasant for this time in May, about 70°. I am sitting at a table in the shade along with my wife, my three children, my parents, and a couple of my closer coworkers. Suddenly, my wife gets up from the table, and I wonder where she's going. Then, I notice that someone is turning down the stereo. I turn just in time to see my wife step up to the microphone. The crowd begins to quiet, and she starts out by thanking all of them for coming and making this day such a special one for me. Then, she turns and looks at me directly. I think I see her tearing up just a little, and then, in a calm and loving voice, looking into my eyes, she says…

"Dear, you have been such a wonderful and loving husband. You have created an environment in our marriage that has allowed us to grow our relationship, communicate openly, and share our thoughts and feelings with each other without fear of rejection or judgment each and every day.

You have spent quality time with me as often as possible, and, throughout our marriage, we have never stopped dating each other. You have set an excellent example for our children as to what a good and loving husband and father can and should be.

You always speak to me in loving tones and you seek to lift me up. You listen to me carefully and intently, never interrupting, always seeking to understand what is in my heart. I truly feel that nobody understands me better than you.

You have been my greatest supporter, my biggest fan, and you are my very best friend. You have been supportive of me in all of my endeavors, my desires, and in my responsibilities.

You have prayed with me. You may not know it, but over the years there have been many quiet evenings when I could overhear you praying for me. You have served me willingly as my husband. But most of all, Honey, you have loved me unconditionally, and for that I love you. Happy Birthday."

Now it's your turn. Print out 5 to 7 copies of the following page and write your own Role Tribute Statements for you most significant roles. You may opt instead to simply type them using a computer. Whatever works best for you is fine.

Role Title:_____

   Key Person(s):_____

    Role Tribute Statement:_____

_____

_____

Value: Intellectual Growth

Value Statement: I grow intellectually.

Clarifying Statements:

I listen with an open mind to what others have to say and take in what I think might enhance my world. I value diversity and love to challenge my mind. I read things relating to all aspects of my life and seek to internalize worthwhile things. I seek opportunities for education that will help me learn and grow.

Value: Generosity

Value Statement: I am generous.

Clarifying Statements:

I remember the generosity of my parents and seek to ensure that their examples will live in me always. I seek opportunities to help others by giving of my time, talents, and financial means, and I expect nothing in return. As I give feely to others great joy fills my heart and my life.

Value: Financial Security

Value Statement: I am financially secure.

Clarifying Statements:

I live a three-fold financial strategy, 1. Save, 2. Invest, 3. Give Generously. I spend less than I earn and save at least 10% of my income each month, no matter what. I have liquid savings sufficient to meet all of my expenses for at least 1 year. I contribute to my long-term retirement savings each year as part of my preparation for retirement and the future. I recognize the difference between saving and investing. In addition to saving I also invest wisely for an even greater return. I spend several hours per week working on my finances and enhancing my financial knowledge. I also give generously to family, friends, charity, and the poor & needy.

Value: Physical Fitness

Value Statement: I am physically fit.

Clarifying Statements:

I maintain a body-fat percentage of 16% or less. I exercise 6 days per week: 3 days X 30 minutes for cardiovascular endurance and 3 days X 30 minutes for muscular strength. I eat a healthy, well-balanced, nutritious diet, consuming no more than 2,500 calories per day on average. I get plenty of sleep and rest, at least 8 hours each night. I engage in regularly schedule recreational activity, and I lead a vigorous lifestyle.

Value: Happy Marriage

Value Statement: I am a loving husband.

Clarifying Statements:

I love my wife. I communicate effectively with her, seeking first to understand her heart and mind before seeking to be understood. I am patient in listening, continuing in the communication until she feels understood. I consider her thoughts, feelings and needs. I enjoy her company and express my appreciation to her sincerely and often. I make it a point to do things for her and with her that I know she values and appreciates. I plan for and create the time needed to spend quality time together, not leaving it to chance. I date my wife regularly, showing her the same love and attention that I did when we first started dating years ago. I respect her and acknowledge that she is a unique, dynamic and changing human being, never to be taken for granted. I value her opinion, her example, her contribution, and the great and wonderful impact she has in my life.

Value: Service

Value Statement: I serve others.

Clarifying Statements:

I seek to serve and help others at every opportunity, being of assistance whenever and wherever possible. I strive to be a good example and I am kind to all. I serve others, I'm friendly, I'm kind, I'm helpful, I'm cheerful and strive to lift the spirits of those around me. I'm thoughtful, I'm a good listener, always seeking to understand. I give of my time and talents. I sacrifice my own desires for the good of others. I'm caring. I work to help those in need. I go out of my way to help those in need. I'm courteous, enthusiastic, positive. I help others to see the positive side of things. I'm quick to respond to requests for help. I strive to see others as I know God sees them.

Value: Self-Reliance

Value Statement: I am self-reliant.

Clarifying Statements:

I live within my means. I am wise with my earnings. My finances are in order. I am frugal and careful in my spending. I plan and prepare carefully for my financial future. I have a budget and live by it. I have sufficient for my needs both now and many months into the future.

www.ingramcontent.com/pod-product-compliance
Lightning Source LLC
Chambersburg PA
CBHW051857170526
45168CB00001B/148